SINOSTAN

SINOSTAN

CHINA'S INADVERTENT EMPIRE

RAFFAELLO PANTUCCI

AND

ALEXANDROS PETERSEN

OXFORD
UNIVERSITY PRESS

OXFORD

UNIVERSITY PRESS

Great Clarendon Street, Oxford, OX2 6DP,
United Kingdom

Oxford University Press is a department of the University of Oxford.
It furthers the University's objective of excellence in research, scholarship,
and education by publishing worldwide. Oxford is a registered trade mark of
Oxford University Press in the UK and in certain other countries

Published in the United States of America by Oxford University Press
198 Madison Avenue, New York, NY 10016, United States of America

British Library Cataloguing in Publication Data

Data available

Library of Congress Control Number: 2021946456

ISBN 978–0–19–885796–9

DOI: 10.1093/oso/9780198857969.001.0001

Printed and bound in Great Britain by
Clays Ltd, Elcograf S.p.A.

For Alexandros and Allegra, who will miss meeting him

Preface

This is a book that was started by two and ended by one. It took me a while to get to the end for various reasons, but now I am here, I feel I owe the reader an explanation and perspective before they embark on the text.

When we started this project almost a decade ago, we were heading off on an adventure we were both sure was going to initiate something interesting which we would get to work on for the next few years. Our initial immature vision did not have the grandiloquence it ended up with, and if I am honest, we mostly saw this as a way to spend a good chunk of our time criss-crossing the heart of Eurasia. We both enjoyed visiting remote cities in Central Asia or distant Chinese border posts. Sitting in shared taxis where we knew we were getting ripped off as we traveled along remote borderland roads, in dark bars near dusty borders drinking beer (or at Alex's insistence whatever whiskey they had), or in random institutions meeting curious Eurasians.

I have innumerable tales (and a few pictures) of these different journeys we took. The time we pulled up near an old nomadic marker in Xinjiang in the middle of the desert, to suddenly have a fleet of dark cars appear from nowhere, pull up, discharge a small army of Chinese men with short haircuts and sunglasses to some sort of odd meeting while we tried to make ourselves small in the vast emptiness. To a meeting in Kazakhstan where an older professor took a shine to us, offered us lunch at a local mock Soviet restaurant and proceeded to try to set us up with one of her younger female colleagues. To a grim hotel bar in Mary where we tried to chat to wired Iranian truckers as they were more interested in picking up Turkmen prostitutes. Later that same trip we forced ourselves to drink two bottles of Turkmenbashi brandy in our rudimentary room at the Hotel Aziya after we realized that the seals were leaky, we would never be able to get them onto a plane in carry-on, and it seemed a shame to let the great man's drink go to waste. We suffered the next day as we bumped around Ashgabat. Fortunately, it was not the terrifying car ride we had outside Dushanbe in a crowded shared taxi where a previously lively car went completely quiet as ominous music came onto the radio with a low, deep beat and a monotone voice intoning ritualistically and menacingly over the top. We got to the next petrol station stop, joked we might be about to be sacrificed in some way, and questioned if we should keep on in this ride. We did and survived.

Sadly, however, as we were completing the first draft of writing this text, Alex was brutally murdered in Kabul. He had moved shortly before to teach at the American University there and was out at dinner with a colleague. I got the message in Canada, where I was working on a different project, from a mutual friend in Kabul.

After the devastation of his loss had sunk in, I was left with a dilemma about what to do. We had advanced far enough into the text that we had something substantial to start taking to publishers, but it was incomplete and it felt strange to be doing it alone. I also got swept up in the hubbub of life. A new job, a house, and more. The text sat in the back of my mind as I got swept into more projects and work. I was lucky enough to get to keep traveling to Central Asia and China as part of my work, with a growing portion of my time also spent in India and Pakistan. I have not been back to Afghanistan since Alex's passing.

All of this gave me more material, stories, and experiences. It also gave me more time to think and to place the narrative in a bigger context than the one we had initially envisioned. But the core of the idea was one that I had developed with Alex and it felt appropriate to continue to publish it under both of our names as a result.

However, the book is not the same one that we started with. The emergence of the Belt and Road came as we went along and opened up a new link between Central Asia and China's broader foreign policy. China under Xi Jinping has also transformed into a more aggressive and pushy force on the world stage. The initial book was developed with a view to offering policy ideas for Washington about what to do about China's rise in the region. The biggest issue we encountered at the time, when trying to address that, was a general lack of interest in Washington about the region.

Washington's level of interest has not particularly changed (and arguably in fact it has decreased). But what has transformed is the world's relationship with China. And I cannot speak for where Alex would have ended up on this. He likely had a more Washingtonian perspective on Beijing and might have been less forgiving than me. I recall a heated debate we got into in a taxi in Beijing where we concocted the title for the book (it has remained the same since then). I initially felt Sinostan felt a little too aggressive, but was eventually won over. The deal was sealed when our taxi got into an accident and we ditched it to find alternative transport to our dinner.

At the time of writing this Preface, things had become so polarized that conflict between the US and China did not seem an impossibility. As an American-trained researcher with deep personal and professional contacts there, Alex would have seen his role as being to advise the more confrontational perspective emanating in a bipartisan way from Washington. But he would not, I think, have liked the return to Cold War rhetoric. He was deeply sensitive and empathetic toward others' perspectives, and I would suspect have articulated a fairly nuanced view. He had discussed a number of times getting a job at a university in Xinjiang where he felt he would gain a better understanding of what was really going on. He always saw both sides of the story, and while he was an excellent analyst and writer who always articulated a clear view, it came from a place of knowing the other side well—often through personal contact. Unfortunately, we will never know for sure what he thinks of the world as it is currently shaped, and all I can do is hope that I have done him justice in terms of at least representing what I thought was our common perspective on what was going on in Central Asia.

The other major event which took place as we were in the final stages of production of this text was the fall of Kabul to the Taliban, something which marked the end of the two decade American-led experiment to transform Afghanistan. I am confident that Alex would have shared my sadness at what has happened and worried for the country's future. But the change came at such a late stage, I have only been able to lightly include reference to it in the book. The overall analysis of China's role and vision articulated in the text, however, is broadly speaking unaffected by the change, though of course Beijing's need to play a more proactive role in Afghanistan is now sharper than ever. It also remains to be seen how much Afghanistan will find itself being dragged into the great power conflict framework that has come to increasingly dominate international affairs. Should this happen (and there are indicators that it might), the entire region will suffer as a result.

I owe a debt of gratitude to a number of people who supported this project over the years. First and foremost, Allan Song and his colleagues at the Smith Richardson Foundation who have been consistently and generously supportive of the project from the outset. Crucially taking a chance and getting us going at the beginning, and then helping me with the push to get the final text out. The now defunct Foreign Policy Initiative and the very much more active Carnegie Endowment were supportive hosts for the grant that helped us undertake the research. And the think tanks where I worked for the lifetime of this project—the Shanghai Academy of Social Sciences (SASS), the Royal United Services Institute for Defence and Security Studies (RUSI) in London, and finally the International Centre for Political Violence and Terrorism (ICPVTR) at the S. Rajaratnam School for International Studies (RSIS) in Singapore—were patient employers while I worked on the text among other things. While there are innumerable colleagues, friends, and others that have helped and contributed in little (and large) ways along the path, my former RUSI colleague Sarah Lain merits a particular mention as we traced a number of these Central Asian routes together on later research trips and projects. She may well recognize some of the stories, and our work together elsewhere has covered topics explored in this book. I apologize for not listing everybody else, but after almost a decade of research the list is long and incomplete.

I owe a particular note of thanks to Alex's parents Effie and Christian who have endured my lengthy delays in getting us to this stage and to Effie for playing such a substantial role in the final production of the book; my own mother Leslie Gardner who acted as agent for the book and fed Alex's insatiable appetite when he came to London; and, finally, my beautiful wife Sue Anne, who has been a constant support, came along with us on a number of trips as our photographer, captured images of Alex looking mysterious in Central Asian markets, and helped build the website we had established to promote the work. She is an often unmentioned third character in our adventures. We have her to thank for finding the Tashkent Xinjiang Expo among other things. And her photos remain among the best memories of our trips, some of which are included in this book (and many more which can be found online).

A quick final note on style. I have chosen to write this text using the first-person plural. It seemed the tidiest way to capture the fact both of our names are at the top of the book. It also gave me a way of including meetings we were at together, those which only he attended, some which others attended as well, and those which subsequently only I participated in. This choice was made for the simple reason of streamlining the text and making it an easier read, though I am aware some may question accuracy as a result.

This book is of course dedicated to Alex's memory. I hope he will forgive that I have also made mention of my delightful daughter at the outset, but given the charmer he was I am sure he would not object. And I know she would have enjoyed meeting him. To those who are interested in reading more about Alexandros or his work, or would like to learn about (or contribute to) the scholarship program that was set up at King's College London in his honor, please visit https://www.kcl.ac.uk/warstudies/study-with-us/alexandros-petersen-scholarship

It is strange to get here by myself. I hope those who knew Alex feel I have done his memory justice. He was an inimitable personality, a great friend, and an excellent traveler. I must sadly claim any mistakes or errata as only mine.

Raffaello Pantucci,
September 2021

Contents

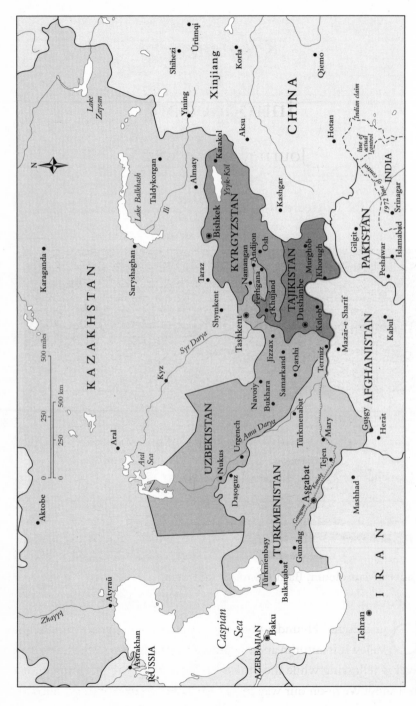

Central Asia

Introduction

Journey to the west

Trader's Mausoleum, Bash Gumbaz, Tajikistan

Our battered Hyundai huffs and puffs through Kyrgyzstan's Alay Valley. It is autumn and the grass along the banks of the Susamyr River is yellowing while the peaks that loom above are gleaming with fresh snow. We're on our way from Osh, Kyrgyzstan's southern hub in the fabled, tense Ferghana Valley, to Irkeshtam, the closest border post to China.

It is late 2011 and we are in the early stages of a project. Our aim is to track China's footprints across the Central Asian steppe and we've read that the once gravelly, uncertain road to the border is in the midst of being leveled and tarmacked by a Chinese company. We're also looking out for that crude indicator of trade, trucks. Chinese lorries or Kyrgyz, Tajik, or Uzbek vehicles are filled with the cheap Chinese goods that have flooded Central Asian bazaars—and much of the world's markets—in recent years and increasingly altered the geographical and economic orientation of the region. But there aren't many on the road. It's election time in Kyrgyzstan, and the last election cycle ended in revolution and ethnic violence (not for the first time in the country's history). Chinese traders at the markets that are fed by the traffic along this road tell us that they have asked their suppliers to wait at the border until the elections are over, quite literally until there is stability in the marketplace. One tells us how during the 2010 troubles the situation got so bad that the local Chinese embassy organized a bus to evacuate those who feared getting caught up amidst the strife between ethnic Kyrgyz and Uzbeks.

It does not take us long to stumble across the Chinese road workers' camp. A dusty collection of prefab dormitories, it nevertheless proudly displays the company's name, logo, and various slogans in large red Chinese characters. The Kyrgyz security guard is fast asleep on his cot. The camp is deserted except for a young engineer from Sichuan. Confused we are able to communicate to him in Mandarin, he explains that they work six months out of the year, when snow doesn't block the passes. Next year, the road will be finished, something confirmed on the large signpost in front of the building that boasts deadlines the workers seem confident they will keep. He says his friends that work on building Chinese roads in Africa get a better deal.

Our Hyundai struggles to climb out of the valley as the road abruptly falls into disrepair. Not only that, but we have to dodge bulldozers and trucks full of dirt: we have found the road workers, distinctively Chinese in their military style green overcoats with shiny golden buttons. They're slowly reshaping the mountains, molding them into smooth inclines that can be paved.

As we reach the ridge crest, we realize that the reshaping could go on forever. The mighty Pamirs unfold before us. These were the last mountains on earth to be mapped. They are the great natural barrier that divides Turkic Kyrgyzstan and Persian Tajikistan. The range touches China at one end and Afghanistan at the other. As we make it across the frozen wastes below these daunting peaks, we can't help but feel that we have almost made it to the roof of the world.

In the middle of a dusty plain atop these heights we find the infam-ous Sary Tash: the setting for numerous 19th-century Great Game moments and now known primarily as a smugglers' den for heroin and hashish funneled out of Afghanistan. Does the South London junkie know that his or her fix came through such spectacular scenery? A dusty hamlet with little to recommend it, there is no reason to dwell here, though signs of China can be found everywhere. Chinese newspaper scraps are blown around while smashed bottles of Wusu, a beer typical of Xinjiang, are scattered by the side of the roads: evidence of the Chinese part of Central Asia just the other side of the border that we are heading toward.

We press on to Nura, a hamlet made up entirely of identical, brand new white trailers. The old Nura was destroyed in a 2008 earthquake. Our driver, who thus far had demonstrated no interest in us or his surroundings, suddenly pulls out his telephone and without telling us what is going on, stops to pray at the memorial to the 225 victims. Just beyond is the pre-border checkpoint, a human-sized, camouflaged tin can with an improvised chimney. The guard on duty looks very young and the AK-47 slung over his shoulder quite obviously lacks a magazine.

A little later, we find the trucks the road is being built for: hundreds of them. Crowded at the border, they are evidence that we have reached Irkeshtam, a haphazard collection of trailers, ramshackle coffee and provisions shops, and burnt out cars: a Central Asian truck

stop. The toothless kids playing in front of the one spartan shop want
us to take their pictures as we try to get pictures of our surroundings.
A border guard catches one of us taking photos and forces us to delete
our pictures. We do get a chance to quickly snap the Chinese customs
building on the other side of the barbed wire fence and the contrast
is total: the Chinese post is new and well-built, like a space ship from
the future landed in shabby Irkeshtam.

One of the truckers, a cheery Chinese Uyghur in a baseball cap, is
eager to chat. The roof of the world is his workplace. It takes three
days to drive a 30-tonne load from Kashgar, in China's Xinjiang province, across two borders, through Kyrgyzstan to Uzbekistan. We ask
what he is hauling, and he vaguely replies about assorted Chinese
goods. He's far more interested to hear about the fact that we are from
Shanghai and what economic prospects there are in a Chinese city
that is almost as far away from his home in Kashgar as is Europe. He
and his colleagues cross this border repeatedly, bringing around a
hundred loads across every week. That is when there aren't elections
on or Chinese holidays that have closed the border.

We are reminded of a meeting we had earlier in the trip. Sitting in a
classroom in Bishkek, a university professor told us how some Kyrgyz
speculate that China is paving their mountains for more than just trade.
The thickness of the asphalt, they say, is capable of carrying not just
trucks but Chinese tanks. This is a not uncommon rumor, but not one
borne out by reality as far as we can tell. Most observers would agree
that fears of military invasion are unfounded. But, this might be because
China already has a stranglehold on the region and Kyrgyzstan's economy. Certainly, the large fortress-like embassy that towers over its
American neighbor in Bishkek (and that is full of empty offices, we are
told on our first visit in 2011) suggests a longer-term play is being made.

Later in Bishkek, a former Kyrgyz cabinet member told us that the
country's economy would collapse without China. With a dramatic
flourish from the plush sofa in an international hotel, he tells us the
markets of the south would be "decimated" if the Russians had their
way and there was a Customs Union stretching from Belarus and

Ukraine over to Central Asia's borders with China. According to him, the little prosperity manifested in Kyrgyzstan is due to its role as a re-export center for Chinese goods headed for Kazakhstan and Uzbekistan, its richer neighbors, and Russia. Years later after Kyrgyzstan joined the Union, the impact of this choice was still unclear, with reported trade in goods dropping and then rising again (and continuing in this see-saw pattern). The focus now seems to be on concerns over the volume of contraband or untaxed goods being sneaked into the Union through Kyrgyzstan's weak border posts. But what remains is a tension in Bishkek between the rival economic pull of China and of Russia.

Regional mega-bazaars like Kara-Suu, outside of Osh, and Dordoi, in Bishkek, are made up of fields holding thousands of containers, bursting with clothes, electronics, toys, tools, toiletries, and pre-packaged foodstuffs—even Muslim prayer books manufactured in China and trucked through remote mountain passes like Irkeshtam. Those trucks need good roads, and hence our eagerness to see them for ourselves to properly understand the wiring that China is laying through the region.

Kyrgyzstan is not a resource-rich country by most measures, but Chinese mining companies are active throughout its expansive countryside, exploring and extracting, sometimes with disastrous environmental consequences. Some of these mining operations have been attacked by raiders on horseback—most likely locals angry that their peaks have been defiled and their streams have turned black, while they see no direct benefit. More cynical observers tell us that the problem is more political—the companies exploiting the mines have simply failed to pay off the right local official, and the angry riders are rented thugs to intimidate the firm into paying up. Certainly, Chinese firms are not the only ones who suffer from this problem. But, whatever the obstacles, the Chinese companies are determined to push on, and they need good roads to transport their goods.

Kyrgyzstan does have some oil but, until relatively recently, did not have the capacity to refine it and turn it into fuel. Kyrgyz drivers were dependent on their old colonizer, Russia, to refine the oil and ship it back to them for consumption. But a new future is on the horizon. A Chinese firm has now built a refinery in Kara-Balta, and while the project was beset with issues around corruption, complaints over pay by local staff, difficulties getting fuel to process, and even reports that they are built on top of an ancient burial ground, the project shows how Chinese investments could have a strategically game-changing effect on the ground in Central Asia.

Of the Central Asian states, Kyrgyzstan is the one that is most obviously dependent on China. And yet clear and coherent political influence is hard to identify. We hear anecdotes of the Chinese embassy leaning heavily on the government when their nationals or companies get in trouble. The deference Kyrgyz leaders show for their Chinese counterparts in public fora is not uncommon for the region (where face and respect are crucial), and the excitement we see Kyrgyz leaders evincing for any investment opportunity is again not exclusive to China (but particularly striking is their excitement for some Chinese initiatives that others feel are unlikely to succeed). Russia remains dominant in various ways, and leaders still look to Moscow when they have problems. During the most recent bout of political turmoil in Kyrgyzstan in 2020, no-one looked to Beijing to step in to help resolve the situation. Yet, it was clear that China was going to be important in the aftermath. Influence is difficult to identify fully in any situation, and in our quest to track China in Central Asia, it has proven the most elusive element to pin down.

But we have witnessed the roof of the world being paved by Chinese workers. And we have noted that China's economic stakes in the region depend on politics. Trade flows are reduced during uncertain elections, spats between governments make cross-border infrastructure more complicated and community tensions cause problems for projects and factories. Chinese support is provided in the form of gifts, bilateral loans as well as support through multilateral organizations (both Chinese led and international). The result can be that energy security is provided for a small dependent nation as well as employment in a country that needs jobs. The public perspective is mixed: some learn Mandarin seeing an opportunity, while many complain about crass Chinese workers and environmental damage. Kyrgyzstan, like broader Central Asia, is benefiting from China in some ways; the question is how will China cash in this chip? And what is it that China sees as its long-term responsibility to the region?

★   ★   ★

The consequences of what China is doing in Central Asia have ramifications well beyond the Eurasian heartland. When we started exploring this question through on-the-ground research in 2011 and 2012, we hadboth been already looking for some time at the question of the growing Chinese influence in the region. What was striking was the degree to which it was possible to see a dynamic and active Chinese foreign policy that had deep local roots, a history that went back to the end of the Cold War (and in many ways much earlier), and which was slowly displacing Moscow from what was a traditional Russian sphere of influence. The development of the Shanghai Cooperation Organization (SCO), the rapid construction of pipelines, the opening up of infrastructure, roads, power lines, and routes into the region from China all marked a pattern of activity which, while never defined clearly as a policy emanating from Beijing, had all the markings of a coordinated surge into the region.

And then in September 2013 President Xi Jinping gave his keynote address in Astana at the Nazarbayev University, announcing the creation of a Silk Road Economic Belt.[1] A month later, this was followed by a speech in the Indonesian parliament in Jakarta in which he announced the 21st-century Maritime Silk Road.[2] Brought together, these formed the 一带一路 (pronounced *Yi Dai Yi Lu*) or (eventually) the Belt and Road Initiative (BRI).[3]

By choosing Astana as the location for the inauguration of this foreign policy concept, President Xi was highlighting the centrality of

Central Asia to the idea which has gone on to become the defining vision of his reign's foreign policy outreach. Here was a region which was usually seen as a Russian-controlled space, and yet it was here that President Xi Jinping, the newly minted and boundlessly confident Chinese leader, was launching his defining foreign policy idea. The question we sought to understand was what this meant for Central Asia, Western national interests, and more generally the rise of China. Our conclusion was that it is in Central Asia that you can see an outline of what China's future foreign policy is going to look like, and get a feel for how China is going to manage some of the problems with which it is confronted.

The policy implications of this for the United States and the West was at the heart of the question we sought to address when we started doing the research for this book. Here was a part of the world that has traditionally been considered a second-rank concern for American and Western policymakers, who saw it as a residual part of the Soviet Empire. When we started in late 2011, the Asian policy in Washington was dominated by President Obama's "Asia Pivot," which appeared to presage a period in which the United States would refocus its attention on the Asia Pacific to the detriment of its Transatlantic connections. Seeking to tap into the prosperity which was clearly emanating from Asia, the "Pivot" was a signal that Washington was trying to move on from the troubled Bush era of Middle Eastern wars.

The focus of this "Pivot" was the Pacific Ocean. And the key adversary was China, though not clearly so in the first instance. When President Obama first came into office, he characterized himself as "America's first Pacific President." In a speech in Tokyo in late 2009 he highlighted how "the Pacific rim has helped shape my view of the world." As he put it, "the United States does not seek to contain China, nor does a deeper relationship with China mean a weakening of our bilateral alliances. On the contrary, the rise of a strong, prosperous China can be a source of strength for the community of nations," he added. "And so in Beijing and beyond, we will work to deepen our

Strategic and Economic Dialogue, and improve communication between our militaries."[4]

Fast forward a few years, and everything seemed to change. With the Middle East proving impossible to ignore, Russian foreign interference sinking the "reset" President Obama had advanced with President Medvedev, and many of the residual problems of the Bush administration still hanging over, the "Asia Pivot" seemed to lose some of its momentum. This all happened as President Xi ascended to the throne in Beijing, heralding a more confident China that was keener to assert global leadership and shake off its previous mantra of refusing to become involved in international affairs. Chinese island construction in disputed waters in the South China Sea moved forward at an ever more ambitious rate, and the Chinese navy launched its first aircraft carrier. In parallel to all of this was the rhetoric of the BRI which grew to become an all-encompassing foreign policy concept: a central organizing concept around which huge parts of the Chinese bureaucracy started to plan.

The Obama administration's response was the Trans-Pacific Partnership (TPP), an ambitious trade agreement that pre-dated the Obama administration but was given a substantial boost during his term. Reflecting the intent for the agreement to be focused on China in an adversarial way, President Obama highlighted in his speech after signing the agreement in Auckland, New Zealand, that "TPP allows America—and not countries like China—to write the rules of the road in the 21st century."[5]

This narrative carried forward into the Trump administration. While President Trump may have overturned the TPP, he continued to make prominent the China threat backed by bipartisan support in Washington. The Pentagon identified China and Russia as the two priority adversaries on the world stage, while President Trump pushed tariffs and economic confrontation to the top of his agenda with Beijing. Evidence could be found everywhere in Washington of pushback to the BRI—groups of senators, calling for the administration to take a more hostile position,[6] repeated statements about "debt traps," dismissive statements by senior state department officials of Chinese investments into South Asia,[7] and eager antagonism by Secretary Pompeo as he visited China's neighbors in Central Asia.[8] Unable to compete directly with Chinese money, Washington pushed "blue dots" of investment and boosted the Overseas Private Investment Corporation (OPIC) to offer alternatives to BRI investment.

And all of this has been carried through to the Biden administration, highlighting an issue on which President Biden appears to be consistent with his predecessor. At the G7 Summit in Cornwall in June 2021, the leaders agreed to push forward a Build Back Better World (B3W) vision which was intended to act as a positive alternative to BRI. Thin on details at the time of writing, it echoes many of the earlier attempts to respond to Chinese economic vision. These constant attempts to offer alternatives to BRI on the economic front came alongside other geostrategic efforts by Western powers. Another initiative pushed forward in the dying days of the Trump administration was to revive the Quad of the US, India, Japan, and Australia. Both the Trump and the Biden approaches to this construct came at a moment when all of the members of the Quad were locked in conflict with China, making it more appealing and giving the meetings greater heft than they had previously had. Separately and at various times, both India and Japan have started to advance their own alternative strategies to counter the BRI. Yet the focus continues to be on the seas, with the US navy and its allies pushing back on Chinese dominance, while Washington strengthens its relations with China's maritime neighbors.

But this focus on China's maritime relations and power projection is overlooking history. One of the most consequential myths about China's geopolitical posture has been its prominence on the seas: but China has never been a naval power. Aside from Zheng He's naval peregrinations in the early 15th century, Chinese empires have traditionally been focused on land power. And even Zheng He for all his skills as a naval adventurer was eventually shored by the *Hai Jin* edict (of 1613) that marked the Chinese Empire's retreat from the sea. The focus for Chinese imperial dynasties was to maintain the integrity of their massive state. Within the Chinese military structures, the People's Liberation Army Navy (PLAN) was always considered a secondary project, with much of the spending and institutional strength focused on the immensely corrupt, but much more powerful People's Liberation Army (PLA). Under President Xi there has been something of a redressing of this power balance within the Chinese military with an exponential growth in naval assets. But China remains very focused on its land relationships, being aware that these have the potential of exposing China's unstable border regions to threats.

By focusing on China's activity on the seas, however, the West has largely overlooked one of the most consequential geopolitical shifts of the past few decades. Beijing's gradual shift to prominence in Central Asia is reflective of a transformation regionally that has happened largely outside the Western gaze and attention. There has now been a reawakening with regards to China and its power, but its impact across Eurasia has been less well examined. Yet, it is from what is happening in Central Asia that one can gain insight into what China's possible global impact might look like. In geopolitical terms, China's rise is manifested on land, in Eurasia, far from the might of the US Pacific Fleet and Washington's rimland allies. Far even from the influence of other Asian powers, such as India. China's geopolitical rise is in Central Asia. Western policymakers should be dusting off their early 20th-century geographer and strategist Sir Halford Mackinder rather than their Admiral Alfred Thayer Mahan.[9]

The fixation with territorial authority is something that persists to this day with the Chinese Communist Party's preoccupation with domestic economic growth. This is mostly a survival mechanism, to prove Party ability and therefore justify its continued dominance, but it has also had the effect of warping Chinese foreign policy to serve domestic interests. This is not entirely surprising. Governments have to worry first and foremost about their public's interests at home. This is what keeps them in or out of power. In much the same way as the

American political cycle warps America's foreign policy attention, China's domestic preoccupations mean that the government is largely focused on domestic policy with foreign policy coming a poor second. And when foreign policy is the focus, it is mostly in service to domestic policy. Even in China's relationship with the United States, the first (and often only) foreign relationship Beijing worries about, the root is to strengthen the leadership's hand at home, be it through economics or the political optics of talking peer-to-peer with the current dominant superpower.

Seen through this lens, Xinjiang is the golden thread tying Chinese domestic and foreign policy together in Central Asia. Given foreign policy is ultimately an expression of domestic policy for China, Central Asia is an extension of Xinjiang policy. China's westernmost province, Xinjiang (whose name literally translates as "New Frontier") is China's piece of Central Asia. Far from the center, rich in natural resources, but largely empty and burdened with minority tensions between ethnic Han and native Uyghurs that periodically erupt into violence, Xinjiang has long been a concern to decision-makers in Zhongnanhai, China's ruling enclave at the heart of Beijing.

These ethnic tensions regularly cause headaches, but they most prominently burst into the world's attention in July 2009 when rioting in the capital Urumqi led to more than 200 deaths. Sparked off by protests in the city against reports of Uyghur workers in Guangdong being abused, the trouble escalated into rioting in which mobs of Uyghur marched around the city beating hapless Han to death. The next day was marked by counter-riots by Han, angry at both the Uyghurs and the failure of the authorities to protect them or to resolve the province's longstanding problems. In a demonstration of the severity of the problem, President Hu Jintao was embarrassingly dragged away from attending a G8 Summit in L'Aquila, Italy, to take charge of the situation.

In the wake of the violence, Beijing decided it was time for a new approach. A number of senior leaders in Urumqi's security establishment were dismissed, and in April 2010, longstanding local party boss

Wang Lequan was also eased out of his position. The rhetoric was that he had been promoted to deputy chair of the Political and Legislative Affairs Committee in Beijing, but in fact it was less a promotion and more a lateral move. Replacing him was Zhang Chunxian, the former governor of Hunan province, who had received plaudits for his work in bringing economic development to that province. The capstone of this revitalized strategy for Xinjiang was a May 2010 work conference on the province after which a number of key strategies were announced: internally, richer provinces were given responsibility for parts of Xinjiang; national energy companies exploiting Xinjiang's rich hydro-carbon wealth were ordered to leave more money in the province in taxes; and Economic Development Zones (EDZs) were established in Kashgar (the southern capital of the province) and Khorgos (a land-crossing with Kazakhstan). Furthermore, emphasizing the importance of external trade for the province's development, the decision was made to upgrade the annual Urumqi Foreign Economic Relations and Trade Fair to the grander China Eurasia Expo, with then Vice Premier Li Keqiang dispatched to represent Beijing.

But while China sees economics as the long-term answer for Xinjiang, in the short and medium term, security has taken the lead. The 2009 riots were followed by a period of escalating violence linked to the region—in October 2013 angry Uyghurs attempted to mow down tourists and then detonate a bomb in Tiananmen Square, lead-ing to the dramatic image of a burning car under the iconic image of Mao Zedong that overlooks the square. In March of the next year a group of Uyghurs started attacking the public outside Kunming's main train station leading to thirty-five deaths. And in April 2014 as Xi Jinping left the region, a pair of suicide bombers blew themselves up after stabbing a passersby in Urumqi's main train station, just one in a series of violent incidents in Xinjiang. President Xi had just given a rousing speech to party cadres in which he called on them to take more strident action to suppress violence and extremism in the region. He was responding to the escalating attacks and in the years after this, a growing push was seen toward increasing the security footprint in the region. The menacingly named "strike hard" campaigns took on a new vigor as China deployed vast amounts of people, hardware, and technology to clamp down on what they perceived as extremism. Keen to pull the problem up from its roots, the government concluded that to deal with this issue, it would have to undertake a mass re-education campaign across the whole province. The result has been a camp system unseen in recent times that seems to sweep up a vast proportion of the region's population, along with a series of policies that observers increasingly point to as an attempted genocide of the Uyghur community within China. The approach looks like an attempt not only to subjugate Uyghurs but also to somehow eradicate their different identity.

However, while the dominant current narrative is focused on a security crack-down, in Beijing's view in the longer term economics is the only answer to stability in Xinjiang. Chinese officials recognize that to ensure long-term stability, they not only need total ideological control, but they also have to offer economic opportunity. And for the policy of developing a land-locked province like Xinjiang to work, the areas in its immediate periphery need to be prosperous enough to be able to trade with it, while also not being a source of further instability. Bordering on Pakistan, Afghanistan, Tajikistan, Kyrgyzstan, Kazakhstan, Russia, and Mongolia, Xinjiang is in the middle of a neighborhood rife with potential trouble, both in terms of militant Uyghur networks posing a threat to these countries and in terms of these potentially unstable regions possibly creating problems that might overspill into China or disrupt any trade corridors. All of this has meant that China has a keen domestic interest in economic and security developments in Central Asia—stretching from the five post-Soviet Central Asian states to Afghanistan. If the strategy to stabilize Xinjiang is to work, China needs to make sure Xinjiang has a stable neighborhood with which it can trade.

This concern is reflected in China's approach to Central Asia, where a combination of security, economic, and cultural efforts have been instituted across the region. What is interesting is that there is little evidence of this coming together as a complete and considered strategy, but rather there have been a series of separate efforts that taken as a whole present a picture that is far more comprehensive than is often appreciated—or even realized—amongst Beijing's policymakers. It is also not clear that China is entirely aware of the incidental impact of its regional activity in reshaping Central Asia or necessarily how it is being perceived by regional states. So focused are Chinese actors on Xinjiang stability and on extracting what they want from Central Asia, it is unclear whether they have taken pause to consider the knock-on effects of their approach. With Russia's influence in the region suffering and with the persistent perception across the region that the United States and Europe consider it a secondary concern, the field has been left open for China.

The result has been that China has carved out for itself an "inadvertent empire" which is gradually being transformed into one of the regions most closely linked to China. While domestically focused, lacking a clear strategy, and attempting, as Chinese actors do in much of the world, to keep a low profile, China has nevertheless quickly become the most consequential actor in Central Asia.

Understanding how this has happened, what it looks like on the ground, and analyzing the long-term consequences both for the region and for the world are the key issues at the heart of this book. Given the importance of Central Asia policy in delivering on security and stability in Xinjiang, it is an approach that from Beijing's perspective needs to deliver success. It is also a region in which China sees opportunities to test out approaches and ideas that can then be developed elsewhere. And Beijing is clearly well aware of Mackinder's theories. In 2015, China's ambassador to the United Kingdom, Liu Xiaoming, wrote an article in the *Financial Times* in which he complained about the negative associations to China's BRI that Mackinder had engendered. According to the ambassador, "Mackinder's theory captivated generations of geo-strategists who saw Eurasia as the 'heartland' of the world's most populous and pivotal region. More recently, however, it has prompted needless scepticism about China's new Silk Road initiative."[10] This defensive posture masks a reality that China has placed Mackinder's "heartland" of Central Asia as the model for Beijing's current approach to the world. Understand how and why China is doing what it is doing in Central Asia, the logic of this text goes, and you will understand how China might act in the world.

★   ★   ★

The first wave of research for this book was conducted in 2011/12. After that both of us traveled repeatedly around the region (to all five Central Asian countries, India, Pakistan, Russia, Iran, and Afghanistan, as well as to other parts of the globe where we found Central Asian expertise) and around China, talking to people, and collecting stories and information about China's rise in Central Asia. At various times we lived in this region or in China. One key topic we kept coming back to, and which ultimately had a very direct impact on our joint project, was Afghanistan.

As we first wandered around, in 2011 and 2012, prying into the underexplored relationship between China and Afghanistan, we discovered that a large question mark loomed over all our conversations: what was going to happen post-2014 when President Obama had said the US was going to withdraw from Afghanistan. Whether it was an awkward meeting at the SCO's unfortunately acronymed RATS (Regional Anti-Terrorism Structure),[11] a cup of coffee on the veranda of the Segafredo Café in Dushanbe, or informal discussions over lavish meals at PLA linked Chinese think tanks in Beijing, the focus of people's attention was on what was going to happen post-2014.

The year 2014 proved, however, to be an arbitrary marker. President Obama did indeed draw down American forces to an extent, but he did not evacuate in the manner that had been suggested. In fact, by the end of his term in office, American forces in Afghanistan numbered 8,400, almost 3,000 more than expected. The dilemma that President Obama had faced was subsequently presented to his successor who, notwithstanding his bombast about wanting to remove America from foreign entanglements, found himself making the same set of choices as President Obama. Where President Trump failed, President Biden appeared to instead be more forcefully willing to deliver, carrying through on an agreement with the Taliban that President Trump's administration had pushed through. At the time of writing, the US and its allies were rapidly moving toward the exit and completing their departure as Taliban forces took Kabul and control of the country and the regime installed by Washington melted away.

Seen from Beijing, Afghanistan is an irritating problem that the West has left on China's doorstep. Repeatedly during our travels we encountered Chinese experts and strategists who would push back on Western expectations for what China should be doing in this country. But as we put it to a roomful of PLA linked think-tankers in Beijing, "the west may have broken the Afghan tea pot, but it is quite clearly on China's side of the table." The point was that it may be North Atlantic Treaty Organization (NATO) and American forces intervention that had led to the current state of affairs in Afghanistan, but the end result remains on China's borders and in the heart of Central Asia.

And while talking to officials in the ministries and to the expert community in Beijing there seems to be a recognition of this fact, there is still a lack of clarity about what exactly needs or can be done about it, or whether China is able to deliver some conclusive resolution to what is going on. In time it became clear, however, that China had been taking the question of Afghanistan ever more seriously, although this has been largely focused around ensuring that Beijing is insulated from any potential violence or instability that might emanate from the country. China has not yet taken on the decisive role that it could play. The result is an approach that pushes tentatively forward on all fronts: China has signed bilateral agreements with Afghanistan, done deals with the Taliban, opened trade routes, supported police training missions in the country, worked in multilateral formats (like the SCO, through the Istanbul Process, as well as with America, India, Pakistan, and others), undertaken joint training projects with the US, Germany, and India, provided aid, helped build infrastructure, provided military support, and played an encouraging role in supporting

China's state-owned firms to invest in the country. China has also invested in strengthening its secondary borders with Afghanistan— pouring military aid and support into border forces in Tajikistan's Badakhshan and Pakistan's Gilgit-Baltistan. It has even gone so far as to deploy forces in Tajikistan and had soldiers appear in training missions in Afghanistan, as well as train Afghan forces at home. Yet while together this is considerably more than it was doing before, it remains unclear whether China has a defined end goal in mind or a plan for how to achieve it. The takeover by the Taliban is only going to complicate things for China going forward.

Afghanistan sits awkwardly in China's greater vision for Central Asia. Within the academic community in China there has always been something of an absence of experts focused on Afghanistan: people have been either Russian-speaking Eurasia experts or South Asian linguists focused on India or Pakistan or on maritime relations. Few speak Dari or Pashto or have any experience in the country. There are some notable and brilliant exceptions to this—some of whom were kind enough to give their time to talk to us, but they are part of a limited cadre.

Within the relevant ministries the same problem applies. For the Foreign Ministry, Afghanistan's location places it at the edge of department boundaries. The responsibility of the Asia Department, it sits on the fringe of their geographical terrain, bound in with the department focused on India and Pakistan, but distinct from the Central Asian department or the West Asian Department. And looking at the greater Chinese economic vision for the region, the reality is that if you are trying to rebuild the old silk routes from China to Europe, you do not need to go through Afghanistan. The road to Europe can pass through Kazakhstan, Kyrgyzstan, or Uzbekistan to get to Russia and then on to European markets. And to the south, Pakistan presents itself as a corridor directly linking China with the waters of the Indian Ocean, and from there a world of commercial opportunity.

That said, Afghanistan is very much part of China's inadvertent empire in Central Asia: and in many ways the issues that Afghanistan presents China are emblematic of a key theme of this book. China's search for natural resources and its eagerness to build infrastructure to connect to those resources, create more efficient trade routes, and open Xinjiang up to the world has given it a political role in Afghanistan and a geopolitical profile in the region whether Beijing wants one or not. Further compounding their need to do something, there is the fact that their entire regional effort in Central Asia and Pakistan will be undermined if Afghanistan returns to being a source of regional instability. As one of China's Afghan experts put it in 2018, from Beijing's perspective, China's concerns around security in Afghanistan start with the potential spillover into Pakistan, then the spillover into Central Asia, and finally Afghan security in itself. And of course, as a Chinese Ministry of Foreign Affairs official from China's Asia Department told us gnomically with a raised eyebrow, "we share a border with Afghanistan."

This is the story across Central Asia. China is a neighbor to whom the relationships are important but not central to national policy. This has reduced Beijing's attention toward the region, and while the BRI has given it a broad vision to operate under, it lacks a clear strategic plan with obvious end goals other than to make China more prosperous and stable by 2049. Chinese actors are focused on individual parts of the overall engagement in the region, but the whole is greater than the sum of the parts. A growing volume of strategic thinking has taken place, instigated by the prominent dean of Beijing University's School of International Studies Professor Wang Jisi who wrote an important article in 2011 calling for China to "look westwards" and to "march westwards." Written initially as a call for China to rebalance its fixation with Washington through focusing more on its land borders, and as an attempt to move the policy discussion beyond a response to the "Asia Pivot," the paper proved in time to be the pathfinder for the broader BRI.[12] Since then, there has been a blossoming in silk-road-studies–related research and writing in China, though it is not clear that any of it particularly answers the question of what kind of power China will be within its own neighborhood.

Prior to the announcement of the Silk Road Economic Belt in 2013 there was no evidence of China having a strategy toward the region. The multifaceted engagement that we found across Central Asia is one that has come together in a scattershot fashion—with economic development taking on a momentum of its own and Beijing policymakers finding themselves trying to tidy up afterwards. Many of the senior thinkers and experts that we spoke to in 2013 (before the speech in Astana) repeatedly decried the absence of a strategy, and few seemed to hold much hope that the SCO might develop into the international player it once aspired to be.

As time went on, this strategic drift continued. Concerns about American encirclement through being based in Afghanistan retreated. In Central Asia, Beijing found itself increasingly drawn in and dependent on the region if its plans for regional stability in Xinjiang were going to be achieved. This had a consequence on the ground. No other outside actor is as comprehensively involved, as dynamic in its engagement, or as obligated in the long term in all six Central Asian states, including Afghanistan. Central Asian governments and business leaders see this and it is with China that they increasingly throw in their lot. Kyrgyzstan, for example, often feels like it has no choice but to do so. Turkmenistan has made a specific choice to partner with China, despite being courted by many outside powers, and has subsequently discovered the difficulties emanating from wedding yourself to a single partner in international and economic relations. The experience of other countries in the region lies somewhere in between these two experiences. But it is not clear that anyone in Beijing has developed a coherent plan on how to carry forward and execute the complicated policy that would be required to ensure China's desired goals in the region.

But the web of connections that China is forging across the region is of global consequence. This is not simply a modern-day interpretation of Mackinder, it is transformative for Central Asia and for how China's BRI is going to play out around the world. The Silk Road Economic Belt in Central Asia is the concrete realization of the "New Silk Road" vision that was articulated by US Secretary of State Hillary

Clinton. The BRI over time is going to increasingly subsume the Asian Development Bank (ADB)'s Central Asia Regional Economic Cooperation (CAREC) program of work, as well as other development visions in the region. American diplomats in Beijing, speaking when we started this research, were confused by the rejection of their New Silk Road plan while increasingly noticing that it is part of the Chinese strategy anyway. The key difference between the strategies articulated by the US and international development banks is that unlike for the former, for China this plan represents an extension of its domestic strategy. In developing Central Asia, China sees itself as helping Xinjiang to grow, become prosperous, and ultimately to stabilize. This makes it of great importance to Beijing, and therefore something which China will find ways to make work. This means it is providing the world with an example of what China's intentions are in foreign lands and the different tools they will deploy to advance that policy.

Key to Central Asia is the reality that Beijing is operating in a pliant environment where the powers involved find themselves obliged to choose between Moscow and Beijing. Outside powers like Iran, India, or Turkey have all played (and continue to play) roles of variable influence, but it is really a story of Chinese versus Russian engagement. And while Moscow may worry about their loss of influence in Central Asia, ultimately both the Kremlin and Zhongnanhai are too focused on their geostrategic positioning together on the international stage against the West to be willing to let themselves be torn apart by Central Asia.

The SCO is able to reduce some of the great power rivalry between Beijing and Moscow. So far, the reaction of Russian leadership to China's inadvertent empire has been a quiet acquiescence, despite the creation of the Eurasian Economic Union (EAEU) or customs linkages that might erect tariff barriers against Chinese goods. Beijing has embraced these efforts. One Ministry of Commerce official told us how the creation of the EAEU was in fact a facilitator for Chinese trade with the region—rather than erecting barriers, it had created a

single tariff area, reducing transit costs and simplifying things for
Chinese goods to get from the Kazakh border to the Belarus border
with Europe. In 2015, highlighting their willingness to cooperate,
Presidents Xi and Putin signed a joint statement declaring their intention to link the two projects up. Illogical as a concept (the EAEU is an
organization with an executive body and secretariat while the BRI is a
foreign policy concept advanced by President Xi), the statement nonetheless highlighted their eagerness to show proximity to each other.

It also highlighted in many ways the deficiencies of the SCO. Severely
lacking in institutional capacity, the SCO has the potential to be the
most inclusive international organization in Central Asia, and it is
gradually expanding its geopolitical influence. It recently welcomed
India and Pakistan as full members, Iran is now on the path, and it has
an ever-expanding roster of regional powers as either "Observers" or
"Dialogue Partners." The SCO's real test will be how, in practice, it
addresses the future of Afghanistan and it is here that China's role in
Central Asia most affects immediate US policy. The prospects are
dim—at a regular annual conference on the organization in Shanghai
in 2013, we were abruptly told that "Afghanistan is America's mistake
and problem to resolve." Any sense of the SCO assuming responsibility or doing more in the country were dismissed with the view that
"Afghanistan's problems are too complicated for outside powers to
understand." This attitude has persisted throughout the research
period for this text. In March 2020, a former Chinese ambassador to
Uzbekistan penned a long article for a prominent foreign policy think
tank in Beijing under a headline that roughly translates as "A Well-
Deserved Imperial Graveyard" in describing the failures of American
policy in Afghanistan.[13]

The truth is that neither China nor the SCO are likely to take
"responsibility" for Afghanistan. Beijing has already shown the limits
of its optimism that the SCO might be a useful conduit for engaging
with Afghanistan with the creation in 2017 of a Quadrilateral
Coordination and Cooperation Mechanism (QCCM), a grouping
bringing together the chiefs of military staff of Afghanistan, China,

Pakistan, and Tajikistan. Focused on border security between the four powers, its mere existence reveals China's frustration with the SCO. Chinese investments, security concerns regarding Xinjiang, and Beijing's close relationship with Islamabad will almost certainly shape the direction of the country in the coming decade.

In the longer term, China's inadvertent empire in Central Asia will have geopolitical consequences for US and Western influence in what Mackinder argued was the most pivotal geographic zone on the planet. Should Washington become solely preoccupied with the Asia Pacific in its China policy, it not only would be missing the more profound manifestation of China's global posture but also could quickly find it far more difficult to cultivate relationships with the countries of Central Asian and the broader Eurasian heartland in the longer term. These powers are all keen for outside Western support, but they find the West a flighty and disengaged partner. China may not be seeking an empire in the region, but it is the only power that is active in a comprehensive, long-term oriented manner. If other outside powers do not also engage, China's lock on Central Asia to the exclusion of others will be not only inadvertent but inevitable. And as Mackinder pointed out, whoever controls this territory, controls the entirety of the Eurasian "World Island."[14]

This book is an attempt to map out the extent of China's influence in Central Asia, using both a bottom–up and a top–down approach to sketch out China's interests, influence, and impact in the region. Drawing on interviews at cold border posts, in regional capitals, and in Beijing's halls of power, it seeks to understand the contours of China's push into Central Asia. In the first chapter we look into the history of China's links and the foundation of China's interests in the region. Chapter 2 looks at Xinjiang and how policy toward the region has been developing. Chapter 3 looks at some of China's biggest investments in the region, mapping the natural resources the country is slowly dominating. Chapter 4 follows the routes that we took around the countries, riding the roads and rails of China's new dominion while visiting some of the many markets. Chapter 5 tells the tale of

China's aspirational soft power in the region based on conversations with the numerous Chinese professors, students, and travelers we met teaching Central Asians Mandarin, as well as the other branches of soft power that China is exerting in the region. Chapter 6 explores the SCO—the infamous expression of "Shanghai Spirit" that Chinese policymakers excitedly talk about as representing a new approach to international relations. Chapter 7 discusses China's growing security footprint in the region, highlighting the long-term foundations that Beijing has already laid. Chapter 8 sketches out the experience in Afghanistan, trying to see what China is doing, what it might do in the future, and how this decision hangs over much of what China is planning and thinking in Central Asia. Chapter 9 places this all in the context of the BRI. The final chapter then clarifies our greater vision of China's "inadvertent empire" in Central Asia and illustrates how China is the future power in Eurasia and one whose influence is only going to grow as its economic links tighten.

This is a conclusion the long-term impact of which is hard to measure but which has repercussions not only for Central Asia but also for the world, as it highlights China's emergence as a global power. During the research for this book, we saw a new leadership ascending in Beijing, projecting a new and confident vision for China in stark contrast to the economically explosive but politically stagnant years of the Hu Jintao administration. Xi Jinping's first visit to a foreign capital was to Moscow, highlighting the importance of that bilateral relationship (and consistent with Chinese recent history). Xi Jinping's first big foreign policy speech was delivered as part of a Foreign Policy Work Conference focused on border diplomacy. His vision for the evolution of China's foreign policy was launched in Astana. Taken together, it is easy to see how Beijing is placing greater focus on its immediate periphery, starting in Central Asia.

It may still be many years before China finds itself able or willing to focus on Eurasia and to prioritize it over its relationship with the United States, but the groundwork it has laid so far means that it has already changed regional dynamics. And the long-term resonance of this change is emblematic of the permanent impact of China's decade of explosive growth. As people shift from talking about China as a rising power to talking about it as an established power, the question becomes *what kind* of a global player it will be and whether it will live up to the "responsible stakeholder" role that former World Bank President Robert Zoellick called on it to become. China's position in Eurasia offers an insight into what its international footprint might look like, offering in microcosm a model of how Chinese foreign policy really works. What should concern international thinkers, businesspeople, policymakers, and strategists alike is how incoherent the strategic thinking in Beijing really is. China may be increasingly dominant in its international posture, but it remains uncertain about how to use this leverage, and it is unclear whether it fully understands what the consequences of this role might be. Power may be shifting to the East, but it remains uncertain whether the new architects in Beijing know exactly what they are going to do with that power.

I

Beyond the Heavenly Mountains

Manas statue on the road near Talas, Kyrgyzstan

In the 1st century BC, *Records of the Grand Historian*, Sima Qian—China's Herodotus—describes in detail the exploits, misadventures, and remarkable intelligence gathering of Zhang Qian, an imperial envoy to the peoples west of China decades earlier.[1] Zhang Qian is credited not only with exploring Central Asia for the first time but also with playing an active role in the region's diplomacy and paving the way for Chinese conquest—despite being taken prisoner for a decade by the nomadic Xiongnu, the Han Dynasty's sworn enemies at the time.

As a military officer with experience battling the Xiongnu (historians speculate they may have been the Hun of Europe), who ravaged Chinese farms and trade routes from the north and west, Zhang Qian was dispatched with a force of ninety-nine men to traverse the perilous Xiongnu territory and forge an alliance with the fabled Yuezhi (possibly the Tocharians described by the Greeks), a more settled people even farther west, also menaced by the Xiongnu.[2] He was quickly captured and enslaved by Xiongnu horsemen, but during the ten years of his captivity he managed to curry favor with their leaders, not least by marrying a Xiongnu woman and fathering a child. Staying true to his mission, he escaped with his family and a guide beyond the Tian Shan (which translates as the 'Heavenly Mountains') to the Ferghana Valley and further southwest to the Yuezhi, who after all this effort were uninterested, or more likely militarily incapable of allying against the dreaded Xiongnu.

Before he forged a path back east, Zhang Qian spent over a year with the Yuezhi, and in neighboring Bactria, gathering intelligence about their governance, economies, and culture, as well as information about a number of nearby areas he never visited, including India, Parthia (Persia), and Mesopotamia. In the Ferghana and elsewhere, he mostly describes what historians have identified as settled, learned Greco-Persian and Indo-Greek peoples who flourished in the area in the centuries after Alexander's conquests. These were polities similar in lifestyle to the Han for which Zhang Qian knew the Chinese would have respect. They were also peoples who, he observed, very much valued the Chinese-made goods that filtered West.

Upon his heroic return (he was captured and escaped again on the way back) to the Han capital Chang'an (modern day Xi'an), he provided the Emperor Wu with intelligence on at least eight distinct civilizations with whom the Chinese had had no previous contact. The paradigm shift this affected in the Chinese world view cannot be underestimated. Zhang Qian had single handedly opened up a whole new world of trade possibilities and cultural contacts for the Great Han. He had also provided ample reason for China to beat back the marauding Xiongnu in order to reach the markets of Central Asia and beyond.

Zhang Qian's solo mission was followed by an outpouring of Chinese diplomacy westwards, with several missions of hundreds of officials and traders departing every year during the 1st century BC.[3] These reached as far as Parthia and Rome, with a number of reciprocal missions and trade delegations making their way to China as well. It was along the routes these envoys established that Greco-Buddhist culture spread from India and Bactria to China, with Eastern Church Christianity making its way to the Chinese court centuries before Marco Polo and that the famed Silk Road had connected the great Eurasian landmass from the Atlantic to the Pacific.

This was China's exposure to, and view of, the western regions that today make up Xinjiang within China and the post-Soviet Central Asian states, including Afghanistan. Chinese school children today learn about Zhang Qian's exploits. When we gave a joint lecture at Xinjiang University in Urumqi, our references to his journeys were immediately recognized. This historical opening up westward in the 1st century BC informs the views of contemporary China when it comes to Central Asia: great opportunities lie to the west, along with attendant challenges. The west is wild. What lies beyond the Heavenly Mountains excites everyone's collective imagination.

★ ★ ★

The Talas Valley in northwestern Kyrgyzstan is not only the supposed birthplace of the Kyrgyz peoples' national icon and Chinese-slayer, Manas. It is also the site of the most fateful battle in the history of Central Asia and one of the defining moments of world history. In the summer of 751 AD, on the green, windswept plain between two glowering mountain ranges, the Arab-led armies of the Abbasid Caliphate decisively defeated the troops and allies of China's Tang Dynasty.[4]

Only twenty-two years after the death of Muhammad in 632 AD, the vast, ever-growing armies carrying the banner of Islam crossed the Oxus into what is now Uzbekistan. By the first decade of the next century they had conquered the great trading cities of Bukhara and Samarkand. In the east, from the base established at Kucha in the Tarim Basin from which China sought to pacify the west, Tang envoys, traders, and military expeditions fanned out across the Heavenly Mountains and the Pamirs, encouraging alliances and forcing tributary relationships from the then largely Persian-speaking peoples of what is now Kyrgyzstan, Tajikistan, and easternmost Uzbekistan. Apart from securing trade routes west, these arrangements with local rulers were key in the ongoing struggle against the Tibetan Empire, which at the time threatened to cut off the Tang from their westernmost possessions in modern day Xinjiang. One of these vassal states was Ferghana, in the fertile valley that still bears that name, so that in 750 the Arab military governor at Samarkand, Ziyad ibn Salih, sat only a couple hundred miles from Tang officials to his northwest.

When he tried to expand his dominions into Ferghana by deposing the local Chinese vassal and installing his own, the protectorate general across the mountains was alerted and the celebrated Chinese-Korean Commander Gao Xianzhi led a force of 10,000 Tang regulars to reassert Chinese authority in the valley. It should be said that Arab sources flip this tale on its head, writing that the son of the deposed ruler of Ferghana's neighboring state, Chach, sought assistance from the Arabs against an expansionist Ferghana supported by the Tang.[5] But, whatever the spark of the conflict, the Tang forces, together with 20,000 local allies met a far larger force (Chinese sources say 100,000) of Arab-led Persians, Uyghurs, and Tibetans on the Talas plain.

Here again sources differ as to how exactly the battle was conducted, but by all accounts it was hard-fought, bloody, and long, lasting five days. It seems that whether it was predetermined or spontaneous, at some point in the fray, the Tang's local allies turned on them and attacked them from the rear at close quarters. This proved the decisive blow, as Chinese forces were caught in a cauldron of carnage, with their only hope of escape being a disorganized retreat out of the valley and across the mountains once more. It was a tactical rout with profound civilizational consequences. Not until the 21st century would Chinese influence be felt so strongly on the western side of the Heavenly Mountains. Chinese Tang armies continued to push further into the region, but the An Lushan rebellion (755–763 AD) within China turned the Tang dynasty in on itself as it faced internal upheaval distracting it from dominating Central Asia.

With victory assured for the armies of Islam, Central Asia's gradual conversion was cast in iron, although the nomadic peoples of the region would wear their religion lightly. The lucrative trade of the Silk Road continued to flourish, but until the Russian conquest of the mid-19th century, most of Central Asia would be culturally and religiously tied to its neighbors in the south. West of the Heavenly Mountains, previously flourishing Buddhism, Manichaeism, Eastern Church Christianity (often erroneously labeled Nestorianism), and Zoroastrianism would almost completely dry up.[6]

A popular story recounts that it was Chinese prisoners of war, taken at the Battle of Talas (751 AD), who brought paper-making technology to Samarkand and thus to the greater Muslim world and eventually Europe.[7] This seems apocryphal, as paper-making was well-known in Central Asia before 751 AD. But it does seem that encountering the Chinese on the battlefield fascinated the Arab and Persian invaders of Central Asia, sparking renewed interest from the west in trade with the East. At least ten embassies from Persian-speaking peoples were represented at the Tang court in Chang'an—modern Xi'an—during the century surrounding the Battle of Talas. Islam and the cultures of the Middle East would eventually find their way across the Heavenly Mountains as well, serving as distinct markers of identity for the layered Indo-European-Turkic peoples of Xinjiang to this day.

The memory of the Battle of Talas is one of the poignant historical events that for many Central Asians places China firmly as an "other," an external, vaguely menacing power across the mountains and deserts, more myth than reality: a power that must eternally be guarded against.

In modern Talas, known today in Kyrgyzstan more for its purportedly
elegant young women than for the medieval clash that sealed the
region's fate, townspeople joke about the Russian and Western historians and archaeologists that occasionally pass through trying to
pinpoint the exact location of the battle. Their opinion of the Chinese
are similar to those of other Kyrgyz: they view them with a sort of
resigned suspicion, with a mixture of resentment, about the preva-
lence and power of the Chinese, and gratitude for the opportunities
afforded by the small-scale trade in Chinese goods. None we spoke to,
however, would acknowledge the past long-term presence of Chinese
in the area or the idea that this land could ever have been considered
part of China's domains. Nursultan, a young man with yellowish eyes
eager to practice his English, said "if the Chinese were here, we drove
them out. They have left no trace."

As we crisscrossed Central Asia, however, we came upon relics of a
Chinese presence before the contemporary period. High in the Pamir
Mountains in one of the most remote parts of Tajikistan's already isolated Badakhshan region, outside the ethnic Kyrgyz village of Bash
Gumbaz, we came across what was said to be a Chinese general's
tomb (though we later heard other theories about this historical arti-
fact). The imposing, yet crumbling, mud-brick structure was so battered by the wind and snow of countless winters that there was no
way of determining its origins on the spot (although subsequent
cross-referencing with history books and ethnographic accounts
seemed to corroborate the Chinese link—whether it was the tomb of
a merchant or a general, however, was unclear). The enthusiastic
villager who took us to the spot told a tale of a punitive Chinese
expedition force that had entered the region and had met with much
success until its general had died. His soldiers had buried him on the
foothills of a craggy mountain, the villager said, and built a substantial
mausoleum with three pillars atop his grave. This was surrounded by
local graves of a much younger provenance, however our self-
appointed guide made a point of mentioning that since it was considered by locals to be a Chinese tomb, it had not been maintained and

did not serve as a place of pilgrimage the way many mountain tombs do in that part of the world.

On the road from Kazakhstan's commercial center Almaty to Khorgos, the main border crossing between China and the rest of Central Asia, we stopped in Zharkent, a sleepy farming town, to see what had been described to us as a Chinese mosque. From the stories we had gleaned, it was unclear whether this was a Dungan mosque or one that had simply been built by Chinese authorities for the local population in the late 19th century (the Dungan people are Chinese Muslims and are known as Hui in China). As the border between the Chinese and the Russian territory in Central Asia was unclear at the time, both scenarios were plausible. It turned out that in fact this magnificent structure was the product of a key border treaty made between the two powers at the time: the Treaty of Kulja. Under the terms of the agreement, locals could choose to live under the control of either power; and so a group of over 75,000 Uyghurs and Zhungar Mongols had decided to follow a Russian garrison to found the new town of Zharkent in 1881, in what is now Kazakhstan.

Once established, and being increasingly prosperous as a trade conduit from Xinjiang to Russia, the town's mainly Muslim citizenry pooled their funds to build a mosque unlike any other. It would act as a symbol of their faith in Islam but also signify their links to the East: an elegantly appointed compound with a multicolored pagoda as a minaret. Designed by noted Chinese architect Chon Pik, the wooden structure was built entirely without nails and consists of the central mosque, pavilions, a Koran school, and an imposing gate with its own tower, all in the Buddhist-inspired style of the late Qing. To Western eyes, it resembles the palaces of the Forbidden City and would almost certainly not be taken for a Muslim house of worship. Like many religious structures in Central Asia, it served as a museum and warehouse during the Soviet period, but since independence it has been restored into a jealously guarded community mosque. We were reluctantly told by a groundskeeper that entry for non-Muslims had been allowed while it was a museum, but not anymore. We had to content

ourselves with peeking over its low walls and marveling from afar at
its distinctive "floating roofs" in the midst of an otherwise nondescript
early Soviet-style neighborhood.

★ ★ ★

The Zharkent mosque is a poignant example of how in this part of
the world the dividing lines between China and Central Asia are
blurred. That is to say that Central Asia as a geographical and cultural
region exists both in the six (including Afghanistan) post-Soviet states
and within China, in the Xinjiang Uyghur Autonomous Region.
Parts of Xinjiang have long been under Chinese rule, but have only
recently evinced any sort of Han character, despite the presence of
pockets of Han for millennia. While tracking China in Central Asia,
we had to remain cognizant of the fact that part of Central Asia is in
China. The topic of Xinjiang's identity and fate is sensitive in China
as well as in the greater Xinjiang Muslim diaspora, whether Uyghur,
Dungan, or the substantial Kazakh, Tajik, and Kyrgyz populations that
live in China (or Pakistani and Afghan traders who have settled in
China). Initially, being for the most part nomadic tribes, the peoples
of Central Asia had lived across the region, rather than within the
tidily defined borders that we know today.

Modern Chinese control of Xinjiang began in the 16th century,
when the Qing Dynasty sought to arrest the growing power of the
Zhungharian Mongols in what is now northwestern Xinjiang.[8] It was
in fact these same Zhunghars who were enemies to both settled and
nomadic peoples of the Ferghana Valley. The Manchu Bannermen, as
the shock troops of the Manchu-dominated Qing were called, sought
for more than a century to split the alliance that had been formed
between the Buddhist Tibetans to the southwest and the largely
Buddhist Zhunghars to the northwest—an echo of centuries-old
strategies dating back to before the Battle of Talas. By the mid-18th
century, the Bannermen had crushed the Zhunghars and extended
Qing control to Kashgar, just the other side of the Pamir and Heavenly
Mountains from today's Tajikistan and Kyrgyzstan.

As the conquest had been about keeping a nomadic menace at bay rather than being a push for outright colonization, the Qing governed with a light touch, maintaining the local power structures dominated by the traditional elite of *khojas* and *begs*.[9] Some Han Chinese did settle in the region during this time, especially as agriculture gradually replaced nomadism and animal husbandry, but many Uyghurs do not look back on this period as one of Chinese control, rather merely as one of greater influence from the east. As the Qing prospered, trade was revitalized along the old Silk Road arteries, and Han merchants could once again be found as far west as the Ferghana. The Khanate of Kokand, in today's eastern Uzbekistan, Kyrgyzstan, and Tajikistan, became a key trading partner and briefly a vassal. But, the Qing Dynasty was not destined to shape Central Asia.

Global international politics had changed dramatically since the last time Chinese had been spoken in Ferghana bazaars. To the north and south, two previously unknown powers were converging. They would not only wipe self-governing Central Asia off the map but also threaten to divide and conquer the nominally Chinese dominions in the region as well. Britain and Russia had only come to blows much farther west, in the Crimea, but the Cossacks' relentless thrust south and east into what is now Kazakhstan and Turkmenistan in the 19th century alarmed the viceroy of Calcutta as he sought to maintain British links to the Middle East through Afghanistan and British-dominated Persia to the north and west. The so-called Great Game, about which much has been written by explorer-spies of the time as well as latter-day arm-chair adventurers, was most illustratively played out in Xinjiang, at the British and Russian legations to the Qing at Kashgar. With the advent of Russian and European intervention—punctuated by the Opium Wars of the mid-19th century—the Qing grew increasingly weak in the east and found that exerting control over the already lightly governed west became increasingly difficult. Chinese Central Asia was reduced to a mere backdrop for the global imperial struggle.

Russian emissaries negotiated a series of trade concessions in the west as well as along China's Pacific Coast. Regional politics were

increasingly manipulated by the two foreign diplomatic missions—
British and Russian—undermining Beijing's authority and fostering a
power vacuum. Then, as the Qing were at their weakest, a son of
Kokand crossed the Heavenly Mountains to lead a brief rebellion at
Kashgar, which spread throughout almost all of modern Xinjiang and
lasted for thirteen years, from 1865 to 1877. Yakub Beg, who is still
today venerated by many independence-minded Uyghurs, declared
allegiance to the Caliph in Constantinople, and cemented the Muslim
Turkic identity of the region in opposition to the Chinese "other."[10]
The Qing were able to suppress Yakub Beg's emirate by 1877, but they
had to negotiate unfavorable terms with the Russians, who had taken
the opportunity to annex large parts of northwestern Xinjiang. The
borders of Chinese territory in the west were not fully demarcated
until after the dissolution of the Soviet Empire.

It was during this time that the great explorers of Inner Asia, Nikolai
Przhevalsky, Sven Hedin, Aural Stein, and others, probed the deserts of
today's Xinjiang, mapping remote regions for the first time in history
and carting away the cultural riches of ancient Greco-Buddhist cities
buried beneath the sands of the Taklamakan desert. The so-called Silk
Road collections at the British Museum, the Louvre, and the
Hermitage, while understandably eliciting nationalist ire in China, are
some of the few relics rescued from destruction during China's tumultuous mid-20th century.[11]

After the Qing Dynasty collapsed in 1911, Republican governors of
Xinjiang were known more for corruption and petty conniving than
geopolitics. Stories abound of Japanese spies undermining central rule
across what was by then, at least on paper, an official province of
China. Han administrators were known for their aloofness and refusal
to speak local languages. When traveling through the region, the
American Sinologist Owen Lattimore claimed that these officials had
expressed the view that "the time had come to set about the business
of making all natives either turn Chinese or get out."[12] This suggestion seems implausible, especially given the very tenuous hold of the
Republican government on the region at the time. In 1931, as the

Japanese invaded Manchuria, discontent and localized revolts were rife across Xinjiang. When the vassal state of Kumul in northeastern Xinjiang was summarily abolished and its khan replaced by Han administrators, a three-way conflict broke out between forces loyal to the Republican Xinjiang governor, Kumul Uyghurs, and a Chinese Muslim (Hui) warlord.

Taking advantage of the chaos in the northeast and the struggle between Republican and Communist forces in the east, in 1933 Uyghurs in Kashgar once again rebelled, this time declaring themselves an independent state: the Turkic Islamic Republic of East Turkestan (TIRET). However in reality, this period was marked by a lack of authority that saw various warlords—Chinese, Turkic, Hui, Kyrgyz and Kazakh—competing for spoils. To reassert a façade of control, the new Republican governor, Sheng, "dealt with the devil" and invited the Soviets, who had just swept through former Imperial Russian Central Asia, brutally crushing nascent independence movements, to take effective military and economic control of most of Xinjiang. Sheng declared himself a Marxist and the Chinese civil war in the east gave way to Japanese occupation. While it was never officially annexed by the Soviets, the province effectively remained under Russian[13] control until 1950, when Chinese Communist forces took back control of Xinjiang while Moscow was preoccupied with Central Europe and the new Cold War.

With the borders of modern China as we know it having been established, Xinjiang was largely left to itself. In Chapter 2, we will go into greater detail about Beijing's policies toward the region, but first it is important to touch upon the nature of Xinjiang's relationship with Central Asia during the Cold War period in particular. A distant border of both empires, the line between China and the Soviet Union at Xinjiang's frontier was remote from both Moscow and Beijing. From Beijing's perspective, Central Asia was largely seen as a region with which Xinjiang could trade. The Chinese leadership saw the region's ethnic links to Central Asia as providing an opportunity which could be taken advantage of to help the region prosper.

During the Soviet invasion of Afghanistan, the region became a staging point of one of the many paradoxical relationships fostered during that conflict when China provided support for the American-marshalled, Pakistani-controlled, and Saudi-funded mujahedeen fighting the Soviets in Afghanistan. Building on the relationship forged in the wake of President Nixon's ground-breaking trip to Beijing in 1972, the United States negotiated Chinese support and basing rights to establish listening posts in Xinjiang which they could use to monitor the Soviet Union and support efforts in Afghanistan. In addition, Chinese-made weapons were funneled through to the fighters via Pakistan, helping strengthen a bond between China and Pakistan that later became a major regional lynchpin of the broader Belt and Road Initiative.

However, back during the Cold War the current vision espoused by Xi Jinping was on a distant horizon. Beijing's internal tumult during the Mao era largely consumed the leadership's attention, with Xinjiang and Central Asia relegated to a distant concern as China focused on Cold War conflicts to the east and south. Washington loomed as an adversary at various points, and continued to consume Beijing's attention. It was not until the collapse of the Soviet Union that the region started to grow in importance once more, principally through the vehicle of the Shanghai Cooperation Organization—which will also be handled in greater detail in a later chapter. At this stage, the key aspect to remember is that China is a Central Asian power, and one whose history and peoples are interlinked with those of the Central Asian countries themselves. This is not to give Beijing absolute primacy over the region, but it is an important factor to remember when seeking to understand China's regional interests.

On its West, China's Xinjiang Uyghur region borders Afghanistan and three
Central Asian countries

2

Developing the new frontier

Lake Karakul, Xinjiang, China

Xinjiang is one of China's most fascinating regions. Naturally beautiful, ethnically diverse, culturally and minerally rich, it is in many ways one of the main reasons why we started undertaking the research that drives this book. As inveterate consumers of Eurasian literature, we were both struck by the way in which Xinjiang acts as a crossroads of the continental landmass, yet is firmly placed within

China. This is not to deny that Xinjiang should be part of China, but rather it has a place at the heart of Eurasia which is often forgotten because it is within China's borders. In the future, the roads emanating from Xinjiang may be determinants in the flows of trade and power across the Eurasian heartland. From Beijing's perspective, it is the key to understanding the how and why of what China is seeking to achieve in Central Asia. As Wen Jiabao articulated to an audience we sat in at the imposing new auditorium of the Second China Eurasia Expo, Xinjiang and its capital Urumqi were to be the "gateway to Eurasia."[1]

To understand China's approach to Central Asia it is useful to first understand China's own relationship with its westernmost province of Xinjiang. China's piece of Central Asia is in many ways the sixth Central Asian state with a resident Uyghur community that is closer in ethnicity, culture, and language to the Central Asian countries it abuts than to what we traditionally think of as Han Chinese. The current borders of the region were defined in 1949 when the People's Liberation Army (PLA) pushed out the remnant Kuomintang forces from the region. The years leading up to 1949 were chaotic to say the least, as the central government in Nanjing struggled to control the region. Home to warlords and regular turmoil between different communities, it was an area in flux for decades as rival power centers sought to assert control of this remote region. Its final gasp of independence came in 1944 with the creation of the Soviet supported Second East Turkestan Republic (ETR), based in the region around the city of Yining. This was short lived, however, and by 1949 the districts that made up the ETR had joined the now Communist-led China.[2]

With the conclusion of the civil war and the Communist victory, something needed to be done to tie the distant and restive region back to Beijing. Aware of the region's history as a source of potential problems and its geographical distance from Beijing—the old Chinese saying goes "the hills are high and the Emperor is far away"—the Communists' approach to governing Xinjiang was markedly different from their predecessors. Acknowledging the reality that this was a restive province with few tangible links to the east, but imbued with an ideology that declared Xinjiang an indelible part of China for over 2,000 years, the new authorities in Beijing set about creating links that would never fade. The primary mechanism for tying Xinjiang to the east was and still is the Xinjiang Production and Construction Corps (XPCC). At its core a centrally controlled set of military units, the XPCC is responsible for internal and external security, including border protection, as well as agriculture, animal husbandry, industry, trade, and transport.[3]

The idea behind the XPCC and its control of the region was in many ways a reproduction of the approach that the ancient Romans had taken in dominating distant lands. Aware that the only way to truly guarantee loyalty was to have your own people there, Roman emperors would offer generous land concessions and opportunities to their legions who had conquered those territories. Some of the men would return to Rome, while others would take up the offer and stay to marry local women, establish families, till the land, and reinvent themselves. This cadre of men would become the ground forces who would help to reconfigure the ethnic make-up of regions and impose a permanent Roman presence at the further corners of the empire.

The XPCC replicated this approach by demobilizing many of the PLA cadres who had helped reclaim Xinjiang from the Kuomintang and creating an institutional structure around them to control the region.[4] This provided Beijing with a means of maintaining authority and increasing Han control, but also a way to focus efforts on developing the region and try to ensure its long-term prosperity and stability. As a region that was naturally rich in minerals, in a country with an already very crowded coast, it was an attractive area to maintain control over. During the years of the Cold War, especially after the Sino-Soviet split, during which the border (disputed as it was) with Soviet-controlled territories was remote, the XPCC's focus was on the conversion of Xinjiang from a generally pastoralist society to an agrarian and then industrial one. Before Communist control, around 6,500 square kilometers of land had been cultivated. By 1960, this figure was 30,000.[5]

The human migration westward, initially under the auspices of the XPCC, is one of the main means of Chinese control over the region, and is also one of the main sources of anger regionally. In 1953, Han made up about 6 percent of Xinjiang's population. Ten years later, Han constituted approximately 33 percent. Today, the Han population stands at just over 40 percent according to official census figures and appears to be growing as a proportion. The population that is increasingly finding itself under pressure is the Uyghur minority who used to dominate most of the territory. The Uyghur community sees their own country being transformed into something over which they have no control and in which they increasingly see themselves as a minority (it is worth noting that there are a number of other minorities also present, including large ethnic Kazakh, Kyrgyz, and Tajik populations, among others).

At the same time as the Uyghur community in Xinjiang has felt itself lost, its men and women have increasingly spread out around the country, working in jobs on the other side of China. In mid-2009, stories started to circulate of an incident in Guangzhou where some Uyghur women had allegedly been mistreated. These stories filtered back to Xinjiang where large protests were gathered. Accounts vary as to where exactly responsibility lies, but as these protest groups moved through the city they became violent, and mobs of angry Uyghurs rampaged around the city killing any Han they could find. Around 200 Han were reported killed before authorities were able to restore order.

The next day, angry Han counter-protested, furious at the authorities' massive security failure. Their anger was fanned by a series of images widely circulated via mobile telephone displaying images of disemboweled women accompanied by inflammatory statements about Uyghur atrocities. Marchers pushed through downtown Urumqi, the counter-protest culminating in a shouting match outside the local Chinese Communist Party (CCP) headquarters. One of the more dramatic images to emerge was that of the Xinjiang party chief Wang Lequan trying to calm the crowd from the top of a car as the angry group threw water bottles and other detritus at him. As a man who had ruled the region for almost fifteen years—a period unheard of among regional Chinese party chiefs—he was infamous for his strongman tactics and iron rule. Rumors of corruption swirled around him. One Chinese friend joked that he was an infamously "good son of Shandong," the region in which he had been born and whose companies had done remarkably well in Xinjiang's economy. He was close to then President Hu Jintao, having been part of his Communist Youth League faction, and sometimes described as his protégé.[6]

This relationship was what made the situation all the more complicated for the senior leadership. As the rioting was playing out in Urumqi, President Hu was in L'Aquila, Italy, for a Group of Eight (G8) Summit. Right when he should have been enjoying his time in the sun as helmsman of one of the world's great powers, he had to abruptly leave the summit and head back to China to manage this situation. Few others in the Chinese leadership could give orders to a man like Wang Lequan, and the total loss of local control demonstrated by the riot and counter-protest represented a massive failure of state control.[7] This humiliating moment became a major turning point in Beijing's policy for the region, the repercussions of which continue to be played out to this day.

It was not the first time in recent years that Beijing had faced large-scale violence in Xinjiang. In 1990, a protest in Baren, Kashgar prefecture, southern Xinjiang near China's border with Kyrgyzstan and Tajikistan, resulted in an unknown number of casualties after a group attacked a local police station. Reports suggested there had been talk of declaring independence. Official reporting suggested some sort of Afghan-linked network had been responsible, while other reports claimed it was in fact an outburst of local anger.[8] Then in February 1997 another outburst took place in Yining (also known as Gulja or Ili). Again, the roots of the clashes are unclear: government narratives pointed to "separatist" action while locals claimed it was a response to oppressive measures being imposed by local authorities. At least nine protestors were acknowledged to have been killed, but some reports indicated dozens had been gunned down, and there were reports of summary executions of captured protestors. Following this outbreak of violence, there were also reports of fatal bomb attacks in Urumqi, leading to further crackdowns.[9]

But while these protests took place at a sensitive time for China— 1997 was the year in which Hong Kong was handed over to China by the United Kingdom—their impact was relatively limited. Few had heard of Xinjiang, and China was not the big news story that it is today. An event in a far-off corner of the country might have had resonance in Beijing, but the world and country were focused on other things.

The context in 2009 was vastly different. China's ascent as an economic force on the planet was one of the dominant themes of international discourse. The age of sacred terrorism as defined by al Qaeda was ongoing, but large spectaculars seemed to be receding into the background. Great powers and their interactions were becoming the narrative of the day. China as the economic force that was going to manufacture our future was the driving vision, with the CCP riding the surf of wealth accumulation in order to drag China toward ranking with the first powers. Within this context, for the leader to have to abruptly exit the international stage to manage a clash on the country's fringes was an embarrassment and seemed like a problem from an earlier age.

In the aftermath of President Hu's return, there was a dramatic rethinking of policy for the region. This played out in a number of ways. In the first instance, there was a major reshuffle in leadership as the old guard was moved aside for new leadership. Urumqi Party Secretary Li Zhi and Xinjiang Public Security Bureau (PSB) leader Liu Yaohua were both sacked soon afterwards, being held responsible for the failure of authorities to respond quickly enough to the incident. In April 2010, Wang Lequan was moved aside, although nominally to a more senior position in Beijing as deputy secretary of the powerful political and legislative committee. While on paper this was a promotion, the move was widely seen as a punishment for the failures of the year before. It was also something of a repudiation of the

approach taken in the region that he had presided over, which suggested a major change might be coming in the government's approach
with Xinjiang. First, a new governor was appointed—Zhang Chunxian,
formerly of the historically poor and underdeveloped Hunan province, who was also well-known (at least, this was the narrative advanced
in the press) to be a man who understood modern communication
methods and would therefore be able to help the region respond to
the emerging problems it was facing.

However, in some ways far more importantly, a conference was held
in May of the following year which sought to develop a new work
plan for the region. The Xinjiang Work Conference was hosted by Li
Keqiang, who was at the time a vice premier tipped for a senior role,
and drew on President Hu's statement in the wake of the riots that
"the fundamental way to resolve the Xinjiang problem is to expedite
development in Xinjiang." Following the conference, a number of
new policies were announced, including the pairing of nineteen of
China's wealthier provinces or cities with parts of Xinjiang. In addition to sending between 0.3 and 0.6 percent of their annual budget
as aid, the wealthier provinces were made responsible for providing
technical support, including posting municipal staff and cadres to
Xinjiang for a year where their job was to help mentor the locals.[10] In
2012, Shanghai officials told us that while these positions were difficult posts, they were guaranteed ways toward promotion.[11] When we
visited later that year, we met senior Urumqi officials who originally
heralded from Xi'an.[12] Full of ideas and able to talk in terms that
would be attractive to international investors, these were clearly cadres
who were angling to rise within the CCP bureaucracy. There is a
tradition within China whereby those who serve in what are considered challenging or "hardship" posts receive high promotions—Wang
Lequan was widely reported to have been elevated to the Politburo
(China's central decision-making body) as a result of his time in
Xinjiang; Hu Jintao had risen to the top having served in Tibet.

Each of these cadres would bring their own approach to developing
the region. Shanghai sought to help the parts of Xinjiang it was

responsible for to emulate its own success as a financial center. The
Shanghai government would take groups of international and domestic bankers out to the region to help the locals establish how they
could turn Kashgar into a financial hub. Some of the foreigners who
had been invited told us how underdeveloped Xinjiang was, and
scoffed at the idea that it could become a financial hub of any sort. In
Tashkurgan, Tianjin officials sought to replicate their own industrial
success by creating an industrial hub—a somewhat fanciful idea if one
considers how very far off the beaten track the city is. In 2012, we met
a group of Chinese businesspeople in Tashkent a number of whom
were from Guangdong companies encouraged to go out to the region.
They had then followed the natural logic of exploring the opportunities in neighboring Central Asia. Few saw much opportunity, with
one grumbling about how poor the local populations were and how
difficult life in Xinjiang was. But these men were the frontline of
Beijing's attempt to bring some of the prosperity that had transformed
China's coasts to its inland regions.

Beijing also increased its budget for expenditure on the region and
ordered the large natural resource companies that mine Xinjiang's
hydrocarbon wealth to leave 5 percent of tax revenues in the province.
A new calculation was used to assess this price, with tax collected on
the basis of energy price rather than volume—meaning that at times
of high energy prices, the region would also receive more revenue.
Previously, everything had gone to Beijing or Shanghai, where the
companies tend to be listed or headquartered, which had been a
source of substantial resentment to Xinjiang natives and had reinforced
a narrative among Uyghurs of a parasitic state robbing them of their
wealth. The fact that energy firms tended to suffer due to issues of
corruption only served to accentuate this narrative. One of the biggest figures to be brought down in the anti-corruption campaign
President Xi Jinping initiated when he came into office was Zhou
Yongkang, a Politburo member who had previously served as chief of
CNPC (China National Petroleum Corporation)—overlapping with
Wang Lequan's time as party secretary of Xinjiang, a region where the

company had significant interests. Having been pushed out from Xinjiang, the committee in Beijing at which Wang went to work was headed by Zhou. These sorts of connections only serve to further stories of corruption and plunder.

The cities to spring up around where the oil wealth is concentrated are among the wealthiest in China. In 1955, China's biggest onshore oil field was discovered in Xinjiang's north. A city emerged nearby soon afterwards, named Karamay ("black gold" in Uyghur), which by some reports became the wealthiest city in China per capita for some time. In 2008, when oil prices were at their peak, gross domestic product (GDP) for the area around the city rose to RMB (renminbi) 66.1 billion. In 2015, the GDP per capita was calculated as being the second highest in China at $27,601, compared to $16,524 in Shanghai and $12,189 in Urumqi.[13]

Yet, the percentage of Uyghurs in Karamay and Xinjiang's wealthiest cities has always been low. Go to Xinjiang's west, where most Uyghurs are concentrated, and the wealth is nowhere to be seen. Kashgar has only recently been modernized as a city, and continues to suffer from underdevelopment. Any modernization that has come has been at the expense of the country's Uyghur heritage, with its old city rebuilt and cultural sites destroyed in favor of generic buildings ubiquitous across China or others designed with a mock ethnic feel to them. The richer cities in Xinjiang tend to be majority Han, and are often controlled by the XPCC. Shihezi, XPCC's capital in the north of the region, houses one of Xinjiang's most affluent universities and acts as a second, regional, capital. Prior to traveling to Xinjiang, we asked a prominent Beijing expert to suggest ideas as to whom we should arrange to meet. When we mentioned we were going to see some experts at Xinjiang University, he dismissed them and told us the only serious experts to visit were in Shihezi University, as they tended not to be drawn from minorities and were linked more closely to the Party. This off-handed racism highlights one of the key issues in Xinjiang, where locals are looked down upon and minorities are seen as being outside the realm of prosperity in the region. While we did meet senior Uyghur officials, the over-whelming majority were Han.

Seen from Beijing, part of the problem was a massive lack of invest-ment into Xinjiang's infrastructure, leading to another key pillar of the work plan to help the region undertake "leapfrog development" as Xi Jinping later put it. A frantic construction project was launched, focused on building infrastructure to connect the different parts of the vast region. Covering around a sixth of China's landmass, Xinjiang has a sparse population and pockets of substantial underdevelopment. Infrastructure around the region has historically been poor with long distances covered by only limited routes.

In the wake of the 2009 riots, there was a palpable increase in investment in infrastructure around the region. In October that year, China Telecom announced a RMB 15 billion investment over a five-year period, while November saw the start of construction of a high-speed train line between Lanzhou and Urumqi to help connect the region to China's growing network of high-speed trains. A giant bul-bous train station was planned for Urumqi. The May 2010 work plan was part of an acceleration of this investment. In its wake, CNPC announced it planned to invest RMB 300 billion during the twelfth Five-Year Plan (2011–15). The country's leading coalmining firms, Huaneng Group, Huadian Group, Luneng Group, China Coal Group, China Poly Group, and Guodian Group all reportedly announced investments of some RMB 100 billion during the same period.

Finally, three special economic zones (SEZ) were established in Kashgar, Khorgos, and Alataw—the latter two being border posts with Kazakhstan, in a bid to replicate the success of previous SEZs in places like Shenzhen. As part of our travels, we sought out these loca-tions to understand better what was going on in these SEZ, and the areas around them. The source of repeated news stories in the Western press (both then and now), our best approach we thought was to get up close and see what we could discover. The view from up close was as opaque in many ways as it was from far away. During a round of meetings in Urumqi in 2012 as part of a delegation, we got to meet some XPCC officials who would proudly highlight their role in managing the SEZs in Khorgos and Kashgar. Our interlocutor was a fierce female colonel who did not brook idiotic questions and laid out the clear plans that the *bingtuan* (兵团 "The Corps", the last two characters of the full Chinese name for the XPCC) had for the development areas, and offered to take any willing businesses around them. Following up on this later, we got no response, and ended up trying to head out to see them ourselves.

At their core, these SEZs are a reproduction of the projects that have transformed China's coasts. The idea is that what has worked on the coasts can work in the west to help develop the region and provide employment. It has in time become the standard mantra for Beijing to try to help expand prosperity in neighboring countries. A number of Belt and Road countries are currently exploring economic zones. But out in Xinjiang, it was not clear to us how much this was working. In Kashgar, we were only ever able to see construction sites, and while in Khorgos we were able to get much closer and even into the site of the border itself, there was very little to see beyond the usual clusters of border louts hanging about helping people out with odd-jobs, and rather misbegotten groups of people shuffling back and forth with goods on their backs. When we visited in 2012, the site was largely complete on the Chinese side but unfinished on the Kazakh side. While we never made it back again, subsequent reporting has shown how the site is now finished on both sides, but the trading that is going back and forth remains fairly limited. Large markets built in Khorgos seem to still be largely filled with products bought by Kazakhs who then carry them back across to sell at the markets. As we wandered around the largely empty buildings, people did not particularly rush to sell us products, staring instead at their phones or televisions. When we did find people to engage with, they were uninterested Han from the inland, selling products to travelers from across the border. Those we met at some of the nearby larger cities, like Yining or in Urumqi, later would report little had changed, and in fact, most researchers we met who had been to Khorgos on

similar research trips would state that while the infrastructure was
impressive, it was not clear how much it was actually being used.

★   ★   ★

Our trip to Khorgos started in Yining, the site of the 1997 clashes.
Close to the border with Kazakhstan, it is reportedly majority Kazakh.
However, our Uyghur cabbie begged to differ, proudly telling us of
how Uyghur the city was, and a Uyghur police officer proved the most
helpful person when we sought to locate our hotel.[14] The journey
from the city to Khorgos showcased the infrastructure construction
that was driving the region in the wake of Beijing's plans to redevelop
Xinjiang. Crossing the Yili river on a giant new bridge, the entire route
and journey was peppered with brand new constructions and buildings. At one stop, we picked up a guide to a newly built China Southern
Airline hotel—a grand building with a cavernous reception where
there was still plastic on the chairs and the toilets showed evidence of
having just been installed, with the plastic wrapping still visible.

Underlying tensions were palpable. At our hotel in Yining, a police-
man at the front desk repeatedly asked where we were from, what we
were doing, and so on as if on a loop. It did not take long to figure out
he was using the old interrogators' trick to see if we would slip up in
our tale, but this was new to the girl at the front desk who, exasperated by his repetitive questioning, finally said, "he just told you" only
to be told rudely to "shut up." This was in contrast to the friendly IT
man who came to fix the Internet, who heralded from Shanghai and
seemed very uncertain how he had ended up in this misbegotten
corner of his country. None of the Han Chinese we met expressed
much comfort about the region they were living in. And our Uyghur
guides were uniformly negative about the Han Chinese, with one
taking great pride in spitting on any signs he saw in Mandarin. This
young man had managed to become fluent in Mandarin and English
as well as in his native Uyghur; he was someone who should have
been thriving in this new economy China was building—yet he
found his opportunities regularly blocked and was stuck shuttling

foreigners around the region instead. When we asked him why he did not travel, he complained that he had been unable to get a passport, and told us stories of others who had faced similar problems.

These contrasts were found throughout Xinjiang, nowhere more so than in Urumqi, the regional capital which in many ways can boast the title of being Central Asia's beating heart. Xinjiang's capital is a gritty metropolis that could claim to be one of the most cosmopolitan cities in the great expanse between Shanghai and Istanbul. On the surface it resembles most second-tier Chinese urban landscapes—a testament to the lightning speed of economic development that has occurred over the past decade in what used to be a bleak backwater. But its myriad advertisements, signs, and business placards appear in Mandarin, Uyghur (written in Arabic script), as well as Russian, Kazakh, and Kyrgyz (all written in Cyrillic). Its museums boast of the region's diversity, and while it has become a largely Han city with only light touches of Uyghur and other minorities remaining, it is the bustling center of China's push into Central Asia.

On the street, in the immense electronics, clothes, and kitchenware (indoor and outdoor) markets and in the twenty-four-hour all-inclusive spas used by many traders as cheap hotels, you come across such diversity as Guangzhou businesspeople, next to uncertain Pakistani merchants from Peshawar, and rubbing up against entire Russian families, dressed in white as if on vacation in the Greek islands. Overnighting in the city on our way to Central Asia, we stayed at one of these twenty-four-hour spas where the discerning customer can enjoy computer games, swimming pools, saunas, films, and endless bouts of food, drink, and entertainment at very reasonable prices. We had the added bonus of being continually mistaken for Russian traders. At the markets we found a mix of entrepreneurs and salesmen from across Eurasia, Farsi-speaking Tajiks, or the many Turkic-speaking peoples, seeing how far their language would get them with the Turkic Uyghurs of Xinjiang.

All these people are in Xinjiang to do business. Elderly shuttle traders with overstuffed cargo bags will fly or bus back to their local markets in a remote region such as Karakalpakstan to resell plasticky Chinese merchandise at inflated prices to shepherds, farmers, and housewives. Take a plane from Urumqi airport and you are fighting for space alongside these traders who have packed and weighed their goods into masking-tape-wrapped packages that are exactly the right weight to be allowed onto the plane, but with little consideration to the space into which they have to cram themselves and the other passengers on the plane.

Mid-range container owners come to fill a couple rail carriages with air conditioners, laptops, or nylon carpets to take back to the bazaars of the Ferghana Valley on the train, where they will resell their items in bulk to retailers in affluent Kazakhstan or Russia. Urumqi has all of the brands and services available in China's major east-coast cities. It is just that they appear a bit more rough and ready: the latest Samsung smartphone is still in its bubble wrap, the flashy BMW is still on the transport truck. For those who have to come to the city to oversee deliveries, usually only a few visits are required before the deals are set up and then you can manage the business from afar. Across Central Asia we would meet energetic businesspeople who would report their desire to avoid returning to Urumqi unless they had to—something that was only accentuated as time went on and the security clampdown in the region got tougher.

The official population of Urumqi is around 3.5 million, with the overwhelming majority Han Chinese. But as with most Chinese cities, unofficial estimates sometimes add another million or two to that number. Apart from cultivating it as the capital of the autonomous region, the central government has boosted Urumqi's commercial credentials at the expense of Xinjiang's more historically traditional Silk Road trading cities of Kashgar and Turfan. To fly anywhere in Central Asia from the east, one will almost certainly fly China Southern through Urumqi. Whether it is intended or not, many flights onward to Tashkent, Almaty, Kabul, or Kashgar require an overnight stay in Urumqi. On our many trips across the region, we spent

a number of nights sampling this first hand. Flights were late or canceled, meaning missed connections and the pleasure of sharing a
China Southern hotel room in downtown Urumqi with some random Eurasian traveler. In one case, a shameless buxom Russian
babushka peeled off her clothes in front of us, on another some rapid
mandarin with the receptionist kept us in a private room away from a
shambolic-looking Afghan trader returning home after what looked
like an unsuccessful visit (everyone else ended up having to share
rooms). This stopover, however, has the effect of unexpectedly introducing all sorts of newcomers to Central Asia's commercial hub.
China's major railway and pipeline arteries heading west into Central
Asia, Russia, and the Middle East converge at Urumqi and fan out to
China's major urban centers from there.

Ever since the 2010 work plan conference, central planners in Beijing
have annually concentrated a lot of resources to underscore this point:
underwriting the China-Eurasia Expo, the region's premier trade fair
and aspiring Davos. During the year we attended, the six-day event
included speeches by Premier Wen Jiabao and a host of regional leaders,
from the Central Asian states to Pakistan, Turkey, and even the Maldives.
A smattering of professional former senior figures attended as well, most
notably former UK Prime Minister Tony Blair. Tens of billions of dollars'
worth of deals were reported as having been made, with everything from
Kyrgyz kalpak hats to Chinese tractors on display. A mock-up giant toy
Transformer by the heavy equipment manufacturer Sany stood guard
over the large stand selling the Chinese heavy vehicle firm's trucks. PLA
officers attending the meeting walked past it marveling at its size and the
imaginary potential adversary they might one day have to face.

The Afghans touted their mineral deposits, the Kazakhs their oil,
and local Xinjiang potentates repeatedly stressed the opportunities of
investing in Xinjiang. We visited as part of a UK delegation, with the
senior British investment coordinators reporting how eagerly Xinjiang
officials had lobbied them to bring large delegations to discover the
opportunities in the region and beyond. Once out in the region, the

British firms were somewhat at a loss, unclear about what these
opportunities might be—something further confused by the fact that
most of the employees were in fact Han Chinese and predisposed to
be fearful of this region so far from the eastern seaboard of China that
they knew and heralded from.

Sat in meetings in Urumqi with the delegation, it was clear that the
driving message was one of opportunity in Xinjiang that was there for
the taking. One of the main opportunities was the access the region
provided to the Eurasian heartland. As articulated in the twelfth Five-
Year Plan adopted by Beijing in March 2011, "Xinjiang will serve as a
base for our 'opening up' up the West." This narrative was repeatedly
laid out during this visit and many subsequent visits to Xinjiang. The
key for Beijing was to ensure economic prosperity in the region, to
help quell the anger between the ethnic communities in the region.
As banners screamed around the Expo site and across the city,
"Harmonious Development Cooperation Win-Win." Eager businesspeople from Chinese firms operating in the region and active across
Central Asia rushed up to swap business cards and establish links with
British firms that might be interested in working in the region.
Subsequent visits to the region, as well as encounters with Xinjiang
delegations in the UK and elsewhere emphasized this point.

And in some western capitals, the idea appeared to resonate. The
British government under David Cameron and George Osborne's
tutelage embraced the idea with the chancellor, Britain's finance minister, George Osborne, even going so far as to visit the region as part
of London's attempt to engage with this opportunity. He visited factories and companies that were exploring opportunities in the UK, while
also seeking to understand what the region might offer the UK as a
potential target for investment. German car-maker VW went further
and undertook to establish a joint factory for its saloons in Urumqi
with its joint venture partner SAIC. This particular deal was not one
that VW was initially very keen on, with the then CEO reporting that
the Chinese authorities and SAIC had been very persuasive in their
attempt to get the company to open the factory.[15] SAIC was under

pressure itself to do more business in Xinjiang, and was keen to show it would help advance the central government's edict that the wealthier parts of the country help the poorer ones. Years later some of this effort was painted in a more negative light, with VW accused of using forced Uyghur labor in its supply chains to support the factory.[16] At the same time, some of the investment that Chancellor Osborne had sought was materializing in Manchester in the form of real estate projects undertaken by the Xinjiang Hualing Group.[17]

★ ★ ★

Over time, reports of forced labor have become more common.[18] Postings found on WeChat suggested they were even being trafficked around the country to work. As these stories came out, greater pressure emerged internationally to try to clamp down on economic contacts with Xinjiang, with accusations emerging that almost no part of the supply chain that touched Xinjiang was untainted. This is a major problem for China, which sees economic prosperity, in part linked to Central Asia, as the long-term answer to Xinjiang's stability.

At the same time, in the medium to short term there were difficult security issues to be addressed. During our visit in 2012, there was evidence of a heavy security presence around the Eurasian Expo—something unsurprising given the level of participation at the event we were attending. But subsequent visits showed an increasingly beefed-up security presence across the region. By our visits in 2016, the airport had multiple layers of security—a cordon that stretched back to the departure airport in Shanghai where those flying to Xinjiang were subjected to additional, enhanced searches. Once in the city, street corners were protected by armored personnel carriers with circles of heavily armed police standing firmly to attention. In the historically minority-dominated Erdaoqiao sections of the city, outside the city's biggest mosques there were teams of fierce-looking armed police, while airport-style security had become *de rigueur* to get into most buildings.

As time went on this was upgraded even further, with iris scanners added to the usual bag checks, as well as all-pervasive CCTV with facial recognition technology, and dramatic measures like banning matches in parts of the region (after reports emerged of an incident in which people used the powder in match heads to create an explosive[19]). After knives became a regular feature of terrorist attacks, shops started to brand them with quick response (QR) codes which were linked to people's identity (ID) cards,[20] meaning in the event of an incident the knife could be traced back to the original purchase. Petrol purchases were similarly linked. Rumors circulated that this was in turn linked to individual car usage, theoretically meaning the government has all the data required to be able to track any discrepancies between purchase and usage. A growing number of cameras in Xinjiang monitoring roads were apparently outfitted with automatic number plate recognition (ANPR) software which could be used to track vehicles. A foreign traveler who wanted to drive around the region in the mid-2010s told us of how he had run out of petrol in the region's empty northern regions and had struggled to buy petrol as the shop owner would not sell it to him in the absence of a formal Chinese ID. He had had to wait until a friendly Han driver took pity on him and let the traveler buy petrol on his card.

Beijing's efforts to assert control stretch in many other directions as well. For example, everything in Xinjiang operates two hours later than in Beijing, though the official time is the same as in Beijing's. This makes for oddly confusing schedules at extreme times of the year, and an additional problem of having to verify whether meetings are set to be at Beijing or Urumqi time (people tend to specify—something that took a while to work out when we first went there and led to some missed meetings).

Culturally, central government has also sought to assert control through a rebuilding program to modernize the region's housing infrastructure. In February 2010, the government in Urumqi announced a RMB 3.54 billion ($520.6 million) to demolish old houses and relocate 10,000 families. To compensate the displaced people, the local government announced they would invest RMB 1.2 billion ($176.5 million) to renovate what the domestic press called "shantytowns." Mostly housing the variety of different ethnic groups resident in Urumqi, the "shantytowns" dated back to the 1930s. Visit Urumqi today and you will find a city not dissimilar to most other Chinese cities with only elements of Uyghur decoration maintained across the city. This push to destroy local cultural institutions goes far beyond Urumqi. Most famously, Kashgar's old city has been largely destroyed and rebuilt in a push going back decades that we watched unfold over the years we visited. The reason that was often given was to make the areas safer and more accessible to emergency services, something that is likely true when one considers how small and crooked many of the roads in the old city were, but it is not clear that it is being done with the consent or support of all locals. More recently, a push to subjugate religion has extended to destroying mosques and religious cemeteries. Close analysis by researchers using satellite imagery shows the degree to which this has been done across the region. In some cases, mosque structures have been reappropriated for other purposes, but in many cases they have simply been destroyed.[21]

But it was the stories from locals about tension between communities that were the most depressing. A Han couple we met on the plane flying to Urumqi from Shanghai, eager to show us the beauty of their region, preferred to take us to artificial minority sites rather than genuine Uyghur areas, complaining of how dangerous the Uyghur areas were. Our Uyghur driver on another occasion spent most of a long car ride telling us how malicious the Chinese were, how some Chinese "you just want to wring their neck" and spitting when he saw signs of the Party or Beijing's dominance. Long-term Han residents resented the growing security state, fearful of the consequences of it and feeling the same pressure that their Uyghur neighbors felt from the police state that was being built around them. Han we met outside Xinjiang who were originally from the region had little desire to return. Clashes between communities seemed regular enough that people took little notice when they did occur. On our way to Yining from Urumqi, we watched as a middle-aged Uyghur man lost his temper with security guards who were manhandling his wheelchair-bound mother. He started attacking the security guard with his mobile phone, which led to a fight; the two men had to be pulled apart by police, leaving blood splattered all over the floor. All around them, however, the airport operated normally, with check-in continuing and people muttering to each other about the depressing normality of such events. The Uyghur man at the center of the spat seemed to be simply someone who had reached the end of his tether, but who was now clearly caught up in what had been turned into a formal security incident.

The repeated instances of violence in the region have meant Xinjiang has always been under a relatively heavy security regime, though not in a way that is uniformly applied across communities. Regular "strike hard" campaigns have taken place in response to instability and violence—mostly targeted at subjugating the Uyghur populations through the heavy deployment of security officers. But in recent years the level of security and policing in the region has grown exponentially, with thousands of security officials hired. According to figures by expert independent academics James Leibold and Adrian Zenz, in 2015 around 9,000 security positions were advertised in Xinjiang, a number that jumped to just over 30,000 in 2016, and doubled again during the first half of 2017 to just over 60,000.[22] Across the region, an ever-tighter and more pervasive network of police stations has been developed, with closed-circuit television (CCTV) installed with greater frequency and the establishment of what are described as "convenience police stations"—smaller bases for police and security forces to operate from among the people, providing a greater degree of coverage.[23] Visiting in 2016 and 2017, you could see these smaller police stations almost everywhere in Urumqi, including some in mobile caravans that appeared to be only semi-temporary.

Large-scale patriotic military parades, oath-taking ceremonies and training of security forces have become commonplace, while the distant corners of the region near Xinjiang's borders with Central Asia are policed by armed soldiers and police, with drones buzzing overhead. Tashkurgan, capital city of the Tajik Autonomous County and the last stop before the border posts to Afghanistan, Pakistan, and Tajikistan, is dominated by a military base on its fringes, with regular patrols through the city. Historically significant, thanks to a stone fort that overlooks the town (which also gives the city its name—Tashkurgan roughly translates as Stone Fortress in Turkic), the vista from the fort looks down the sweep of a valley that links China to South Asia, highlighting the strategic importance of the city. The fort now sits as a pile of rubble on top of a hill open to tourists, while the soldiers deployed there are focused on internal threats rather than foreign ones.

The biggest threat that China increasingly sees internally in Xinjiang is driven by the Internet and social media. Always a challenge to access in China, the Internet is perceived as even more problematic in Xinjiang. In the wake of the 2009 riots, the local government placed an almost total clamp down on all communications in and out of the region. When we visited in 2010, people would report that it was still impossible to send pictures via phone messages—Han we spoke to would tell of how around the time of the riots hideous pictures showing Goya-esque images of murder and torture had been circulating along with accusations of these being the acts of Uyghur. Businesspeople would report having to go to neighboring regions to send communications or use faxes to get word to suppliers or customers who were not in the province. This was a major topic of conversation during our visit in 2012, accompanying a business delegation, with everyone asking how it was going to be possible for them to be able to communicate with the rest of the country, their head office, or the rest of the world if they were to start doing business in the region. Sitting across the table from us during a meeting in an Urumqi government building, a senior official from Xi'an who had been sent to the region to help it develop, firmly said that this was an exceptional situation that would not happen again.

In fact, while the Internet clampdown was not repeated in the same way in the years after the 2009 riots, partial clampdowns did take place, some restrictions imposed after the riots stayed in place, and there was a gradual tightening of all control of communications in and out of the region. People with whom we were accustomed to talk slowly became quieter and quieter, unable or unwilling to maintain communications in an environment that was increasingly penetrated and controlled. The fact we were foreigners no doubt made it harder, but as time went on it became clear that all communications from the region were being made difficult.

In late 2015, stories emerged that people who had used virtual private networks (VPNs), a tool used to get around China's Internet firewall, or had downloaded foreign messaging or social media applications, suddenly found their phones cut off. To get the phone reactivated, they had to report to a police station and ensure their ID card was properly linked to their online activity and to stop using VPNs or accessing certain foreign applications. By 2017, local authorities made it mandatory for people to download an application on their phones called Jinwang (meaning "web cleansing"), which was ostensibly to be a "web filter" to protect the user, but it was reportedly intended to stop people accessing "terrorist information" according to local authorities in the region who had issued the orders to install it. Credible reports in the media started to circulate that police were stopping people at checkpoints to ensure that they had downloaded the application. Failure was met with arrest in some cases. The application was not just a web filter, but also reportedly a way to give authorities remote access. People whom we would meet from Xinjiang, increasingly meeting them outside the region, would complain of how difficult it was to get over the Internet blocks, how most people had multiple phones, and how police were developing ever-more comprehensive tools to track you down.

But the most terrifying response at the regional level was the mass detentions that began to be reported in 2016 and 2017, when stories started to emerge of what were called "re-education camps" being opened across the region. As part of new regional Party Chief Chen Quanguo's efforts to stabilize and control Xinjiang, a network of camps was created across the region, where people suspected of any manner of anti-state activity were sent to be taught the error of their ways. In many ways, this was an enhanced version of the political re-education camps that have always played a role in China, and that in the past were solely focused on ensuring adherence to Marxist ideology. These camps in Xinjiang appear to have taken in many thousands of people (with some reports, including some from the United Nations (UN), suggesting the numbers may be up to a million). The camps seem to be an approach that built on Mr Chen's earlier innovation of "convenience" police stations and a net-like web of tools to control and pry into most aspects of citizens' lives. Additional programs included sending Party cadres to live with Uyghur families, to further deepen the monitoring and to try to stimulate integration. All of these were tools that Mr Chen had previously deployed during his time in Tibet, when he brought a superficial calm to a region that has long proven complicated for Beijing to manage.

Independent reporting is difficult to verify, but there can be no doubt of the existence of these camps, in part as a result of reporting that emerged from Kazakhstan in 2018. As a growing number of stories emerged of ethnic Kazakhs from China or those with families and other links in China getting caught up in these camps, there was an increasing volume of complaints by Kazakhs to the government in the Kazakh capital of Astana (since renamed Nursultan).[24] The local authorities felt such pressure from these stories that they found themselves having to raise them during formal bilateral engagements with Beijing. Kazakh courts started to hear cases of Chinese-Kazakhs who had fled across the border and sought asylum in Kazakhstan, which had started to acquiesce to their requests for asylum. In one case, a Chinese-Kazakh woman was able to effectively fight her extradition to China after complaining that she was going to be persecuted and incarcerated unfairly if she was sent back. Among the most frightening claims she made was that she had seen and experienced forced sterilization, as China sought not only to subjugate the Uyghur communities through re-education in camps but now also to stop them

reproducing. These horrific reports were difficult for us to verify
independently, though growing numbers of credible news and research
organizations have sought to do so. China's aggressive denials have gone
so far as to personally threaten the researchers involved, but the story
has persisted and was one we heard repeatedly from independent voices
in Central Asia. The published reports were damning in their objective,
detailed analysis.[25] This is in some ways a repeat of earlier historical
reports of Uyghurs complaining about birth control methods being
imposed upon them. During the 1990 uprising in Baren, Kashgar
prefecture, one of the complaints made by angry locals was over the
imposition of birth control policies by Beijing, seeking to force Uyghur
women to be sterilized and to abort fetuses. At the time of course such
birth control policies applied to everybody after the first child.

The tensions generated with neighboring Kazakhstan (and to a less
public degree with Kyrgyzstan and Tajikistan, which also have diaspora communities in China) represent a potential threat to China's
vision for joint prosperity between Xinjiang and Central Asia. China's
neighbors are already deeply concerned about Chinese dominance,
concerns which are only likely to be exacerbated as time goes on.
Beijing's dominating behavior in Xinjiang points to a potential pattern of activity that they fear might spill over their borders. During
our travels, we would regularly hear such fears voiced in dark terms
from Central Asians, though the worries tended to be fairly unfocused
and mostly about what worrying lessons their governments might
learn from the Chinese experiences in using such draconian measures
to control their populations. We rarely found much sympathy or concern for the plight of Uyghurs, though there were sometimes fears
about fellow Kazakhs or others caught up in China.

The problem for Beijing is that if the fabric tying these two loca-
tions together is the people, and they are now pushing back, it becomes
very difficult for China to guarantee a smooth ride in strengthening
links with Central Asia as a means of stabilizing Xinjiang. If the public
are unhappy, this will affect how the local governments respond. While
the Central Asian governments are (with the exception of Kyrgyzstan)

one-party systems, they are sensitive to internal public opinion. And if it turns dramatically against China, they will be responsive. This is, for example, visible in the shrinking willingness of Central Asian governments to sign up to letters circulated through the UN expressing support for Chinese policies in Xinjiang or Hong Kong. They are unlikely to condemn China, but increasingly they are unlikely to want to actively support the country. This is a problem for China. From Beijing's perspective, this security response to local unrest is only part of the picture. The longer-term answer to stability in Xinjiang is economic investment and prosperity, which for Xinjiang is intimately reliant on good relations with the region it abuts in Central Asia. If the communities on the ground are unwilling to play along, and the central authorities in the Central Asian capitals are only willing to withhold their private views up to a point, China finds itself with a key complicating element in its plan to enhance Xinjiang's prosperity.

Our narrative does not seek to discount China's understanding of its own territory. The key point for us here is how China sees Central Asia as intimately linked to China, and the importance of Xinjiang within China's policy for the region. We assert that when considering China's role in Central Asia, this is as much a domestic question as it is a foreign policy one, and it is tied to a particularly complicated part of China. This is a key aspect which distinguishes China's policies toward Central Asia from its policies toward other parts of the developing world, such as Africa. China–Africa relations do not have the same underlying domestic imperative. Hence our central claim is that China's Central Asia policy is primarily a component of Beijing's policy for Xinjiang, predicated on domestic security concerns and economic development imperatives. To understand Chinese activities, old and new, beyond the Heavenly Mountains, it is crucially important to understand the central government's goals to the east of the range.

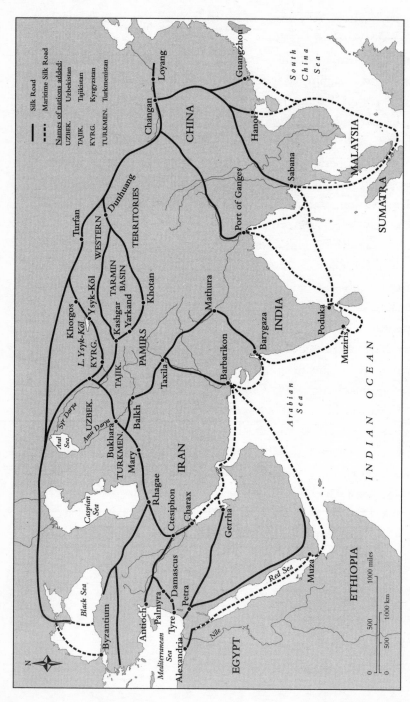

The modern East–West connections across the Eurasian heartland are notably similar to the network of interlinking corridors that formed the ancient silk road

Turkmenistan

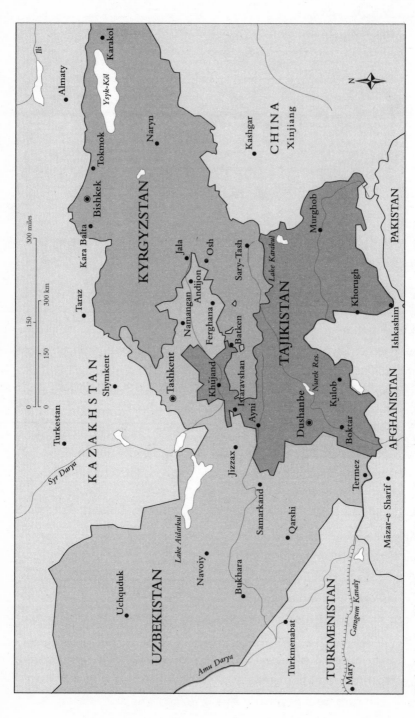

Today's national borders do not reflect the spread of Central Asian peoples across the region

3

Cake, heaven sent

Turkmenistan's southeastern desert, not far from the border with Afghanistan, is a forbidding place. Its bleak, dusty vistas are punctuated by the ruins of ancient *caravanserais*: rest stops on the old Silk Road. But the silence of that long-lost East–West artery is now regularly broken by the rumble of Chinese truck convoys. These are not ordinary tractor-trailers: they move slowly carrying massive loads of natural gas extraction equipment. According to Turkmen officials, the shepherds' bridges and village roads have had to be reinforced because of the weight of the trucks. The equipment is headed to one of the top five natural gas fields in the world. Formerly known as South Yolotan-Osman, in 2011 the field was renamed Galkynysh, or "renaissance" in Turkmen. The name is apt because this gargantuan reserve of natural gas is the prize motivating China National Petroleum Corporation (CNPC) to revive the old Silk Road, only this time by pipeline.

Silk Road scholars often point out that there was never one route from China to Europe through Central Asia. The old Silk Road was a network of interlinking corridors that formed a spider's web of connections, east–west and north–south across Eurasia. CNPC and China's energy strategy for Central Asia looks notably similar. It is anchored by two main arteries—the Central Asia–China gas pipeline that runs all the way from Turkmenistan's south to China's east coast cities (more than 10,000 kilometers) and the Kazakhstan–China oil pipeline, which runs from Atyrau on Kazakhstan's coasts with the Caspian to Alashankou in China.

But these are just at the core of what is a much wider web of energy connections across the region. This goes from energy pipelines, oil and gas fields, uranium mines, new solar furnaces, wind farms, electricity power, refineries as well as much more. And for Beijing, the land beyond the Heavenly Mountains is not just a source of energy resources, but also copper, zinc, gold, and food. For China's central planners and extractives firms, Central Asia is an opportunity waiting to be harvested.

Beijing's appetite for Central Asia is most clearly visible in oil and gas. It is also often the main thing that people focus on when they are looking at China in that region. Beijing's unslakable thirst for natural resources to feed its endlessly growing industrial machine is the most obvious point of connection between Central Asia and China. The topic is also one that lends itself easily to the "Great Game" discussions that often dominate any research or writing about Central Asia—geopolitics in Eurasia is a rich topic that draws people in with visions of buccaneering adventure and strategic games playing out across far-off lands. China has in many ways mastered this game, with energy being one of the first plays it made across the region.

Even before CNPC had completed its Central Asia–China gas pipeline, it began building and talking about building additional spurs from that main line not only to the major energy producers of Turkmenistan, Kazakhstan, and Uzbekistan but also to energy-needy Kyrgyzstan, Tajikistan, and Afghanistan. The long-term vision we were told from Beijing's perspective was not only to source gas from Turkmenistan but ultimately potentially to sell it around the region.[1] By Chinese standards the volumes are small, but they provide important geopolitical leverage for CNPC and Beijing, which is supplemented by other infrastructure that China is building in the region.

CNPC seems to have taken a page from Gazprom's playbook. Russia's state-controlled energy monopoly used its stranglehold on Moscow's former colonies in Central Asia to extend the Kremlin's power over the region. Up until the early 2000s, Kazakhstan,

Turkmenistan, and Uzbekistan were largely dependent on Gazprom-controlled Soviet-era pipelines for export of their gas through Russia and on to Europe. The Russian middle man not only added a hefty price markup but also dictated prices, terms, and gas flows to the holders of the gas. It was this domination that prompted cautious, avowedly neutral Ashgabat to invite CNPC not only to build a major pipeline on its territory but also to have rights to natural gas production sharing onshore in Turkmenistan in Bagtyarlyk, in Gumdak, and later in the Galkynysh.

The discussion between the Turkmen and Chinese dated back to Li Peng's time and visit to the region in 1994. In 2000, President Jiang Zemin visited and signed a bilateral agreement with Saparmurat Niyazov, the self-proclaimed Turkmenbashi (father of the Turkmen) to open up Turkmen gas to China. Gumdak was finally agreed in 2002 following an example that had been set by Kazakhstan when in the late 1990s they signed an agreement with CNPC to develop some of their aging oil fields near the Caspian. Signed in 1997 between the Kazakh authorities and CNPC, it took just under a decade for the pipeline linking China to the fields to be completed and for work to start. Since then, it has pumped more than 100 million tonnes of oil.

Premier Hu Jintao set CNPC's wider gas pipeline plans in motion in 2003 when he visited Kazakhstan to secure Astana's cooperation for what was dubbed at the time the "Pan Asian Global Energy Bridge," with explicit plans for connections through central and western China, Central Asia, and Iran to the Gulf.[2] At the time, Galkynysh's riches had not been confirmed and Turkmenistan was mainly viewed by CNPC as an addition or a thoroughfare. Their energy deals in Turkmenistan were substantial, but Kazakhstan was seen as the key play in the region. But when Gaffney Cline, a respected British energy auditing firm, announced that Turkmenistan's southeastern gas fields gave the country the world's fourth largest reserves, CNPC doubled down on its plans to make the small desert country the hub of its regional wheel of energy infrastructure.[3] The Central Asia–China gas pipeline was duly built in eighteen months, the fastest built pipeline

of its size in history. Gas started flowing in 2009, with capacity set to
more than double to a massive 60 billion cubic meters a year by 2015.[4]

Things have not played out exactly to schedule. On our first round
of talks with experts about China's extraordinary push to dominance
in Turkmenistan, people would excitedly talk of the many "strings"
that were being planned. Discussions around Central Asian energy
always have a somewhat hysterical tone to them as people enjoy the
high-power geopolitics and technical complexity of the projects in
the region. The initial four "strings," or individual pipes, were different
routes traversing Turkmenistan, Kazakhstan, Uzbekistan, northern
Afghanistan, and Tajikistan, with spurs in Kazakhstan, Uzbekistan, and
Kyrgyzstan, as well as a "trans-Turkmen" connection to the Caspian
Sea, where it has been consistently speculated that CNPC or other
Chinese state-owned enterprises (SOEs) are contemplating offshore
extraction.[5] These are the resources that have for almost two decades
been mooted as part of the so-called Southern Gas Corridor to
Europe. But, while Western energy companies and governments
dithered over the scope and political niceties of the Nabucco, Trans-
Adriatic, and Trans-Caspian pipelines, as well as their many competing
projects, CNPC and Chinese diplomats in Central Asia had rammed
their project through and now they sit in the hot seat of Eurasian
energy geopolitics.[6]

But as can be the case with such ambitious concepts, it did not all
go according to plan. While the first three pipelines were built and
pumping quickly, the fourth, "Line D," proved difficult. Numerous
different reasons were provided—from technical issues, disputes over
the route, to the more basic reason that China did not need the gas.
Talking to Chinese businesspeople in 2015 their perspective was that
the hold-up was a product of the Tajik government asking for spurs
the Uzbek authorities did not like (the suggestion made was that this
would increase Tajikistan's energy independence, something which
Uzbekistan at the time had no interest in supporting). Chinese oil
executives were even more cynical and pointed to local government
incompetence while complaining about their boredom over being

deployed in the country. When in late 2016 we had meetings in
Ashgabat, the authorities there instead suggested that the key issue
was Chinese demand. Sitting across the room from us talking in mysterious non-specific terms, they suggested the country was finding
China a less-than-reliable partner.

In fact, it was more likely a recognition of the danger of having a
single customer whose moods or appetites might change leaving
Ashgabat with a natural resource it could not cash in on. For them,
the lesson was to start to look to other clients, something that they
struggled to do, lacking consensus on the routes across the Caspian,
still being in dispute with Russia, and stuck with a cash-poor Iran on
the other side. This led to a very noisy push by the Turkmen authorities to start the process of building the Turkmenistan-Afghanistan-
Pakistan-India (TAPI) pipeline to try to create a new market. But
while Ashgabat was able to mobilize some resources to start this
process, it lacked credibility. One story we had been told during our
travels was that China was interested, but we struggled to pin down
details. In mid-2018, a story leaked into the media from a Pakistani
official who claimed that CNPC had expressed an interest, through
feasibility studies, in supporting TAPI. Possibly part of a bigger regional
play by the company seeking to strengthen its regional role, it suggested the bigger energy vision the firm has for the region. While not
impossible, it seemed unlikely that CNPC would be eager to embark
on a leadership role in a project that has been long mooted and tra-
verses complicated and unstable territory to supply two powers locked
in conflict, one of which (India) is an increasingly angry geopolitical
rival in the region.

By winter 2017, the volumes of gas coming down the pipelines to
China were not adequate—Chinese officials complained that the
Uzbek and Kazakh authorities were tapping into gas from the lines
meaning the volume that was getting to China was down. One result
was that CNPC had to issue warnings for factories to use less gas, and
electricity production using coal-fired plants was ramped up. All of
which meant that by mid-2018 the process of building Line D was

back on the agenda, placing China once again as the major purchaser of Turkmen gas and retaining its controlling stake in the region's gas energy infrastructure. The sagacity of this decision was once again starkly thrown into question when Chinese demand once again abruptly dropped off in early 2020 in response to the Coronavirus outbreak leading to an abrupt loss of income which translated directly into cash shortages in Turkmenistan and queues at ATMs. At the same time, the Turkmen leader soon afterwards visited the fields and announced the opening of new gas pumping stations and two new CNPC wells. While discussions over Line D have persisted since then and Turkmenistan is reported to have cleared its debts with China, it is still unclear when the pipeline will actually get completed, with Chinese domestic gas production increasing as well as various other sources. The key issue is that while Central Asian producers continue to see themselves as steering the conversation about selling hydrocarbons to China, Beijing appears skillfully able to continue to control the terms of agreements leaving it in the driving seat.

★ ★ ★

As CNPC's major gas artery snakes southwest through a growing latticework of routes, its main oil artery winds northwest to Kazakhstan's myriad oil wells. While Western companies spend decades and tens of billions of dollars trying to get offshore mega-projects online in the Caspian Sea, Chinese SOEs have artfully snapped up production rights for already established Soviet-era fields, upgrading them enough to ensure that the oil flows eastward.[7] They have also taken advantage of good relationships in Kazakhstan's relatively open investment climate to buy into subsidiaries of KazMunaiGas (KMG), Kazakhstan's state-controlled energy company, or buy some of the country's energy concerns, such as Aktobemunaigaz, outright. CNPC now controls more of Kazakhstan's oil output than any single Western company.[8]

Visiting Aktobe, Kazakhstan, in 2013, we found a city which was heavily influenced by China, and yet where the Chinese footprint was almost completely invisible. Going around the city, we would ask where the Chinese workers were or where the city's Chinatown was, and the response we got was that such a thing did not exist. When we finally spoke to some Chinese engineers, they mentioned that their main residence at the time was outside the city in an old Soviet-era sanatorium that had been remodeled as accommodation for them.

The Kazakhstan–China oil pipeline, also a staggeringly rapid endeavor in operation since 2006, connects refineries in Xinjiang to Kazakhstan's northwest, the traditional oil-producing region. Its transit volumes have increased by 20 percent a year since its inauguration. In April 2013, CNPC announced plans for further expansion of the pipeline,[9] and by 2019 the operator reported that it had delivered a total of 10.88 million tonnes of crude oil to China over the course of the year and that 130 million tonnes had since been commissioned.[10] As an overall proportion of China's oil imports this volume is relatively modest, but it is a consistent amount that China is able to rely on.

However, CNPC's most remarkable oil extraction projects in the region are those in Afghanistan's northern Sar-e-Pul province. While output is tiny compared to that of CNPC's operations in Kazakhstan, the Kashkari, Bazarkhami, and Zamarudsa blocks have been the first to pump oil in Afghanistan since the US-led intervention in 2001. When we visited in 2013, the crude oil was reportedly being trucked in convoys across the border to Turkmenistan to be refined. Years later, people reported this was instead happening in Afghanistan, though we were unable to ever verify this. Understanding what was actually taking place was impossible, and local Afghan officials were never able to provide a clear answer.

We heard varying reports about how the project was initiated and the problems it had encountered along the way. When starting the project, CNPC had partnered with the Karzai family (related to modern Afghanistan's first president, Hamid Karzai) linked Watan Group as a way of trying to mitigate some of the problems they had observed other Chinese companies encounter and to strengthen their relations with relevant power brokers. A likely astute political move in Kabul, it was something that had angered the dominant figure locally, notorious warlord General Rashid Dostum (who also served for some time as vice president). This led to problems for the company on the ground. One long-serving foreign oil executive based in the region who was friendly with the CNPC managers running the site, told us how at one point the Chinese engineers had been stuck in their encampment as armed men on motorbikes swarmed around their site in a scene reminiscent of the film *Mad Max*. In an attempt to bet on the region for the long-haul, the Chinese SOE arranged security relationships with local militias and reportedly doled out cash to key regional authorities.[11]

A public goal that CNPC was repeatedly reported as pursuing was to help build a refinery in northern Afghanistan, something that would not only help resolve the question of where the hydrocarbons would be processed but would also help the country take a step toward energy independence. For CNPC it also appeared as though the project might be integrated into the broader Eurasian energy network that the company is establishing as a further "string" of the Central Asia–China gas pipeline network.[12] Chinese pipeline executives we spoke to would talk about how the company was exploring opening an office in Afghanistan to service this project, but it was unclear this ever opened or that the refinery project was ultimately delivered.

The uncertainty around the office did not inspire much confidence about CNPC's appetite, but the broader concept linked the potential project into the company's regional interests, something which clarifies their reasoning behind going into Afghanistan in the first place. The project was reportedly one that their engineers in Turkmenistan pushed the company to undertake, aware of the rich gas field they were already exploiting across the border which came from the same pool of hydrocarbons on offer in the Afghan project.[13] By taking on the oil project, the company, we were told, felt it was establishing a footprint in Afghanistan which would stand it in good stead when the larger gas opportunities came to tender.

When put in perspective, this picture is even more striking. The juxtaposition of China's wide-ranging energy infrastructure projects in Central Asia, particularly in natural gas, with the region's relatively paltry place in China's overall energy consumption is telling. While percentages are quickly increasing, in 2011 around 12 percent of natural gas consumed in China was imported from abroad. In the same year, gas only made up about 5 percent of China's overall energy consumption. With liquefied natural gas (LNG) imports and other sources, Central Asian gas makes up a minute part of China's global energy network. Current plans for the country aiming to have gas account for around 10 percent of its national energy mix by 2020, and to increase to 15 percent by 2030.

By 2018, China had achieved a rate of 7 percent natural gas in its energy mix, with about 30 percent imported. Of this, a big part came from Central Asia, with a smaller portion from Myanmar. As the Russian "Power of Siberia" line starts to produce more gas, and with growth in LNG, the proportion of Central Asian gas in China's mix will decrease. But nevertheless, Central Asian gas will remain an important part of China's energy mix, and one that comes in a far more secure and safe manner than the riskier sea imports of LNG which could get caught in the same Malacca Straits Dilemma that has troubled China's oil imports.

China's preeminent role as consumer of Central Asian energy was confirmed in 2013 when CNPC signed an agreement with KMG, the Kazakh national oil company, to purchase 8.33 percent of the super-giant Kashagan oil field. The decision was made more significant by the fact that back in 2003, China National Offshore Oil Corporation (CNOOC) and Sinopec had joined to try to purchase British Gas (BG)'s portion of the project when the company had decided to cash out. KMG used its right of first refusal role in the consortium to block the purchase and instead bought part of BG's stake while the rest was divided up among the Western oil majors involved in the project (Eni, Shell, Total, ConocoPhilips, and

ExxonMobil—Inpex, the Japanese firm also with a stake in the
project, chose not to participate in this buy-out).

At the time, Nazarbayev was reportedly pushing for China to be
allowed into the project, but the companies were not keen to let the
Chinese firms in, particularly after CNOOC had threatened the
companies with retaliation in China if they were not allowed in. This
use of coercive diplomacy backfired. The exact reasons for the decision by the Western companies to go against the host government's
desires and to proceed in this way were not clear, but it demonstrated
a dramatic miscalculation by the Chinese firm. The situation was,
however, rectified almost a decade later when ConocoPhilips decided
to sell its 8.4 percent stake. Initially it was reportedly intended to be
sold to Indian energy provider ONGC, it was instead purchased by
KMG who then sold it on to CNPC. We were never able to get the
absolute details on what happened, but it only served to confirm the
strategic thinking behind energy purchase and ownership in the region.

This geopolitical dance was as much about nations as it was companies drilling for oil. When we spoke to energy executives in Central
Asia, their conversations would flip between government tensions and
narrow technical issues. From their perspective, any problem was as
much an engineering issue that needed to be rectified as a political
conundrum over which they struggled to have influence. There were
clear geopolitical consequences for Kazakhstan in letting China in
while keeping India out, and they reflected as much the reality for
Kazakhstan about making sure its biggest economic partner, China,
had a clear stake in its interests on Kazakhstan's territory. While Kazakh
authorities were clear in wanting to show that they were able to navigate between these great powers, they were also very aware of the
fact that China was their biggest customer. Given the physical proximity, it made sense that most of the natural resources they were able
to get out of the ground would be sold to feed the insatiable Chinese
market. While ONGC offered a window into the other great rising
Asian giant, physical geography made it a harder sale. This alongside a

persistent Indian failure to materialize as a serious player in Central Asia (despite much rhetoric and posturing) merely confirmed to the government in Kazakhstan that they were better served to continue to solidify the relationships they already had rather than go out on a limb with new ones.

★　★　★

The story of China's engagement in Kazakhstan's wider mineral resource sector is most vividly illustrated by the company Kaz Minerals, which used to be a part of Kazakhmys. A majority copper mining firm with a footprint across Central Asia (but predominantly Kazakh), Kazakhmys is a company that has attracted criticism and suspicion. In early 2014, it split into two, with its more mature assets being placed into a private firm, while the newer growth assets were transferred into a public company which was listed in the London, Hong Kong, and Astana stock exchanges.

Our main interest was the fact that the company had attracted substantial volumes of loans from the China Development Bank (CDB). This came in two separate chunks—first, in 2009 when national sovereign wealth fund Samruk-Kazyna became the vehicle for a substantial government to government loan from the CDB of which around $2.7 billion ultimately went toward Kazakhmys projects. Then later in 2011 the firm went straight to the CDB to gain a further $1.5 billion. The first loan was to develop a copper mine in Bozshakol (in eastern Kazakhstan) and Bozymchak, a copper and gold mine in Kyrgyzstan. The second was to develop a massive copper mine in Aktogay, a site relatively near the Chinese border. When we asked about the first loan, company executives would tell us that the government had secured the loan and then the firm had gone to the national fund to gain access to the facility. This relationship had given the company the contacts and experience to go back next time to the Chinese policy bank and negotiate a second loan directly. The dealmakers in Kazakhmys, a heavily British group, had been impressed by their

Chinese counterparts whom they found to be individuals focused on a very clear outcome using professional methods. Nothing like the characterization of what they had expected from Chinese bankers.

From a CDB perspective, a firm like Kazakhmys, and later Kaz Minerals, which carried with it the CDB loan focused assets when it was spun out from the main company, was an ideal target for national bank loans. The company was not only mining a mineral which China would need to feed its ever-growing manufacturing base, it was also near China. It was a local company, which softened the impression of China taking over its neighbors. And finally, it was using Chinese firms to deliver these projects. So close is the relationship between Kaz Minerals and its Chinese partners that in the year-end audit report for 2015, the company reported that it had reached an agreement with China Non Ferrous Metal Industry's Foreign Engineering and Construction Co., Ltd (NFC), the main construction firm it was using in its Aktogay project, to defer payment of the $300 million it owed the company by three years. In mid-2018, NFC further highlighted the positive nature of its relationship with Kaz Minerals announcing it was going to invest some $70 million into a third project it was going to work on with the company.

For Kaz Minerals, using a Chinese contractor made natural sense for numerous reasons—first, there was a relationship of trust that the two firms had developed; second, it was clearly going to be appealing to their Chinese customers and bankers; and, third, it made it easier to spend the money they had borrowed from CDB. While the first loan through Samruk-Kazyna was all in dollars, the second was $1.1 billion in dollars, and an additional Chinese renminbi (RMB) 1 billion. This gave the company a much easier way of paying its Chinese contractors—as an executive told us when they met with us in 2013. This also provided a further advantage to the Chinese policy bank in that it was able to help the broader Chinese government's vision of getting the national currency (the renminbi) into wider international circulation.

The importance to the Kazakh company of its relationship with China is clear from its balance sheet. In its accounts year ending December 2017, the company reported revenues of some $1.938 billion, of which $1.468 billion came from China. A year earlier, the company reported revenue of $969 million, with $570 million coming from China. The sharp increase in volume and relationship with China show the importance of China to the company, something the firm's official statements repeatedly mention, highlighting the risk of their exposure to China. Yet at the same time, the company and host country, Kazakhstan, clearly benefit from this relationship. The country is able to exploit its natural resources, Beijing will eat up whatever the firm produces, help finance the projects (the overwhelming majority of Kaz Minerals operating budget comes from CDB), and also provide companies that will develop the sites.

This sort of virtuous circle is what China is aiming for in its mineral investments in the region. Money, minerals, and employment—keeping all of these flowing and helping China is ultimately how Beijing would like to see all its investments play out. From Beijing's perspective, Central Asia is a rich area where there are numerous opportunities in mineral wealth which the country will need if it is going to keep up its breakneck growth. While the size of the deals and projects is not always on the scale of the hydrocarbon finds CNPC has undertaken in Turkmenistan or Kazakhstan, or the Kaz Minerals deals in Kazakhstan (similar deals and structures can be found across the region in smaller mining concessions in Tajikistan or Kyrgyzstan, as well as others in Kazakhstan), the point is that from Beijing's and Central Asia's perspective there is a logic to having China as both a creditor and purchaser of their mineral resources. For China, the minerals are appetizing, but so are the potential employment opportunities for Chinese firms and the way in which the contracts signed can help get Chinese currency circulating throughout the region. With a booming economy that needs the minerals Central Asia is rich in, the region is an appetizing looking cake for Beijing central planners.

Authorities in the host countries clearly welcome the projects. The question that is most frequently asked, however, and is the focus of much attention, is how much do the local communities around the project sites actually benefit.

★   ★   ★

Kara Balta in northwestern Kyrgyzstan is an old Soviet industrial hub. The hulking Kara Balta Ore Mining Combine Processing Plant ensured the livelihoods of about 50,000 people for decades until it partially shut down in the mid-2000s. Entire families were uprooted to Bishkek, the country's capital only a couple valleys away. The plant processed uranium from across Central Asia for use in power plants and warheads from one end of the Soviet Union to another. People joked that Geiger counters still register abnormal levels of radiation in most of the town's residential areas. Uranium tailings, waste products from the processing, pollute drinking water with what locals say is arsenic and mercury. But in conversations with residents of all ages, the future of Kara Balta seems to lie in further industrialization: the refining of crude oil. This time, however, production directives will come from Beijing instead of Moscow.

When we first embarked on our research for this project, the Kara-Balta plant was a key Chinese project in Kyrgyzstan. Offering the potential for greater national energy independence, it showed what China might offer the region. But as with all such game-changing projects, it was beset with problems. Visiting in 2013, residents were locked in a struggle with Chinese firm Zhongda over compensation for predicted future pollution caused by the company's oil refinery under construction outside of the town's center. Construction at the time was behind schedule due to this and other delays. Zhongda began the project without proper paperwork under a previous Kyrgyz administration during which it was more of an imperative to grease the palms of the ruling clan. Subsequent governments have insisted on a retroactive authorization process which has included its own set of byzantine requirements and payments—at one point a senior Chinese executive was arrested and stories of corruption, back taxes, and more were levied against the company. But notwithstanding these problems, the underlying logic of the project has persisted. With a reported investment as high as $300 million the project provided direct employment to 500 when it was operating and indirectly over its lifespan to a few thousand locally, offering good opportunities to the community living near the site as well as to Kyrgyzstan more generally.[14]

When we visited, the Chinese takeover of the company that runs the Soviet-era ore plant was greeted with a shrug by most, but the new refinery is a symbol in many minds of China's creeping takeover of Kyrgyzstan's economy. Elmurat, a fading pensioner with a sort of involuntary Mohawk of prickly white hair, logged thirty years at Kara Balta Ore Mining Combine. To him,

> the Russians are not our friends, but we have worked side by side with them for so long they are like step brothers. We all have relatives working in Moscow. They might not like being in Russia but they know Russians...we don't know anything about the Chinese. We don't know what they want, what their plans are, what they will do once this refinery is finished. Our government courts them because they want their money. I don't trust them. I am sure they have secret plans.[15]

Zhongda's plans in the longer term are believed to be to help connect the plant and country to CNPC's larger regional plans. Kyrgyzstan is energy-poor, so oil is currently brought in from Kazakhstan or Russia and the resulting petroleum products distributed in Kyrgyzstan. Despite Elmurat's suspicions, this seemingly local development will have geopolitical consequences far beyond Kara Balta. It was initially suspected by locals that the refinery's products would be destined for Chinese consumers, but this has not proved the case at all, with all of it largely being consumed by the Kyrgyz market. While the project has been repeatedly beset with stories of environmental damage (from reports of local environmental damage to those of dangerous chemicals being brought into the country and potentially leaking in transit or within Kyrgyzstan), illegal sales, tax avoidance, staff disputes, the arrest of senior staff on various accusations, and regular protests that are suspected to have been stirred up by opposition politicians demanding to see the work permits of Chinese workers there, the project has nevertheless made a real difference to the country. Contradicting the common predatory narrative attributed to Chinese investment in the country, during the COVID-19 crisis, the firm continued to pay its workers even though operations ground to a halt.[16]

Zhongda's refinery provides much needed energy diversification for Kyrgyzstan: a geopolitical as well as an economic boon in this part of the world. A long-term expat we met who has followed the Kara Balta issue closely put it to us this way in 2013,

> The Kara-Balta refinery will probably have the capacity to meet at least half of the domestic market's needs, producing "Euro 4" or "Euro 5" grade petrol. That will end Gazprom's monopoly in the country and force the Russian producer to compete with locally refined fuel. Politically, investments of this kind will strengthen Kyrgyzstan's hand in future relations with Moscow. Currently the local economy is characterized by an unenviable reliance on Russia both for energy security and as a source of remittances. By building facilities that provide both local jobs and local fuel, China offers a helping hand twice.[17]

This effect is visible elsewhere in Kyrgyzstan as well. In August 2015, then president Almazbek Atambayev gave a speech at the inauguration of a Chinese financed and built power transmission line in a village called Kemin. The new power line meant that Kyrgyzstan was no longer hostage to neighbors to transmit electricity around its awkwardly shaped country. As the president put it, "Previously, we needed the help of neighbouring countries for electrical power... After completion of future energy projects, Kyrgyzstan will not only meet the needs of the country, but it will also export electricity." Conscious of China's role in this, the president ended his speech saying, "Thanks to partners and friends (like China), who give us long-term loans, we can undertake large-scale projects."[18]

China has reduced Russia's strategic influence in Kyrgyzstan, and helped bolster the country's dependence on its neighbors. Unable to upgrade or develop its own infrastructure, Kyrgyzstan was left with the Soviet infrastructure which ignored national borders and treated the entire region as a single space that would trade on terms dictated by Moscow. As we have noted in our travels across the region, however, while the United States is busy extracting itself from Central Asia, Beijing is slowly but surely increasing its on-the-ground, functionally tied geopolitical clout through facilities such as the Kara Balta refinery and the pipeline network into which it will fit. Zhongda representatives are understandably tight-lipped about these repercussions, but Chinese diplomats in Bishkek at least acknowledge them, even if they smother those admissions in an avalanche of language about "good neighborliness" and "international cooperation." In directly challenging Russia, however, Beijing is underscoring that in energy terms it sees Central Asia as its turf, not Russia's.

But there is a difference in China's approach. While it is not clear that Beijing will directly benefit from the fuel generated by these projects (outside the specific companies involved), it is improving the region's energy capacity. It is also possible in the longer term that Kyrgyzstan might be able to export electricity to Xinjiang, and that CNPC might in the long run find ways of selling oil to the Zhongda refinery. Across the region, there are similar stories as China continues to develop local energy infrastructure using its companies and offering its financing, with the immediate beneficiaries being local markets that receive upgraded infrastructure, or an ability to access other markets more efficiently.

This all contrasts significantly with Moscow's approach. Russian energy giants Gazprom, Rosneft, and Transneft, together with Moscow's diplomats in the various Central Asian capitals, pursued a divide and rule strategy, emphasizing for example disagreements between Kyrgyzstan and Kazakhstan on the price of oil and terms of export. Not only could Russia then play one of its former colonies against the other, but it would ensure that energy needy Central Asian states purchased Russian oil directly—a convoluted, highly inefficient system that suited the Kremlin. China, mainly through SOEs such as

CNPC and Zhongda, is instead seeking to rationalize the Central Asian energy network on its terms. The Kara Balta refinery will create an oil export connection—under Chinese tutelage, of course—that would have always made a lot of sense geographically and economically for both Kazakhstan and Kyrgyzstan. This rationalization also reduces regional bargaining and transaction costs for Beijing. As a long-term expat observer put it, games of divide and rule in the energy sphere just provide a "needless headache" for the Chinese. Kazakhstan and Kyrgyzstan gain greater diversity, but they also gain a new patron.

★   ★   ★

"A natural resource appendage, that's what they call us in your Voice of America, your Radio Free Europe," says a Tajik investigative journalist who specifically asked to remain anonymous. Gesturing wildly in a Dushanbe café as he worked his way through our cigarettes, he insisted,

> Go out to the mines yourself. Look at the conditions. Look at the way locals are excluded or treated like animals. The Chinese don't care about contributing to our economy or our livelihood. They see Tajikistan, they see Central Asia as one big pit from which to extract the resources they need for their economy. The local people don't matter. They pay off our leaders and do what they like. Go and see for yourselves.

At the Zarafshan gold mine near Penjikent in northwestern Tajikistan, 1,500 miners laid down their tools in 2011, citing a cut in wages despite increased inflation. Some of their demands were eventually heard, through negotiations brokered by the central government, but they received nothing close to the sort of compensation they had been demanding: US$500 per month, compared to the just over US$100 they were being paid. When we visited, we were not allowed by supervisors to speak to ordinary miners, but brief exchanges with drivers working for the mine and local villagers confirmed continued resentment and bubbling Sinophobia. This ranged from anger about working conditions to theories that all of the donkeys, dogs, and snakes in the area had disappeared since Chinese workers arrived. It is an almost universal complaint throughout Tajikistan that Chinese are marrying Tajik women, especially the wives of migrant workers in Russia, who are all alone at home. This is a common scare story across the region, though the evidence of it actually taking place is limited: the few mixed couples we met seemed very happy and settled.

In other places, this resentment has turned violent. Also in 2011, the Soltan-Sary gold mine in Kyrgyzstan, operated by a Chinese company with mostly Chinese workers, was overwhelmed by a mob of over 300. Chinese miners and the Kyrgyz police officers who tried to protect them were beaten badly and much of the site's equipment was stolen or damaged. In April 2018, a group of angry locals attacked a gold processing plant near the village of Kazarman in Jalalabad, storming the site and setting fire to vehicles and offices. Firefighters were prevented from entering the site, and eventually the company calculated that its losses were around $2.3 million. Later in 2018, a group of Chinese engineers visiting a site in Batken fell foul of locals who accused them of coming to poison the environment in the area; the engineers were imprisoned in a metal trailer by locals who were recorded as threatening to go and get their knives to "punish" the Chinese. In 2020, during the violent uprising that shook the country in the wake of parliamentary elections, Chinese companies were among a number of foreign firms attacked by angry mobs.

Imported Chinese laborers often fight back. In 2012, the Taldy-Bulak gold mine was picketed by local protestors demanding compensation for environmental despoliation and the reportedly aggressive treatment of villagers by the Chinese company operating the mine. The protestors, who included Kyrgyz workers at the mine, engaged in what local media terms a "mass brawl" in which scores were injured. More than 250 Chinese nationals were evacuated once the Chinese ambassador protested. It is these sorts of incidents that led the Chinese Chamber of Commerce in Kyrgyzstan to warn potential Chinese investors that "resistance from locals traps many foreign companies working in the country in an unstable and risky situation." In July

2015, a brawl erupted between Chinese and Kazakh workers at the Kaz Minerals site in Aktogay, reportedly over the food being offered in the staff canteen.[19] These sorts of large-scale clashes between locals and Chinese are reported fairly regularly across the region, in particular in Kazakhstan and Kyrgyzstan, which is no doubt in part due to the relatively more open reporting and the larger Chinese presence in these countries.

Sometimes these incidents escalate in other ways. When we visited in late 2014, Bishkek was abuzz with a story of a group of sixteen Chinese workers who had gotten drunk and assaulted a police officer and passerby who tried to break up the fight. During the COVID-19 crisis in 2020, a group of Chinese workers in Tajikistan started protesting their conditions and voicing concerns about the way the government was handling the virus response, which led to armed police being deployed to break up the gathering.[20] Visiting Turkmenistan in 2013 we heard stories of how Chinese workers near Turkmenabat were restrained from leaving their compound after some of them were reported as using local prostitutes (a separate rumor we heard years later echoed this when we were told that there had been a spike in unregistered births in the region, which was discovered when someone started asking why some of the children in the area had been given obviously Chinese names that did not appear on local registers. The mothers feared ostracization). Chinese energy sector workers we met in Ashgabat would complain of the boredom they experienced in the country, having few people to connect with and limited access to the Internet. Even WeChat, the ubiquitous Chinese super-application, was blocked.

Clashes and stories of problems between locals and foreigners are universal in the region. In Kyrgyzstan, Western mining companies have experienced raiders on horseback attacking their work sites; and unrest routinely breaks out in the capital Bishkek and elsewhere over the massive Canadian-operated Kumtor gold mine. These attacks are sometimes tied to local politics. As a long-term expat observer said of the Kara Balta refinery, for any nationalist politician looking to pick a fight with the weak central government in Bishkek, the vision of a Chinese refinery that will inevitably employ a significant number of Chinese workers belching out carbon emissions and violating local labour codes is going to be far too tempting a weapon-in-waiting to ignore.

Oil company executives in Astana confirmed that while Western companies are strictly held to the requirements and quotas for hiring locals, Chinese companies such as CNPC seem to get a pass. In Aktobe, in Kazakhstan's northwestern onshore oil region, the daughter of a truck driver who had worked for several Chinese energy companies detailed his acute unhappiness with his treatment. She also pointed out that Chinese companies make it look like they are attempting to meet local hiring requirements by advertising positions for local staff, but that they get around having to follow through by listing requirements such as Mandarin fluency or familiarity with Chinese-built machinery. According to her, this was even true for positions such as cook, janitor, or manual laborer. A possible reasonable explanation for this which was pointed out to us was that a Chinese firm would likely want a chef who could prepare Chinese dishes, something more likely to come from an individual who spoke Mandarin. As with many of the complaint stories we heard, there were often two sides to the story.

The frustration of those working for Chinese companies in the mines or oil fields is compounded by the general lament that older generations—or those influenced by the stories of older generations—make for the perceived benefits that had been afforded to manual laborers in Soviet times. A truck driver in his mid-50s, for example, would recall a time when he received—albeit meager— housing, healthcare, pension, and other benefits from the state-controlled industries before the collapse of Communism. Most importantly, he would recall a work culture that—at least in theory— prized the working conditions and camaraderie of workers over the bottom line. He would also recall the petty corruption that allowed for the drawing of benefits without actually working very much at all.

In practice, in the Central Asian context, while economic conditions were rather desperate in the 1970s and 1980s, extended lunch breaks, chatting and smoking on the job, and short hours were indeed commonplace for those in industry or the extractive sector.

While for many such workers there is frustration across the board about contemporary working conditions, whether they work for a Kazakh, Western, or Chinese company, it is the major Chinese SOEs that receive the greatest ire because their working culture is very much the opposite of this Soviet legacy. Putting in long days of relentless shifts is something that Chinese firms and workers are used to doing, but this stands in stark contrast to local practices. Accusations of China enforcing a prison labor work style is a common myth that locals circulate as providing the only explanation as to why the Chinese workers are willing to work such miserable hours. And truth be told, it is possible that in some cases this has happened. One long-standing Chinese businessman in the region who took a shine to us on our travels confirmed he had met such groups, though he was vague about details and the numbers involved. Certainly, within China, prison labor practices have been known. We were never able to confirm first-hand if this was really happening in Central Asia, but the stories served at least to highlight the complexity of a situation where different work cultures find themselves in conflict.

Chinese firms are equally frustrated about the situation. Local governments relentlessly seek to get the projects done quickly, usually to local political cycles. Chinese firms are keen to accommodate these requests and will therefore ask to have the project done on their terms. At the same time, they are aware of local legislation around procuring local employees, and while they may seek to sometimes get political clearances to overcome these rules, often this is done for pragmatic rather than nationalist reasons. All foreign firms complain about the lack of local intellectual capital to deliver senior roles in complicated mining, extractive, or infrastructure projects. If you cannot find enough locals to fill the quotas but are still under pressure to get the

project done, what can you do? In most cases, you will resort to bringing more people in. And at the lower end of the employment scale,
they are equally happy to hire locals (and contrary to many of the
local myths, a lot of local hiring does happen[21]), but then find themselves frustrated by the quality and dedication levels of the workers.
This leads to clashes between workers and company, as well as the
firm and local authorities, creating a vicious circle in which blame is
spread in all directions.

Sinophobia is not just a kneejerk populist sentiment. Scholars, successful businesspeople, and other prominent figures across the region
express suspicion about Chinese intentions and concern about Central
Asian governments' lack of transparency regarding agreements with
Beijing and investments by Chinese SOEs. There is a pervading sense
among what is still often called the "intelligentsia" that their political
leaders are far more in the grip of Chinese interests than they are
willing to reveal. This is based on more than just traditional uneasiness
about the Han Chinese "other." Their sense is that their leaders are
corrupt and taking advantage of the Chinese investment at a personal
level. Some of which accusations would appear to be true, with court
cases against senior political figures in Kyrgyzstan appearing to show
large sums of money exchanging hands to advance Chinese projects
in the country. In other countries, rumors of similar stories are rife,
though it is often hard to get hard evidence of them—we were regularly told of complicated corruption networks tied to family members
of senior figures.

And then there is the traditional post-Soviet love of conspiracy. On
more occasions than we could count, prominent analysts—often government advisors—and even some serving state officials would pull us
aside (as supposedly sympathetic Westerners) to confide deep, often
paranoid, suspicions about prominent infrastructure projects, business
investments, or Shanghai Cooperation Organization (SCO) programs
involving the Chinese. One prominent Tajik analyst who made a point
of detailing his ties to the presidential administration spent almost two
hours describing the elaborate plots of Chinese companies to prepare

the way for future military invasion from the east. "They are preparing the ground," he said, "for a large-scale territorial grab. We should not be blind to the coming wave." Such "yellow peril" views are widespread.

As Central Asia scholars Marlene Laruelle and Sebastien Peyrouse have observed, the suspicions of such elites are "generated precisely through the dearth of information" on China's activities in the region. For example, a major study they conducted cites scholars in Kazakhstan speculating that their government hides the true control of Chinese companies such as CNPC over the country's energy sector.[22] Sometimes this opacity is understandable given the commercial nature of the projects. But in many cases, this is public money which is being spent and it is not clear where it is all going.

Numerous locals point to the undermining of local manufacturing by cheap Chinese goods on the Beijing-built "Synthetic Road." There are also persistent complaints about the prominence of Chinese businesses, from corner noodle shops to major office buildings, such as a pagoda-styled skyscraper built by a CNPC subsidiary in Kazakhstan's capital Nursultan which houses the local offices of numerous Chinese companies, as well as a hotel and a rotating gourmet restaurant. Nevertheless, it is Chinese activities in the natural resources sector that persistently elicit Sinophobic sentiments among the poor and the wealthy, the educated and illiterate alike. This is because the extraction of resources is inherently linked to the control of territory, and in the Russian-trained Central Asian mindset, this determines power.

Although many of the claims are based purely on rumors, the former Soviet states of Central Asia are rife with conspiracies about land grabs by the Chinese. After all, the spurious theory goes, the Chinese are so many, Central Asians are so few compared to their vast tracts of land, whether Kazakh steppe, Turkmen desert, or the Pamir mountains. This view ignores the reality that Chinese population centers of any magnitude are far from Central Asia and that Xinjiang, in Western China, presents a far more tantalizing prospect of available land with few people on it—at least for now.

But the fear is one based on a conspiratorial view of the world, where hard power and control of resources is what determines national power. And this can seem a more believable argument, as incorrect as it often proves. In a series of border demarcation agreements generated from the Shanghai Five process, which preceded the creation of the SCO (which we will discuss later in greater detail), Kazakhstan, Kyrgyzstan, and Tajikistan did end up ceding some land to China. The most recent of these agreements, fodder for whispers and nudges at conversations in Dushanbe, was the 2011 parliamentary ratification of a 1999 deal that gave China 386 square miles of land previously claimed by Tajikistan in an uninhabited part of the wild Pamir mountains along the border.[23] While officials on both sides praised the ratification as the final resolution of a century-long dispute, commentators and ordinary Tajiks openly speculated that China used its preponderant influence as the largest investor in Tajikistan to nab a piece of resource-rich ground. Gold, rubies, and other precious minerals are to be found there, according to this conspiracy narrative. But geologists we spoke to dismissed these stories, and explained why it would be all but impossible for gemstones to be found there.

But, zooming out, the border readjustment begs the question of why massive China would even bother pressing minute Tajikistan for a relatively small and isolated parcel of land. It abuts China's Tajik Autonomous County, a fairly neglected corner of China in which it is rare to even come across Han Chinese. What could motivate such high-level diplomacy over a few remote, insignificant mountains? Surely, only rich resources of which locals were unaware. Land is a precious commodity that defines nationhood.

In the deadly freezing winter of 2010, almost 1,000 Kazakhs bundled up to stand outside in an Almaty park for hours protesting what they called "Chinese expansionism."[24] Their specific grievance was about a deal in which the government of Kazakhstan would lease large parcels of farmland—up to a million hectares—to Chinese agricultural companies. The large-scale farms, it was thought, would use Chinese labor and export their produce to rapidly growing Xinjiang.

As one protestor put it, "our people are awakening, our land is under threat." That this demonstration was allowed to proceed is notable, because the Kazakh government usually restricts public shows of discontent with major policies. Perhaps it was a test of popular sentiment. Either way, it seems to have achieved results: the land deal is purportedly delayed indefinitely and will probably be canceled. When the government sought to revisit the idea of letting foreigners purchase land in the country almost a decade later, a similar set of protests occurred, in part stirred up by opposition figures, but also as a reflection of local fear and unhappiness. The government remains fearful about the perception of selling its land to foreign powers, especially China.

Similar deals in Tajikistan, however, seem to be going forward on land that has heretofore been considered too salty to be used for farming. A number of pilot projects have yielded a profitable crop through the use of Chinese agricultural technologies, so that 6,000 hectares are now set to be leased to Chinese companies with the stipulation that all produce is to be sold in Tajikistan and not exported to China. Locals pointed out that this had changed the face of some Tajik markets, with produce now available all year round. But the very need for such assistance breeds resentment. As journalist Faromarzi Fosil has written, "if the Chinese and other foreigners build all the roads, power plants, companies, and farms then why do we even need our own ministries?"[25]

★   ★   ★

CNPC representatives and Chinese diplomats tend to emphasize the complementarity between China's natural resource-hungry economy and Central Asian countries' vast reserves of oil, natural gas, and minerals. This dovetailing is one of the key pillars of China's "harmonious" relations with its neighbors to the west, according to officials in Beijing, Shanghai, Urumqi, and Chinese embassies in the region that we spoke to. It is true that the networked approach of SOEs such as CNPC is pursued partly to complement Beijing's resource extraction plans in Xinjiang. Much of Kazakhstan's oil flowing east, for example, is refined in Xinjiang at facilities in Karamay, Dushanzi, Kuqa, and Urumqi. These are complemented by so-called industrial clusters throughout the province, with plans for petrochemical, plastics, and heavy machinery production. The refineries connect through Urumqi to the Western China Refined Oil Pipeline, which runs to Gansu province and from there through various spurs to China's thirsty east coast cities.

But, it is not simply that Central Asia has what China needs. CNPC's pipeline, extraction, and refining network is a major geopolitical asset. While Chinese officials deny that they are playing politics with their pipelines, the consequences are that China has displaced Russia in the latter's traditional backyard, and in the sector in which Moscow traditionally has the most international clout. This is not a small accomplishment. And while allusions to a new "Great Game," similar to that of the 19th century in Central Asia between the Russian and British empires, are probably not the most helpful in understanding the region's contemporary geopolitics, China's quest for "cake" in Central Asia brings with it links to even greater resources in Iran and the Gulf, as well as access to the Indian Ocean and across the Caspian Sea.

CNPC has struggled in its forays into the Iranian energy sector for a variety of reasons, but it should not be much of a surprise if it ultimately uses infrastructural connections through Turkmenistan and Afghanistan to bind itself to Iran. The US push against Iran under President Trump worked to Beijing's advantage within this context, and the decision by European companies to abandon the country by means of sanctions has led Tehran to turn firmly toward Beijing, including by signing a twenty-five-year agreement of cooperation and investment. While the realities of the projects and engagement might be regularly questioned, the overall visual thrust by Tehran to be seen to leaning more toward its eastern partner, China, is unmistakable. Chinese companies have also struck some small-scale resource deals in Azerbaijan, in the Caucasus, on the edges of Europe, and once CNPC has established itself just across the Caspian on Turkmenistan's coast, the Chinese energy behemoth's next steps may well abut the territory of North Atlantic Treaty Organisation (NATO) and the European Union's Eastern Partnership space. CNPC's "rationalization" of a great continent-spanning energy network conjures memories of Sir Halford Mackinder's warnings about the immense potential of powerful Eurasian "organizers." With a continent at their command, he wrote, they would be unstoppable.

4

Silk Road or Synthetic Road?

Female traders at Jalalabad Market, Kyrgyzstan

In Khorgos, on the China–Kazakhstan border, trucks laden with Chinese goods line up along the road, waiting for Chinese and then Kazakh customs officers to give them the go-ahead to continue their transcontinental journey across Eurasia. Many will be heading to the great markets of Central Asia, like Dordoi, Barakholka, and Kara-Suu while others head all the way to Europe. Squeezing through a single lane, the trucks get stuck in lengthy backlogs as they wait in the shadow of the brand new multilane Chinese customs point that sits idle next door. These roads run in parallel to a growing network of railways across the region which start from Urumqi's giant new train station and slowly trace across the steppe to reach Europe's shores. This latticework of transport is the heart of the Silk Road Economic Belt (SREB) China is paving across Eurasia, with its first hub and staging point in Central Asia.

It may seem a cliché to use Halford Mackinder's talk about Central Asia in "Great Game" terms with battling rival powers elbowing each other to assert their influence. Seeing the region as a geopolitical chessboard has long been the remit of armchair strategists and imperial dreamers, but it is also at the heart of Central Asian leaders' strategic conceptions of themselves. The old vision was of the region as a physical battle space for power and control. Those days of power games still exist, but these days they are articulated through markets and flows of goods along roads and infrastructure that is gradually getting rewired to all aim toward China rather than Moscow. Talk to senior Central Asian officials or strategic thinkers and they will discuss multivector diplomacy where they are in the driving seat. Go out on the ground, and the sheer range and depth of Chinese economic engagement suggests a very different story.

The degree to which China's modeling and planning for the Belt and Road Initiative (BRI)[1] and SREB in Central Asia drew on Mackinder's thinking has never been clear. There are echoes of the historical geographer in Wang Jisi's initial writing about China's "March Westwards".[2] And, as mentioned earlier, in 2015, the Chinese ambassador to the Court of St James in London suggested Mackinder was very much in China's mind when he told readers of the *Financial Times* to "take the new silk road as an opportunity not a threat" and started his article directly citing Mackinder. He went on to highlight the importance of transportation networks, citing another more recent geostrategist, Zbigniew Brzezinski, who said "the inevitably emerging transportation network meant to link more directly Eurasia's richest and most industrious western and eastern extremities."[3] In Ambassador Liu's interpretation the core of the project was one of improving connectivity across the Eurasian landmass and building infrastructure for common prosperity. The flow of goods would determine this new Silk Road, most of which was meant to cut across the Eurasian landmass through Central Asia.

We traced as many of these routes as we could during our research. We visited four of China's border posts with Central Asia—in all cases, visiting both sides up close, though we never made the formal crossing due to visa requirements. Taking cars to distant borders in Xinjiang as well as remote routes to the edge of Central Asia, we tried to follow goods as they cut across the continent, exploring markets where we could find them and chatting to traders who were trying to eke out an existence in challenging circumstances. Some were friendly, others accused us of being spies, but none felt themselves part of this Great Game—most were simply trying to make a living. Yet, it was clear that they were all being affected by the bigger transformation that was taking place across their region as the new Silk Road was being paved by Beijing.

The romantic mystique evoked by Mackinder was not lost on everyone. In 2012, we visited Xinjiang University in Urumqi at the start of one of our trips around the region. Upon arriving at the university to meet with some of the researchers, we were surprised to discover that they were expecting us to present to the students. Unabashed, we launched into lengthy presentations weaving Mackinder and Sima Qian into modern narratives to a gripped audience (even though it was done through translation). They came back with specific questions and were eager to understand the US's perspective on the new Silk Road, and specifically what then US secretary of state Clinton had meant when she had spoken about the route in Chennai the year before. What struck us after we left them to trace these routes was how advanced Chinese activity was in the region—the US had spoken about the New Silk Road vision, China was realizing it.

The term "Silk Road" was actually coined rather late in the day by one of the first 19th-century Inner Asian explorers, president of the

German Geographical Society, Ferdinand von Richthofen (who was the uncle of the infamous World War One flying ace Manfred von Richthofen, the Red Baron). He was also professor of Swedish explorer Sven Hedin, who was among the first Westerners to map out vast parts of Central Asia and modern Xinjiang and Tibet. In his own time, von Richthofen was probably best known for the intelligence he provided to the expatriate Shanghai Chamber of Commerce about Chinese coalfields. The Gansu mountain range that bore his name has been relabeled and his meticulous geographical works remain untranslated from the German. His lasting legacy is the notion that was in some ways among the most superficial he contributed, the idea that the network of routes across the center of Eurasia, from China to Europe, the Middle East, Russia, and South Asia, were largely for the silk trade. The goods that flowed in all directions were of course myriad, from Chinese jade to Indian spices and Roman coin. Cultural and religious syncretism flourished, with the melding of Hellenism, Buddhism, and Manichaeism to mention just a few. The Bubonic Plague also swept through the trade network, probably making its way West rather than East.[4]

Today's overland trade network across Eurasia, if it were to be described in a similar fashion, would more accurately be called the "Synthetic Road" because the most prevalent types of textiles that are loaded on its lorries and pass through its customs houses are nylon, polyester, and carbon fiber, manufactured in China. Chinese factories produce not only the t-shirts, jackets, blankets, and curtains common around the world but also Central Asia–specific products such as synthetic Turkmen carpets and polyester Kyrgyz *kalpaks* that are now more widely available than their authentic woolen forbears. For consumers from Kabul to Kazan, it is China's cheap manufactured goods that are in demand and Chinese state-owned enterprises are in the midst of building the transport networks to get those goods to market. This very same Synthetic Road also carries raw materials in the opposite direction and provides infrastructure for a connectivity-poor region—which according to Beijing's Develop the West plan in Xinjiang brings with it economic development and political stability.

This Synthetic Road is a relatively novel one. Contemporary historians point out that until the mid-1990s the route was one which actually ran the other way.[5] Goods imported into the former Soviet Union from the west would be purchased by eager Chinese buyers who remained deprived of such products in China's disconnected western regions. Of course, this was during the period of great growth and opportunity in China, and it did not take long for the route to turn on itself and instead start to feed products—oftentimes fake ones—back the other way. By the time we got to these markets in the 2010s, they were filled with the same imitative junk we would find in the markets back in China. People generally considered Chinese products to be of the lowest quality, but they would still purchase them in vast quantities as the price was so low. As time went on, this balance started to shift with higher end and quality Chinese products showing up in markets. Huawei phones were considered to be of excellent quality at a reasonable price, while Central Asian manufacturers identified reliable Chinese partners to produce cheaper but high-quality white goods. But the lingering quality suspicion remained, with these same Central Asian manufacturers giving the goods European sounding names to avoid the connection with China. Additionally, cheap products from other manufacturing hubs like Turkey could be increasingly found shifting the public's perceptions of the quality ranking among products.

But whichever market we went to—be it those closest to China's borders in Kara-Suu or Khorgos, all the way over to Awaza on the Turkmen Caspian to Aktobe in northwestern Kazakhstan—we found Chinese goods and traders or workers. Not many of them gave much (if any) thought to their role as the modern-day inheritors of the Silk Road or that they might be part of a bigger push by Beijing. We found traders who had recently arrived, some who had been there for decades, and others who had been sent there. Some had settled down for the long term with local partners and lives, while others were

clearly seeing this as a temporary stop in a life of trading. Fortunes
were being built and had been lost by some, while others barely
seemed to understand where they were.

★   ★   ★

A striking thing that we kept noticing as we interviewed and spoke to
Chinese experts and officials in Beijing, Shanghai, or Xinjiang was the
general absence of a clear strategy for Central Asia. Prior to Xi Jinping's
announcement of the SREB in 2013, there was a general sense that
Central Asian relations were largely a question for Xinjiang and that
the issues were about domestic economy and unstable neighbors. In
the wake of Xi Jinping's big speech, the view was largely unchanged
though now it was layered with confusion over what exactly this
SREB and subsequently the larger BRI would actually mean. When
we presented people with our interpretation of what was going on
based on our many discussions and meetings, they would largely stare
back at us nodding, and then say that none of this adds up to a larger
strategy or vision for the region.

But what they would all agree on was the fact that a major foundation for this relationship was the roads and routes that were being
built across the border and growing Xinjiang's economy. Meeting
with experts at the Xinjiang Academy of Social Sciences (XJASS) in
Urumqi before and after the announcement of BRI we met researchers whose work was focused on their neighboring regions and who
all preferred to communicate in Russian rather than English. As long-
time students of Central Asia they had an intimate understanding of
the relationship that Xinjiang had with the region. Talking to us pre-
BRI they were full of discussions of investment and the construction
of special economic zones flowing from the 2010 Xinjiang work plan.
Aimed at jump-starting Xinjiang's economy, the work plan was an
ambitious effort that sought to open Xinjiang up and turn it into the
gateway to the west.

In a meeting with the Xinjiang Production and Construction
Corps (XPCC), we were hosted by a severe female colonel with a

distinct high-top haircut who barked in excellent English about the opportunities the region and company offered. In listing the company's many achievements, she focused heavily on agriculture, both in terms of the experience they had in Xinjiang and their efforts across the borders in Central Asia. Her company, she told us, was playing an integral part in helping build the infrastructure which would help realize regional connectivity, opening up local markets to Xinjiang and vice versa. With military efficiency, she outlined the company's three-stage strategy to any project: visit to lay the groundwork, develop the appropriate frame to deliver the project, and finally to actually start and deliver the project. We had no doubt about how promptly this would happen.

The colonel was in fact articulating what would ultimately become the BRI, and on these early pre-BRI visits to Central Asia we were struck by how regional connectivity seemed to be the driving vision behind China's activity in its neighboring Central Asia. This set the tone of our first wave of regional visits in which we sought to explore and understand the various routes across the region that were gradually rewiring Central Asian infrastructure so that it would go toward Urumqi rather than Moscow. We were keen to uncover China in Central Asia from the ground up, and firms like the XPCC or the thinkers at XJASS were at the forefront of strategizing about what this would look like.

But what was equally striking about our conversations in Xinjiang and similar discussions we had in Beijing and Shanghai was that no-one could articulate to us what the actual plan was. Everyone had a view on the high-level relationships (who was close to whom and why) and could talk about the detail of the programs and routes, but no-one would talk about it as a vision or a strategy. In fact, when we pushed Professor Zhao Huasheng, one of China's foremost Central Asian scholars, in his office in Shanghai he bemoaned the fact that all of China's activity in the region amounted to a series of disparate projects and efforts lacking coordination. Officials and think-tankers we would meet in Beijing downplayed any larger strategy and talked instead of specific connectivity projects and routes. When we pushed them on what China's larger vision was, they would dismiss us as paranoid Westerners and say China had no such ambitions.

This was in stark contrast to many others across the region who had long ago spotted connectivity as the key element to help stimulate the region. The Japanese-led Asian Development Bank (ADB) has long advanced a vision and strategy for the region called CAREC (Central Asia Regional Economic Cooperation). Through this, they funded large infrastructure projects and supported local industry to foster regional connectivity. Trains, pipelines, roads, and more were captured in CAREC's embrace. Even earlier than CAREC was the United Nations Iron Silk Road concept, in which a web of railway lines would be built across the Eurasian landmass from Asia to Europe. And the International Monetary Fund (IMF), Islamic Development Bank, Aga Khan Foundation, and numerous other national aid and multilateral bodies have long seen regional connectivity as the answer to Central Asia's landlocked isolation. Given Xinjiang's essential nature as the sixth Central Asian country, it is in many ways only natural that it would also be incorporated into these visions.

But the discussion of regional strategies will come later. Here we will focus instead on the physical roads, railways, border posts, and markets that we visited across the region which showed how the flow that used to go to Moscow is now quite clearly going toward Urumqi, and how Central Asia's infrastructural hardwiring was always at the foundation of China's approach toward the region. Pre-dating the BRI, the point of creating regional connectivity at its most basic was to open up Xinjiang's manufacturing and markets to its neighbors and therefore help the region to prosper, and eventually to stabilize.

★ ★ ★

In the last week of October 2012, major Chinese state-owned enterprise China Road and Bridge Corporation (CRBC), completed the longest tunnel in Tajikistan. Helping connect Dushanbe and Khujand, two of the country's largest cities, the route was an important one that reportedly cut almost ten hours off of an already grueling journey through spectacular mountains. At the opening of the new Sharistan Tunnel, Tajikistan's President Emomali Rahmon announced that the tunnel now made this "the shortest route between Asia and Europe." The 3.25 mile tunnel was intended to in part replace a crumbling Iranian-built Anzob tunnel, an ill-fated "gift" upon Tajikistan's independence. At the opening ceremony, President Rahmon praised CRBC workers for their ingenuity in completing the company's longest tunnel project outside of China. He also awarded the project manager with Tajikistan's Order of Friendship, while Chinese ambassador to Tajikistan, Fan Xianrong, was on hand to praise the project as a symbol of the close relationship between the two countries.

The connection was badly needed. In May of that year, we had driven through the old tunnel. As many travelers before us have remarked, one feels a certain relief at still being alive upon exit. During the winter we were told the tunnel was flooded and impassable, effectively cutting off Dushanbe from the northern part of the country. In the spring and summer months, it was still awash with water as it poured through cracks in the ceiling and walls, collecting in ominously large puddles on the ground. It is perhaps then not a surprise that the tunnel's concrete was not just cracked, but also lying about in large fragments, dropping unexpectedly from the ceiling and collecting in piles of rubble along the way. It doesn't help that, apart from car headlights, there was no illumination in this crumbling subterranean cocoon. Hapless workers could occasionally be glimpsed through the darkness, like moles with lights on their helmets digging in the dark. Their job: to shovel the rubble to one side or another. One can only imagine the backup in case of a flat tire along the way. One rumor goes that some years earlier drivers stuck in immovable traffic in the tunnel's depths had neglected to turn their engines off, resulting in numerous deaths from carbon monoxide poisoning.

This sort of adventure is now a thing of the past. Friends who have since taken the new tunnel attest to its effectiveness, how well-lit it is, and the fact that they no longer have to take the so-called "tunnel of death" at Anzob. The importance of this type of infrastructure in a country like Tajikistan cannot be underestimated. To go back further in history, prior to the construction of the Anzob Tunnel, Tajikistan was at Uzbekistan's mercy in terms of access by road from Dushanbe to the northern capital Khujand. Given the parlous state of relations between their two leaders and countries, this meant a severing of the country in half. Iran's contribution at the time was a game changer for the country. Infrastructure can be transformative in regions of the world that are still developing, and in particular in ones like Tajikistan that are home to such dramatic topography. In other contexts in Central Asia, China has offered similarly significant projects—like the Kamchiq Tunnel in Uzbekistan which helps get a train from Angren to Pap. Started in 2013 and completed in 2016, the railway line is crucial in better connecting Tashkent with its restive and fertile Ferghana region. At 19 kilometers, the tunnel is the longest in Central Asia and was built with remarkable speed by a Chinese firm using money that the government had borrowed from China Export-Import Bank. It is an important project for Uzbekistan and has saved an unknown number of hours of travel and labor for the country.

This is a common model for Chinese projects in the region. As was highlighted in Chapter 3, Beijing often helps by providing cheap loans to countries, which they can then spend using Chinese companies. This provides for a curious situation whereby money essentially transfers from one side of Beijing to another, with a piece of infrastructure appearing on the other side of the world. The model is not an uncommon one—Japanese and Korean national development banks have in the past offered similar loan structures whereby they provide so-called "linked loans" to countries in which a stipulation of the deal is that companies from the lender's own country are used in delivery of the project. It is a model of business that has been supercharged and globalized under the BRI. In Central Asia, however, it is something that has been happening for some time.

Reflecting on how this process worked in practice, we shuttled around Beijing visiting the China Development Bank, meeting with officials at the Ministry of Commerce and those working at CRBC or China National Petroleum Corporation (CNPC) to hear each one of them talk about how they were working in Central Asia and beyond. Each institution had its own directives and aims, and few had much actual interest in the countries in which they were investing. On the ground in Central Asia, we occasionally met engineers who were fascinated by the countries they were working in, but there was little evidence of this curiosity in Beijing.

Instead, at CRBC they told us with great pride of the accomplishments their engineers had managed in faraway lands as they showed us promotional videos of their work. At China Development Bank they listed the benefits that would accrue to the recipient countries of the loans that they would extend. And at the Ministry of Commerce they would tell of the complexity of navigating these different jurisdictions with all the diplomatic issues that went alongside, trying to negotiate and discuss economic corridors between countries that historically did not get along. The think tanks advising them would tell us of the programs they were running trying to get the companies delivering projects to improve their engagement with local actors. The entire process, we were told, was one that was undertaken with the full cooperation of the local authorities.

In Kazakhstan we met with one of the heads of the national sovereign wealth fund who told us about his discussions with Chinese bankers and how they would work together to deliver infrastructure within his country. Elsewhere we met western executives and international development bankers who would tell us about how impressive they found their Chinese counterparts. ExIm Bank and China Development Bank have now opened offices across Central Asia seeking to strengthen their ability to negotiate and manage the vast sums of money that they lend to the countries.

All these positive discussions in capitals seemed very different from what we ultimately found on the ground. Driving up the winding roads to Irkeshtam or Torugart we found Chinese work crews in distinctive overcoats hammering away. When we tried to engage they were largely uninterested. Similar to the workers described in Chapter 3, there were as many rumors about the Chinese workers as there were workers. And every Chinese worker we were able to talk to was quite open about being there for the paycheck. To them it did not really matter where they were. As long as they were getting paid and were able to send money home, they were content. They had little desire to spend money on their living conditions as they preferred to save more to send home.

We found many of these workers either at airports, as they were leaving or arriving (in one instance we helped them complete entry forms), or as we traveled along roads in the region, taking any opportunity we could to strike up a conversation. Leaving one morning from Osh with a driver whom a friendly local Chinese teacher had helped us locate, we traveled painlessly to Irkeshtam on the Kyrgyz side of the border. The road was mostly tarmacked and, aside from a bumpy part in the mountains, in good condition. As we raced along the empty road we passed the CRBC management office for the road building project. The company was responsible for building most of the road (often as subcontractor to the international projects), funded in part by the ADB, the Islamic Development Bank, and the Chinese government. We quickly told our driver to stop and turn around.

Wandering into the compound we found a few Chinese engineers who said that the project was due to finish in spring 2012. Their entry guard was sound asleep, and only woke up once we were deep inside the compound. They worked from April to October of each year when weather conditions were bearable. An hour or so down the road, we came across their colleagues, Chinese men huddled in heavy green military coats directing large trucks of granite as they worked to pave the road.

As with many borders in the region, there is a gap between the actual border and where passports are checked before you get to the line of demarcation. On the Kyrgyz side, a small camouflage-painted mobile home sat by the side of the road with a simple metal barrier across the road itself. The young Kyrgyz guard manning the barrier waved vigorously at us as we tried to take pictures, though he seemed a lot less threatening once we noticed that his AK-47 did not have an ammunition clip.

The border itself was a dusty parking lot with giant shipping trucks, with 海关 ("Customs") emblazoned on the sides, edging around each other. A lone donkey wandered through the chaos as various truckers and assorted loafers used facilities; shopped at the mini-mud buildings selling food, cigarettes, and other provisions; or had meals at the rudimentary restaurants. One excitable Uyghur-Chinese driver told us that he was on his way to Uzbekistan with a truckload of "stuff"— when asked to specify, he said various electronica and low-end Chinese products. He was more interested to hear about Shanghai (where we had come from) and the business prospects there.

In contrast, the Chinese side of the border was visibly policed, with more solid structures at the actual border post—a big white tiled building and men in warm uniforms guiding the truck traffic. Present in early spring (we visited the Kyrgyz side in October and the Chinese side in April), there was still snow on the ground and written into it on the mountain above the post was the phrase 中国民爱 (roughly translated as "China loves its people"). Unlike the dusty Kyrgyz side, the Chinese side was a small village of concrete buildings with a police station, Sinopec office, restaurants, hotels, and grocery stores. On the road before the encampment was an odd building with a giant football on top of it. Behind it was a walled area with cameras on top that our driver informed us was some sort of military installation.

While the border itself was relatively developed, there was a dramatic contrast in the state of the roads leading up to it on the Chinese side. Likely done by the same company as that on the Kyrgyz side, the road on the Chinese side was a potholed mess and for a substantial period we were drudging through dirt and knee-deep snow. Our driver steadily became more exasperated, chain-smoking his way through two packs of cigarettes as we battled on and his carefully cleaned car turned into a mud-colored mess with a broken bumper. Plowing through a blizzard we saw large trucks abandoned by the side

of the road, battered by the treacherous road conditions. We had been
warned the ride would be difficult, though given the excellent state
of the Karakoram Highway and most infrastructure in China, we figured this could not be that bad. We were wrong: it was a bumpy ride
from almost the moment we left Kashgar.

The reason for this rather surprising inversion in road quality is
that the road to the border on the Chinese side was in the process of
being rebuilt when we first went down it in 2012, due to be finished
by 2013. The construction process was visible along the way as we
saw teams digging holes and moving large pieces of concrete around
to support the road. A city was being built along the way at Ulugqat,
a previously minute village that currently serves as an entertainment
spot for customs officers, and workers on the road and at the border—but is mostly a muddy mess with giant construction sites everywhere. The customs post before the border "dead-zone" on the
Chinese side was a more substantial creation, with a small soldiers'
cabin across the road from a much larger official customs building
with Chinese flags and logos all over it. In contrast to their Kyrgyz
counterparts, these soldiers did have ammunition clips in their guns,
as well as new uniforms that contrasted with our increasingly bedraggled appearance.

Unlike its northern counterpart the Torugut Pass, Irshketam is open
most of the year. One of the key crossing points for China into Central
Asia, it provides a route for Chinese products to get to Kyrgyz markets
as well as travel up into Russia, across into Uzbekistan and beyond to
both Europe and Iran. Much of the material brought across the border ends up in Kyrgyzstan's crowded Osh or Kara-Suu bazaars, an
arrangement that appears to be perpetually under threat. When we
spoke to Kyrgyz officials in 2012, they spoke of their fear of local
economies being destroyed if the Kyrgyz elected to join Putin's
Eurasian Union and a subsequent tariff barrier being erected between
the Kyrgyz and Chinese economies. The Kyrgyz elite worried that
joining a Eurasian Union would mean effectively losing control over

its border tariffs and regulations, and would destroy the rich network of new trade routes that are tying them into China, bringing them cheap goods and enabling a substantial re-export economy. These trade routes are economic lifelines for this fragile state—and for this network the Customs Union has every potential to be a total disaster. As a former Kyrgyz cabinet minister put it to us in Bishkek, it would "decimate" the country's key markets in the south at Kara-Suu and Osh. In his words, "almost every" small business in Kyrgyzstan is reliant on trade with China, and any new tariffs or rules would entirely change the local economy.

At the time, Chinese officials we asked seemed less concerned, partially because the market loss would be negligible in terms of China's overall trade volumes, but also since they believed that the entire Eurasian Union project was unlikely to amount to much. Ambassador to Bishkek Wang Kaiwen put it succinctly to reporters in late November 2013 when he said: "Kyrgyzstan's entry into this Customs Union will not affect trade relations with China." Kyrgyz–Chinese trade, he pointed out, oscillated somewhere between $5 and $10 billion per annum, a figure that was "a small problem" being dwarfed by China's overall foreign trade of $3 trillion. The question of whether "to join or not...should be your decision."[6] China cared little for what decision Kyrgyzstan made, certain that its weight would carry it through any problems that might be created.

Eventually, Kyrgyzstan did join the Eurasian Economic Union (EAEU). In late 2015, the country joined largely as a result of Russian pressure and the offer of a large chunk of money to help the country manage during the adjustment. When we visited markets in subsequent years, we found them diminished. Market vendors in Bishkek where we could find Chinese traders to talk to would complain to us that trade was down. One young Chinese woman whom we persuaded to talk to us complained that the Kyrgyz would harass her in the market and that the opportunities that used to exist in Bishkek had now moved to markets nearer the Uzbek border in Kara-Suu. As the new barriers were raised, traders and markets found it a more challenging environment, though many had found ways of adapting and moving on with their lives.

Looking at trade data, it is clear that there was a rush of Chinese goods into Kyrgyzstan in 2014 as traders sought to get as much in before the tariff barrier went up. In 2012, the value of Chinese exports to Kyrgyzstan was $2.12 billion, a number that increased to $2.5 billion the next year. In 2014, however, it spiked at $5.24 billion before dropping to $1.7 billion in 2015. Interestingly, by 2018 it had risen once again to $4.55 billion, suggesting the initial fears about the decimation of Kyrgyz markets might have been overplayed. The year 2014 also saw a brief spike in Chinese exports to Tajikistan where EAEU membership was not a consideration.[7]

What is notable about China's trade with both Kyrgyzstan and Tajikistan is how one-way it is. Trade back to China is limited and has largely shrunk over time. In contrast, with Uzbekistan, Kazakhstan, and Turkmenistan, given the dominance of commodities exports, trade has remained healthier and in the Central Asians' favor. In Turkmenistan, imports from China have actually declined over time.[8]

One issue, however, that has persisted over time are complaints about getting products back and forth across the border. When we visited Kyrgyzstan in 2012, a local contact encouraged us to meet the head of a local trucker association whom he had discovered complaining about the border and their ability to bring products across. We met a group of Kyrgyz truckers in the lobby of one of Bishkek's international hotels where our local translator struggled to properly understand their accents. They were angry about the fact that they were finding themselves stuck for extended periods at the border with China in their trucks waiting for goods to be loaded onto them. The delays were so bad that it was causing them visa issues with consequent legal trouble. The Kyrgyz truckers we met complained that they were not part of a cartel of Dungan and Uyghur drivers who had connections across the border in China, which allowed them to go to the front of the queue at the goods collection points in China.[9]

This was not the only time we heard frustrations about crossing borders with China with goods. At every border we visited, we would meet people complaining about lengthy transit times and greedy authorities seeking a payout. Chinese traders were always full of stories of petty border corruption, and in at least one instance our driver had to step out to pay a bribe to keep us going on our journey. Within Central Asia, however, the borders with China were often not the biggest problem. In Turkmenistan, spending a night at a hotel near ancient Merv (the only one which would accommodate foreigners), we met Iranian truckers who told us stories of how they had to time-stamp their passports in and out of the country after some of their number had been involved in road accidents on Turkmenistan's roads. Reportedly, in order to allow them to get the journeys done more quickly, drivers would consume amphetamines to stay awake. This would enable them to drive longer distances for longer time, but also tended to make them jittery and, after continuous consumption, made them erratic drivers. The result was horrendous accidents that led to Turkmen authorities imposing regulations that required truckers passing through their country to sleep the night somewhere, with time-stamps on their passports as evidence.

In another instance of trying to cross the border between Uzbekistan and Tajikistan we got to the post to find a huge queue of Tajiks waiting to cross. Seeing us arrive and hearing our accents, the men in the queue gestured for us to go to the front where the Uzbek border guards waved us through rapidly having checked our visas. After watching our bags go through the scanners, the guard who was relishing the opportunity to practice English with us pointed at our bags and said "explosives" in a questioning way. "Of course not!" we exclaimed as he smiled and shooed us on our way. In contrast, as we stood there waiting, we watched as his comrades meticulously rifled through the bags of every Tajik, questioning them aggressively and then taking them into a separate room where they were strip searched.

And at almost every land border post we went to which was open, we found long queues of trucks winding into the distance, laden with goods seeking to get to Central Asian markets or along Central Asian roads to reach other neighbors. As we trudged past on foot we would look up into the cabs and for the most part we would see the faces of Central Asian people, rather than Han, waiting. In Osh in southern Kyrgyzstan, we were told by local authorities that complaints from drivers about difficulties getting back and forth across the border was one of the biggest issues they had to contend with.

Slow border crossings in Central Asia which inhibit trade, are compounded by border spats, animosity between leaders, and occasional ethnic clashes that get in the way of China's vision of trade through the region. According to ADB figures, Central Asia is one of the few places where speed of trade across borders has slowed over time.[10] Unclear borders lead to regular border spats which involve exchanges of fire and loss of life. Awkwardly drawn borders mean that it can be easier to get between cities if you cross a border than if you stay within the country. But if the two governments are in the midst of a spat, this can complicate things. And finally, regular ethnic tensions lead to clashes and flows of refugees back and forth which can also result in abrupt closure of borders. All of which makes it very difficult to envisage the region as an area of free and easy trade which is described as the end goal of China's broader BRI. China can build all the infrastructure connecting the region and countries together, but if the governments have a dispute, the border will abruptly be closed down.

Various regional strategies have been advanced which seek to address these issues, but the degree to which they work is never clear. The Russian instigated EAEU (covered in greater detail in a later chapter), which encompasses Kazakhstan, Kyrgyzstan, and Russia (along with Armenia and Belarus), was intended to bring down border constrictions between member states, making trade transit easier. But problems persisted—with Kazakhs complaining that by opening themselves up to Kyrgyz markets they were exposing themselves to floods of illegal and imitation goods from Kyrgyzstan which had originated in China. A border check established between the two countries in early 2019 pointed to delays at getting goods across the Kazakh–Kyrgyz border, suggesting things were not very smooth.[11]

China also sought to address some of these issues. In 2014, the Shanghai Cooperation Organization (SCO) members signed the Agreement on International Road Transportation Facilitation, which aimed to open up trade routes from China through to Russia. The agreement sought to harmonize road transport arrangements across the entire SCO space.[12] The exact detail and effectiveness of the agreement are unclear. One researcher we spoke to who had visited Kyrgyzstan's southern markets in 2019 found no-one had heard of the agreement and they continued to face the same difficulties going back and forth across borders.[13] Other attempts by Chinese firms to offer tangible opportunities to help facilitate regional trade, like the project to build a trade and logistics center in At-Bashi, Kyrgyzstan, were stymied by local protestors. Signed to much fanfare during Xi Jinping's visit in 2019, the project was to build a logistics center which could service the region and once again make Kyrgyz markets central to the region. Yet, in February 2020 the project was dropped in the face of aggressive local protests with a lack of clarity whether it was the local authorities or the company itself that had withdrawn from the project. Whatever the case, this was a practical example of regional connectivity being blocked, and China's BRI dreams falling foul to local problems.

★ ★ ★

This complicated business environment did not stop hardy Chinese traders. In Bishkek on one visit we met a young Chinese student at the American University in Central Asia who was kind enough to introduce us to her parents. A couple who had lived in Kyrgyzstan for over fifteen years, they had met when he was working for a state-owned enterprise and she was taking Chinese tour groups into the country. Having met and fallen in love in Kyrgyzstan, they decided to stay and build lives there. They started by running a stall at Dordoi,

importing things from China which they sold. This business thrived
and soon they bought another stand at the market, continuing to
grow their business until they had built up enough capital to start to
manufacture in the country. For a while they ran a biscuit factory,
though when we met them it sounded like the factory was not doing
as well as in previous years. Now their most visible enterprise was a
Chinese restaurant where they kindly hosted us and introduced us to
Madame Wang, a glamorous middle-aged Chinese woman with bouf-
fant hair, fake furs, garish jewelry, and heavy make-up. A local fixer of
sorts for the Chinese community, when we asked her how much she
interacted with the local Chinese embassy she laughed and said, while
she had contacts, she had better and more direct ways of resolving any
issues that she or her friends might have.

Wandering around a market in Bishkek we struck up a conversation with a Chinese furniture salesman. Tall and middle aged, he spoke
with the patience of the teacher he had been back in China before
moving to Kyrgyzstan. Curious and bored of selling low-quality office
furniture for the day, he offered to take us to dinner at one of the
better local Chinese restaurants where he spent the meal patiently
correcting our Mandarin while telling us of his experiences in the
country. He had made his start in the country selling animal pelts
which he exported at great profit. But he found the country dangerous, and had fallen foul of criminals and rent-seeking authorities. In
one instance he told us how criminals had taken $100,000 in cash
from him at knife point. Taken aback by the amount, we asked why
he stayed. He shrugged and said there was not much for him back in
China anyway.

In Dushanbe, we were introduced through a Chinese friend to a
small bucktoothed businessman who sent his local interpreter to
come and pick us up from our hotel. He drove us to dinner before
insisting on showing us the factory and compound he had built where
he manufactured fireworks. The key for his business, he told us, was
that he had good relationships with some very senior figures in government who would commission him to produce firework displays

for them. But he also seemed to be making money from the compound he had built in an old factory in Dushanbe where an assortment of Chinese workers lived presumably paying him rent. He seemed to have big ambitions for the country, and saw us as a way in. The next day, he took us to lunch in a restaurant in one of Dushanbe's few tall buildings to a Chinese restaurant where he naturally knew the owner. He brought along a gift of two bottles of Chinese spirits, Baijiu, as a way of thanking us for friendship. Over lunch we learned of how the building that the restaurant was in was owned by one of the President's daughters who had built it as part of some suspicious deal with a Chinese company. On later visits to Dushanbe we were never able to track the bucktoothed man down again, and when finally we heard back from our initial introducer, we discovered his business had failed and he had moved on.

But not all of the Chinese traders we met were particularly there by choice. On a trip to Tashkent, a friend traveling with us joined us by flight directly from China while we came from elsewhere in Central Asia. On her flight from Beijing she met a group of businesspeople who were due to attend a "Uzbekistan Tashkent China Xinjiang Business and Trade Fair" in Tashkent. At the time, there were no direct flights between Urumqi and Tashkent, meaning they had to make a stopover in Beijing (a five hour flight from Urumqi in the wrong direction), before heading to Uzbekistan. While some were Xinjiang locals, many worked for Guangdong companies who had been told by the local authorities there to go and develop opportunities in Xinjiang after the 2010 Work Plan which sought to get China's wealthier regions to help the poorer parts of Xinjiang. Once they were in Xinjiang, they were further commanded to keep going westwards to find opportunities and markets in Central Asia. The event was sponsored by the Xinjiang government, though as they all grumbled, they still had to pay to attend.

We bumped into the Chinese businesspeople around town and helped them purchase fake old Soviet stuff that we suspected had actually been made in China. The next day we visited them at the

conference hall where the event they were attending was being held
and found that we had missed the keynote speeches. Instead, we found
a sparse looking hall dotted with their stands as they sat bored waiting
for Uzbeks to come and engage. They came from a wide variety of
different industries, from retail (one was selling Xinjiang food and
another clothes), electronics (from a Guangdong manufacturer who
had moved out to Xinjiang and was now seeking to sell his products to
locals through the Uyghur salesman he had brought along), to real estate
(a development near Kashgar), power generation (a Siemens subsidiary)
and threshing machines (made by Chinese aviation firm AVIC). These
last three struggled in particular given the lack of passing traffic interested in their goods, and instead for the most part found themselves
fighting off Uzbek children who were keen to play with the display
models they had brought along. We spent much of the day with them
as they groused about how poor the Uzbeks were and what a pointless
market this was, though at the end the tailor made a sale and was
rewarded with huge bundles of worthless Uzbek som. Aware of awkward exchange rates he planned to simply blow the money on "dinner,
drinks and karaoke." At the time the exchange rates in Uzbekistan were
centrally controlled and largely artificial. On one visit, the official rate
was around 3,000 Som to the US dollar, while the unofficial rate was
around 8000. At the time of this visit, it was 1,800 to 2,800—and this
was when you could actually change money.

A few days later, at the introduction of his sister, an academic, we
met with an Uzbek businessman over lunch whose company had
helped sponsor the Expo. He was surprisingly frank about how successful the Expo had been. "Not very, to be honest, but better than last
time," he said. "More Chinese are coming." A former government
employee, he had seen the economic possibilities of China's dynamic
manufacturing capabilities and had chosen to end a flourishing civil
service career at a young age to go into business, with a focus on
China. Though at the forefront of Sino–Uzbek relations, he was not
optimistic about Xinjiang as the gateway for Central Asia. The province made low-quality products, and traders were, in fact, simply

agents from elsewhere in China, something illustrated by the high number of Guangdong firms we encountered. But he admitted that the greater problem was the difficult business environment in Uzbekistan in general. Awkward red tape, worthless currency conversions, and a political environment that took very careful maneuvering meant that it did not matter how many trade fairs were held, things would remain complicated.

We met with the Uzbek businessman again on a visit years later (just before President Karimov had passed away) when the country had started to try to reform its economy a bit. The local currency had lost even more value, but there was an ever-clearer Chinese presence in the country. The businessman had now upgraded his factory and owned a giant showroom where he was showcasing the Chinese vehicles and equipment he was selling. He had recently won a large contract with SinoTruck. He was still bullish on China as an economic opportunity and as candid as we remembered. This time, much of our discussions in Tashkent focused on complaints about the quality of Chinese goods. When we asked him about his experience, his response was honest. Chinese products may be of lower quality, but they were cheaper, and this balanced things out. You could buy more knowing it would last less time but then buying replacements was cheaper, meaning in aggregate it was worth it. And anyway, as he pointed out, the quality was improving all the time. This step up in quality was observable. Every visit showed a greater volume of Chinese advertising, showcasing high-quality electronic products from China and the latest Huawei phones with their top of the range cameras.

The businessman was not the only Uzbek we met who had grabbed the China opportunity with both hands. In Tashkent we were hosted by a generous and successful couple whose husband had made his fortune importing white goods from China. Initially a customs agent, he had noticed the opportunity to be had bringing in products to Uzbekistan, a market that had been closed for many years, and had set himself up as an importer of electronic products. Over time, he had built enough connections in China through events like the Canton fair that he had designed his own brand of goods with a suitably reliable sounding European name. He took us around Tashkent markets, pointing out his products, introducing us to friends and proudly showing off the billboards he had put up to advertise his air conditioning units.

When we approached Chinese traders in Almaty or Zharkent in Kazakhstan, they were equally friendly and would tell us stories of children in faraway universities in America, and of owning numerous properties in Shanghai: stories we could never verify, in much the same way as we could never help with their inquiries about housing markets in London or New York. In one market stall in Zharkent we met a group of Chinese men playing cards, bored as they boasted of the numbers of stalls they owned at the market. As with many markets in the region, Barakholka and Zharkent markets are largely made up of old shipping containers that have been transformed into shops. While most markets also have a central structure to them, as you go away from this, it becomes a field of rusting shipping containers. Owning one of these stands was a highly profitable enterprise, though their long-term viability is unclear. The advent of the EAEU has changed the market flows, and the growing regional use of Chinese online providers like Taobao or Alibaba has shrunk their utility as middlemen.

In a sign of what the future might look like, in Bishkek we met a young Kyrgyz who had set up a website to facilitate access to Chinese sales portals. Aware that these sites were in Chinese and quite difficult to navigate if you didn't know Mandarin or how to deal with Chinese traders, he had established himself as an online middleman for the sites. Meeting us in a brown leather jacket for a coffee in one of Bishkek's many cafes which he had until recently frequented as a student at the American University in Central Asia, he sketched out his plans to build an online empire from Bishkek, linking China and Russia together. Drawing on his linguistic skills, he was moving online what his countrymen had been doing for decades offline in markets throughout the region.

This wave of the future was not lost on policymakers in the region. The SCO in particular has sought ways of facilitating this growing online connectivity, to spread its wings from beyond the security space and to help realize China's ambitions of being a global e-commerce giant. In mid-2019, Alibaba founder Jack Ma met with the SCO secretary general and advanced a plan to invest heavily in the SCO space. Toward the end of the year, this agreement was given teeth through a joint venture between Russia's Direct Investment Fund (RDIF), a government investment vehicle, the Mail.ru Group, mobile phone operator Megafon, and Alibaba. The Chinese firm promised to invest some $100 million into the project, which would mean its payment tools and merchandise would now provide greater access to Russia, while Russian consumers would have greater access to China and the growing parts of Asia which use Alibaba or its subsidiaries. Already, estimates suggest that some two-thirds of all packages traveling from China to Russia and Central Asia are linked to Alibaba or its subsidiaries. The strengthening of this link through these deals further binds Russia, China, and Central Asia together.

The Silk Road was now moving beyond the synthetic, markets and minerals evolution that had developed during the 2010s to reach into e-commerce. For traders in Central Asia, the opportunities were still potentially there, but the nature of the benefits remains unclear, requiring entrepreneurs to be more dynamic like our contact in Bishkek. He saw that his future opportunities lay in figuring out what the new digital and cyber versions of the Silk Road trade would look like, from China to the west and Russia, and how he could make sure he made this trade run through his own website and country.

5

Confucius on the Oxus

"Why do you want to learn Chinese?" we asked the class. "Because I love China!" came one eager response. "Because I want to visit China!" screeched another, in the flat tones typical of a foreigner learning Mandarin. Asking this question at every Chinese school we visited in Central Asia, the answers were invariably different, though driving them tended to be pragmatism about learning the language of the coming power rather than any romantic notions of reading Sun Tzu or Confucius in the original language. One teacher told us the parents usually sent their sons and daughters to learn Mandarin since it would help with business, while most children we asked said that they saw China as an opportunity for work. This was reflected in one class where they were learning the word for business card (*mingpian*名片). At another in Kyrgyzstan, we did a quick poll of which cities they wanted to visit: historic Beijing scored remarkably low, trumped by trading hub Guangzhou or Shanghai with its gleaming commercial towers.

From a Chinese perspective this is of course no bad thing. Increasing the number of traders or locals who speak Chinese will facilitate future trade. More immediately, the many Chinese businesses setting up in Kyrgyzstan and elsewhere in Central Asia will have a ready supply of potential managers—at a number of the schools visited we were told by teachers that this was one of the primary endpoints for their students. One Tajik we met in Dushanbe who had been a Chinese teacher before deciding to go into business told us how big Chinese firms had approached him when he was a teacher. First, they had asked if he had good students they could hire, then they had changed tack and offered him a substantial boost on his teacher's salary to instead come and work for them.

On the demand side, a Chinese engineer who had worked in Turkmenistan told us how it was a shame he was unable to communicate with his Turkmen colleagues, with the only one who spoke any Chinese speaking the language in a manner that was incomprehensible.[1] Some companies try to offer solutions to these problems. In Afghanistan we were told that Metallurgical Corporation of China (MCC), the Chinese firm exploiting a mining site in the country, was dedicating a part of the site for a classroom in which locals could learn Chinese. In Uzbekistan, Huawei sends back certain key local mid-level staff to China—in part as a training trip, but also as a cultural acclimatization effort. They have also established a "seeds for the future" program which aims to offer Central Asian students an education in China and first-hand experience of the firm at its headquarters. It is a global program, reaching across Central Asia. Locally, they offer language classes for those who are working for the company.

Such measures of course serve a dual purpose. At a practical level, they help the company develop its links and capability on the ground. But they also have an additional soft power impact. The great intangible publicly defined by former US State Department policy planner Joseph Nye, soft power remains an elusive concept for Beijing. Talking to officials in the Ministry of Foreign Affairs, they express frustration at how they are perceived internationally, seeing themselves as merely trying to bring China's harmonious world view to a resentful planet. They ask for advice on how to shape their nation's image in the world, vexed as to why a portly dancing South Korean man can utterly reinvent South Korea's image on the world stage, while the billions their firms spend in rebuilding the developing world are seen in an avaricious light. For the Chinese officials, educational institutions, cultural exchanges, language courses are all seen as tools being deployed to help locals and advance China's good name. Following Professor Nye's definition, China seeks to develop its "soft power" through the development of "intangible power resources such as culture, ideology, and institutions."[2] While it is not always clear how effective these efforts actually are, China's "soft power" efforts in the region are multifaceted, with Confucius Institutes (CI) often the most obvious piece. During our visits to the region we tried to see as many as we could and were struck by the added layer of complexity they added to our understanding of the region's relationship with China.

★ ★ ★

He struck a sad figure as we left him in the dust in the middle of Jalalabad. A tall and slightly stooped Uyghur, Mahmut (we will call him) was the CI representative in the south of Kyrgyzstan. Sent from Xinjiang University, he had been based in Jalalabad for over a year and was clearly lonely. Arriving on the recommendation of the CI officers in Bishkek, he rolled out the red carpet for us, taking us around the city's sights and to see the university campus he was based at. A white-washed old building, Jalalabad University has two wings each containing a different cultural center: on the one side, a US embassy sponsored American cultural center replete with copies of *Pulp Fiction*, language courses, books, and films intended to stimulate learning. The most popular element was a computer with Internet connection that they did their best to restrict with twenty-five-minute blocks of time per session (a detail which dates our visit to the city, while also illustrating the transformative effect of the greater online connectivity offered by Chinese investment, which will be discussed later). The Chinese side offered a much less glamorous but practical approach: somewhere in the region of sixty students learned under the tutelage of teachers sent by Hanban, the CI's central command in Beijing. The brightest students were given opportunities to travel to China with photos showing visits to Xi'an, Shanghai, and Urumqi adorning the wall temptingly. For students living in the dusty remnants of Jalalabad, a city that had been torn apart by ethnic violence between Uzbeks and Kyrgyz in 2010 (Mahmut confided that most of his Uzbek students had left soon afterwards), the option of visiting China is no doubt an appealing one, especially when on a sponsored trip.

The CIs are a Chinese version of the UK's British Council, the French Alliance Française or the German Goethe Institut. Government supported organizations that usually provide a blend of language courses, cultural classes, and events to showcase the nation that they represent. According to their website, the primary function of Hanban (the CI's parent institution in Beijing) is threefold: "To make policies and development plans for promoting Chinese language internationally; to support Chinese language programs at educational institutions of various types and levels in other countries; to draft international Chinese teaching standards and develop and promote Chinese language teaching materials."[3]

When we first visited a Central Asian CI in 2012 in Kyrgyzstan, we were told they were not equipped to do any cultural events (the teachers with relevant training were not there) and they were instead focused on teaching students (some of whom would in turn become teachers) to learn Chinese. At one of the more enthusiastic centers in the south, however, we saw students actively embracing Chinese culture, getting their Chinese teachers to help them learn tai chi, and making impressive imitations of Chinese clothing (an oddly ironic turn of events). In fact, at every CI we visited we found evidence of cultural learning to varying degrees, and heard reports locally of the CI supporting and sponsoring events around town with the embassy to advance Chinese culture.

As illustrated by the mandate above, the main purpose of the CIs is linguistic, and across the three cities that we found them in Kyrgyzstan we heard they had roughly 4,000–5,000 students. With two official institutes in Bishkek and two subsidiaries in Osh and Jalalabad,[4] the institutes were described to us as management points from where they would coordinate the delivery of language textbooks (new Kyrgyz–Chinese ones had just arrived when we got there, an upgrade from the Russian–Chinese ones they had been using before) and dispatch teachers sent by the Hanban headquarters in Beijing. Each CI is linked to a Chinese university. In Kyrgyzstan they are connected to the Xinjiang Normal University and Xinjiang University. In Tajikistan, the one in Dushanbe is linked to Xinjiang Normal University while the one in Khujand is linked to Chinese University of Petroleum. The paired university is responsible for dispatching professors who head the various regional branches, both managing and teaching. This created a heavy workload, with one teacher telling us how overworked he and his fellow colleague were in their isolated, dusty city. The postings were only for two years, but two years being underpaid and alone in ethnically tense Osh or Jalalabad (so tense that when we visited, the US had withdrawn its Peace Corps volunteers) can challenge the most optimistic educator.

But they continue, a mix of managers and academics offering pedagogical support to the young Kyrgyz who are attempting the challenge of learning Mandarin. Most of the students have a relatively limited grasp of the language, though one young student in Bishkek clearly distinguished himself from the others. His teacher, a softly spoken middle-aged professor called Zhang from Xinjiang University who would later regale us with stories of religious conflicts played out across Xinjiang and Central Asia, was clearly proud of the young student who boasted of being able to read over 2,000 Chinese characters. Over dinner he said that his interest in learning Chinese was to pursue economic opportunities, but also as a result of his ethnicity. Ethnically Hui (a Chinese Muslim), he had been born and brought up in Kyrgyzstan as part of the ethnically Chinese diaspora that can be found across the region. When asked if he had visited his extended family in China, he said yes, but that he had found them awkward to deal with, in much more of a rush than the laid-back Kyrgyz he was used to in Bishkek. Professor Zhang chimed in at this point agreeing that the hustle and bustle of Chinese cities was far less appealing than the relatively calm Bishkek.

In Tajikistan a similar story played out. Visiting the campus of Dushanbe's Tajik National University, we found the CI in the back of the languages department. A small corridor adorned with red lanterns, the institute boasted one large classroom, a smaller one, and a couple of offices for administrators. Sitting in his office sipping Chinese tea, the Chinese administrator Professor Xin leaned back in his chair and looked out the window at the bucolic Tajik countryside visible from his window, smiling when we asked him whether he liked it in Tajikistan. "Of course I do," he said, back in China he was from Altay, a region in the north of Xinjiang on the Chinese side of the Altai Mountain range. The Tajik countryside reminded him of home. From Xinjiang's wildernesses, he had been dispatched by Xinjiang Normal University and found Tajiks welcoming and calm. He was clearly enjoying his time in the country even though the teaching conditions were difficult. They had no direct Tajik-Chinese language books and were obliged instead to make do through Russian, even though this didn't work that well anymore given the increasingly limited number of Tajiks who spoke Russian. At the time there was only one small Tajik-Chinese dictionary in existence, the product of an enterprising businessman who had seen a gap in the market, but the book was of limited use and additionally it was difficult to procure a copy. Some of the students were keen, but he had noticed a substantial drop-off as time went on—many started, but not all finished their courses.

As we sat there chatting, a pair of pretty young Tajik girls burst in, coquettishly batting their eyelids, asking Professor Xin in simple but fluent Mandarin about whether he had heard back about their scholarship applications to go and study in China. The institute offered twenty to twenty-five places per year and competition was quite fierce. He didn't have any news and he encouraged them to practice their Mandarin with us. Seeing we were not Chinese they rapidly lost interest and only half-heartedly answered our questions about why they were learning the language. Their professor later told us they both seemed quite likely candidates for the scholarships, but they were quite young and might have to wait a year. When we asked about what their job prospects were like afterwards, he told us most became translators or teachers, helping other Tajiks along the difficult path to learning Mandarin.

When we first visited in 2012, unlike neighboring Kyrgyzstan with its two large institutes and two substantial offshoots, Tajikistan had only one institute in Dushanbe that had taught some 1,800 students at every level in the past year. This was an increase on the year before, and there had been steady year-on-year increases for the past five years. At the request of a keen local official who had had a positive experience with China and had approached the Chinese embassy specifically, they had dispatched a Hanban-trained teacher to Panjakent to teach local high school children, though the experience did not seem to be working out. The isolated teacher was apparently lonely at his outpost in the western corner of the country and spent most of his time hanging around the local Chinese company offices seeking company. It was not clear how many students he had managed to pass on his language to. In 2014, a decision was made to formally expand the CI footprint in Tajikistan with the opening of a second campus in Khujand linked to the Chinese Petroleum University. Years later, during the first half of 2020 in the midst of the global COVID-19 pandemic, this CI took the lead in translating Chinese language manuals on managing the disease into Russian to help local doctors navigate in responding to the virus.[5]

As we were leaving the university in Dushanbe we struck up a conversation with a Chinese girl who had served us tea while we were with the professor. It emerged she was one of the younger teachers dispatched to help the Tajiks learn Chinese. From Nanjing, she had learned Russian, having studied it in China and then spent five years in Bishkek. She was starting her first year in Tajikistan and like her director, she liked the country, enjoying the company of Tajiks with whom she could practice her budding Tajik language skills. One of a number of Chinese we met in Dushanbe, they all seemed perfectly happy to wander around the city without any great concern about being singled out for being Chinese. The girl from Nanjing confirmed this, telling us how she had lots of Tajik friends and was perfectly happy and safe in the city.

Isolated Turkmenistan had no CIs, with only rumors of a pair of Chinese teachers apparently working at the foreign studies university. The absence of an institute was not due to Chinese intransigence, but rather the fact that Chinese universities had been unable to make connections with the relevant universities within Turkmenistan. While they are government supported and controlled, CI are intended to be university to university projects—requiring the educational institutions to develop connections that are then approved at a higher level by the Ministry of Education. In Turkmenistan, as we were told in Urumqi by the head of cultural exchanges at Xinjiang Normal University, things were simply very closed.

But in Kazakhstan and Uzbekistan the situation is very different. Both countries are more economically developed and wealthier than Kyrgyzstan or Tajikistan, and the CIs are not needed in the same basic way that they are in the poorer Central Asian countries. With an already established network of well-funded universities that were centers of learning, the CIs in Kazakhstan and Uzbekistan had a very different set of responsibilities. In Astana the CI was based out of the Eurasian University, and we were met by a suited and smiling professor from Xi'an Foreign Studies University. He had been in Astana for about two years and was entering his third and final year in the country. He had somewhere in the region of 660 students currently learning Mandarin, a mix of undergraduates and aspiring teachers. One female student he introduced us to was a keen sinologist who was eager to visit Beijing and Xi'an, fascinated by the complicated language and ideograms. Unlike the CIs we had visited in Kyrgyzstan and Tajikistan, a greater proportion of the students we met were more focused on the value of learning the language for cultural reasons. Rather than solely being fixated on finding employment in China or doing business in the country (though admittedly there were a fair few who still wanted to do that), the focus was on a greater spread of people seeking future opportunity and those seeking to learn Mandarin out of fascination with the language and culture.

In Uzbekistan, the distinction was even stronger. The Tashkent CI was a poor partner to its far more imposing language school at the Tashkent Oriental Studies University. A left-over from Soviet times, the Oriental Studies University was one of the major centers of learning in Central Asia that remained a home for Russian-language Asian and Chinese studies. With over 1,000 students, it also had a number of Hanban-trained professors, though they were far more paranoid about letting us into their school. One, a burly Uzbek-Chinese, had been in the country for years, but had too much paper-work to do to talk to us in any great detail about how things were going.

The CI was located in a squat, slightly run-down building opposite the Kazakh embassy in Tashkent. A small paper figure of a Chinese woman on the wall was all that identified it as a Chinese hub in the city. Inside, a pair of professors from Lanzhou University led a team of young Uzbek teachers who taught children Chinese. Their students were a mixed group of about 120 of all ages, mostly sent there by parents who saw China as an opportunity to be exploited. One told of how she had been persuaded to learn by her grandmother who was now in Kazakhstan, but had previously worked in China and picked up a bit of the language. Using the Chinese name Xiaolong (which literally translates as "little dragon"), the Uzbek teacher showing us his class told of how another child's parents would call the school every day to ask how their son was doing. Showing us the beaten textbook he used, he reported that they were given very little by Hanban in Beijing and had resorted to photocopying the single textbook page by page for each class. The teachers sent from Lanzhou apparently did not come into the office much—we went three times in total and found none on any of our visits. An enthusiastic young man, Xiaolong had difficulty with his students and their language levels reflected this, with most unable to answer basic Chinese questions. We discovered that the CIs in the country had received a boost later, but it still seemed as though the local universities were bigger drivers of Chinese education than the CIs which simply provided some support and contacts with China.

But this all paled in comparison to the CI at Kabul University. Paired with Taiyuan Technical University, the institute had no Chinese teachers when we visited (long before the Taliban takeover). Teaching was led by an Omar, an eager young Afghan who spoke fluent but atonal Chinese and had been left in charge of the institute after the Chinese teachers had left out of concern over the security situation. Adjacent to the languages department, a construction site marked where the Chinese government was erecting a new building to house the institute and Chinese language classes, but this was unfinished when we visited. Sitting in the office with the head of the languages department, using a mix of Spanish, Chinese, and fragments of English to communicate, we heard how China used to be a bigger feature of Kabul University life. According to the department head some thirty to fifty years prior there had been Chinese students at the university, but they had left little mark on the place with the much-reduced CI being all that was left.

Omar eagerly showed us around the building and spaces dedicated to Chinese learning, replete with new (and seemingly unused) computers, projectors, and photocopiers. He only had forty or so students, and they were learning for a variety of reasons. Many were fascinated by China, but most were eager to learn the language for practical reasons. Former students had been recruited by Huawei, China National Petroleum Corporation (CNPC), Zhongxing Telecommunications Equipment (ZTE), and Metallurgical Corporation of China (MCC), while the more entrepreneurial ones would head to Yiwu in China to buy goods to sell in Kabul's dusty markets. There had been a sharp drop-off in Chinese merchants and citizens around the city—the spike in violence from 2008 onward had scared off most, with Hanban finally deciding in early 2012 to pull the plug on sending out Chinese professors. With Omar the only one left, the prospect for those learning Mandarin was quite limited, with most preferring to try English, French, or German—even Japanese apparently attracted more students than Chinese. Chinese companies did invest in building infrastructure for the university, but it was not clear how much educational support atop of this was forthcoming.

The CI and the levels of Chinese language learning in many ways offer a microcosm of China's relations with Central Asia. Largely abandoned Kabul and less-invested efforts in Dushanbe reflect the relatively low interest that Beijing has in those two countries, while Kyrgyzstan is a hub of activity—both in institute and trading terms—as a poor country that needs and takes advantage of all the help it can get. For China, Kyrgyzstan is the highway into Central Asia, and in particular it links up the more distant parts of Xinjiang with potential markets. It is an important entry point into Central Asia, and also a source of potential risk with its porous borders and weak security apparatus. This risk that was amply illustrated in 2016 with the bombing of China's embassy in Bishkek. All of which helps to show why the country merits particular attention from China. In prosperous Kazakhstan, the CIs reside within mainstream universities, offering language teaching and support to those who seek it. A model that reflects the relations between CI and their partners in Western countries—where they are language centers housed in mainstream universities. This reflects the more sober and balanced relationship that exists between China and Kazakhstan. Uzbekistan on the other hand feels it does not need the language schools—while it uses its teachers as support staff in the mainstream universities, it already has established centers of Chinese learning. Again, the relationship is one which the locals benefit from, but are not necessarily dependent on in the same way.

In a particularly colorful experience, we visited a class at the World Studies University in Tashkent where we met an advanced class of undergraduate students. Mostly girls, some spoke excellent Chinese—good enough to be able to see through and correct our own creaky attempts. When asked why they were learning Chinese, some mentioned trade, but most had been drawn by an interest in the culture. The best of the girls was desperately eager to become a presenter on Chinese television and had entered a number of competitions to show off how good her Chinese was. In one, part of a regular "Chinese Bridge" competition in which foreigners demonstrate their capacity in Mandarin before an audience, the Chinese ambassador had particularly congratulated her on her fluency and diction. Clearly the apple of her teacher's eye, when we visited the competition that happened to be taking place while we were in Tashkent, the teacher was furiously applauding in the front row.

The best of the boys had a more traditional route he wanted to pursue—as a diplomat in the Ministry of Foreign Affairs, though he recognized that the Uzbek system was such that jobs in the government were hard to get. Nonetheless, fluent Chinese would help him overcome these obstacles. In between repeating to us the rote phrases their teacher had had them memorize (for example, about how the first thing foreigners like to do when they come to China is eat Peking Duck), they all agreed on one thing: China was the upcoming power. Learning the language would undoubtedly help them.

★   ★   ★

Visiting the other end of the CI in China was a salutary experience in understanding the mechanics of how these institutions saw themselves in China's broader projection into Central Asia. Each of the CIs had a partner institution in China, with Xinjiang hosting many of the larger links. Keen to find out how they saw their responsibilities we reached out to meet with them in Urumqi at Xinjiang Normal University and Xinjiang University.

Arriving to our meeting at Xinjiang Normal University, there was a distinct odor of alcohol at the table. The university cafeteria was abuzz with random people having loud meetings and jabbering on phones. The professor, reportedly the head of international relations at the university, introduced himself briefly before leaving to get his business cards. His colleagues sat mute. Trying to break the ice we made conversation asking what it was they worked on, using a mix of English and Mandarin. "Philosophy," one of them informed us. We asked what kind of philosophy. "Philosophy," he confirmed, nodding sagely. The boss returned, which was the philosopher's cue to leave. The boss apologized that the philosopher had had to leave so early, but he was very busy with other meetings. This set the tone for one of our more memorable meetings in Xinjiang. Having gotten the pleasantries out of the way, we probed to understand why the university had ended up being responsible for the CI in Central Asia.

"Well," he informed us, "we are just simple researchers. For such information we would recommend you go look at official sites and statements." We were caught by this statement, having had our entire substantive question list just shut down. Eager to try to extract something from a meeting which had been awkward to organize in a far-flung part of China, we tried to dig deeper, only to be met by evasive responses about how people-to-people links were key to China's relations with the world. "Global peace" was important we were told. He was willing to share with us that they were the coordinators of some of the Shanghai Cooperation Organization (SCO) educational structures, though he did not offer much detail beyond pointing to the various SCO member state flags that surrounded us in the canteen we were sitting in.

Eventually we discovered the real reason we had been allowed to meet with him in this open cafeteria to enjoy his weak coffee and dry biscuits: "I have never been to England." Apparently, researchers here feel isolated, and want to be more involved in international meetings and conferences. As foreigners he saw us as a good opportunity to make this case and seek introductions to enable his travel. Having clarified his request, he was then apologetic, admitting that he had previously been at a luncheon with some other visitors that had involved drinking. We wished it had made him more loquacious as we wrapped up a meeting, whose entertainment value had superseded its substance. But the entire experience showed us the university's commitment to its obligations under the SCO and to Central Asia. The CIs were seen as a task, one of many the university administrators had to manage, rather than as a tool that was part of a larger strategy. It certainly did not seem a passion.

On a trip years later we met again with Professor Zhang whom we had met in Bishkek. A softly spoken man, he insisted on taking us to lunch with his daughter, to help her improve her English. Over a typical Chinese meal in Urumqi we discovered his real thoughts about

Central Asia and Uyghurs in particular. More of a Han nationalist than we had remembered when we had met him years before in Bishkek, he was of the belief that China was bringing great opportunity to the region and that Central Asians should be more grateful for what they were getting from China. We reminded him of his young student, and he wistfully said the young man had pursued further studies in China. However, he saw him as exceptional, stating that the vast majority of those he came across in Kyrgyzstan (or neighboring countries, as he appeared to have traveled to visit other CIs a number of times and could speak from experience across the region) were relatively indolent. This was a common refrain we encountered among the more outspoken Chinese we found in Xinjiang and Central Asia. They would often comment on how low the work ethic was among locals, contrasting it with Han diligence.

While undoubtedly tinged with racism, this honesty was somewhat refreshing and echoed what we had heard in discussions at the Xinjiang Academy of Social Sciences (XJASS) where they saw the activity that China was undertaking in the region as beneficial to Central Asia rather than necessary to Xinjiang. What China was doing in Xinjiang was something which Central Asia should be grateful for. Few Han Chinese we met from Xinjiang or elsewhere who were in Central Asia were particularly enthralled by the region. Those who were tended to be young, idealistic, and eager to discover the world (which is why the Peace Corps volunteer analogy worked quite well for the young CI teachers). One good friend whom we repeatedly met in Tajikistan had been settled in the region for almost a decade and found Central Asians warm and friendly. But he had left behind a difficult life in Xinjiang as a doctor in a remote hospital, and he also clearly appreciated the rugged terrain that Tajikistan and the region offered. He was in a minority though. Some of the young students sent by Hanban to work at the CIs in Central Asia shared his optimistic perspective on the region, but they were often also quite fiercely nationalistic or found themselves exhausted by what they encountered in Central Asia.

Seen from Beijing's perspective, the value of CIs is to help develop connections on the ground. Teaching language, providing a vehicle to offer scholarships and experiences in China, the CIs provide an easy-to-offer-and-deliver outreach tool. In countries that are aid dependent—like Kyrgyzstan and Tajikistan—they are welcomed in much the same way as similar programs from the West or other countries like Japan, South Korea, or Russia. At the same time, it is not always clear how the Chinese option stacks up in popularity against the others. During one visit to Kyrgyzstan, we were accompanied to our meetings by a smart young multilingual woman who spoke excellent Russian, Mandarin, and English. As well as helping foreigners like ourselves, in her day job she worked in a company that helped young Kyrgyz get placements and study abroad—almost all were keen to head to the UK or US. Chinese opportunities may have more funding and opportunity attached to them, but the attraction was still not strong.

However, the CIs are not the only tool in Beijing's playbook. At the embassy in Dushanbe we were told about cultural events that they were running and how cultural musical troupes were a big success in the country. They had brought over six separate groups in the past year, and the most successful one was from Xinjiang, playing local Xinjiang rather than classical Chinese music. Additional links that were not visibly state supported were provided through a popular Chinese-medicine hospital that lay at one end of Rudaki Avenue, Dushanbe's main drag. Full when we stopped by, it had a Chinese-looking staff member who denied being Chinese but spoke good Mandarin. When pushed about where he was from, he provided an incomprehensible response asking us to come back later when it was less busy. The doctor had been there about a year, establishing the hospital as a business venture that was apparently popular among the local Tajiks. Its primary business was acupuncture and herbal medicines, and it stayed open late every day. Traditional Chinese medicine has received a particular boost in the wake of COVID-19 as President Xi and other senior Chinese officials championed its use to mitigate the virus as part of the wave of "medical diplomacy" that China pushed out in the wake of the virus.

On a different visit to Dushanbe we met again with the CI director who was in the midst of organizing a mini film festival of Chinese cinema in the city. Enthusiastic as ever, he ushered us into seats in the crowded hall, with free water and snacks, as a cultural attaché from the embassy provided some opening remarks in fluent Russian. The audience then sat back to watch the latest blockbuster action film out of China. We stayed with them for a few minutes before sneaking out, but the room was full and people seemed to be enjoying the experience.

At an infrastructure level, Chinese firms have undertaken a number of prestige projects in Tajikistan. The impressive new Ministry of Foreign Affairs has been built by Chinese contractors. An apocryphal anecdote we heard a number of times was that Huawei had installed the telephone system and had left the answering message in Chinese for some time. A lake in the middle of the city separates the Ministry from the main public square where the world's tallest flagpole, a national library and a presidential palace surround a manicured park.[6] All Chinese-built, the most visible stamp of China on the public space is a set of health machines with English and Chinese language instruction stickers on them. Chatting to a group of children playing in the square, using broken English, we asked whether any of them wanted to learn Chinese. Repulsed they all shook their heads, only to then chime in with good pronunciation *nihao* ('hello') and *woshi Tajik-ren* ('I am Tajik'). Up and down Dushanbe's main Rudaki Avenue, old green and white buses chugged along with "China Aid" logos on the side, while Chinese-gifted dustbins are planted at regular intervals along the road.

The practical impact of all of this soft aid is hard to measure, although it seems to mostly be falling on deaf ears. Most Tajiks when we first visited in 2011 and 2012 had little to no view on China. The young and aspiring saw it as a potential business opportunity, although rumors abounded of Chinese mass marrying abandoned Tajik brides (with most Tajik men leaving the country to seek their fortunes in Russia, leaving armies of lonely women behind). However, looking around there was little evidence of mixed race children and when we asked at the Chinese embassy we were told they had only registered one marriage between a Chinese and a Tajik in four years. Instead locals ask whether it is true that the Chinese work crews rebuilding their country or exploiting their natural resources are prison laborers as they had been told. Largely kept in grim camps alongside their places of employment and willing to work long hours, the Chinese laborers tended to keep to themselves. Consequently, opportunities for interaction were quite limited, which had led to rumor and innuendo.

In later years, we found the volume of Chinese speakers in Dushanbe had increased. We met a growing number of young Tajiks who had learned some Mandarin recognizing the opportunity that the country offered. A number worked as local helpers for Chinese businesspeople working in the country, driving them around, providing occasional fix-it jobs as required. Some took on jobs as interpreters or fixers for bigger companies. Sitting on a balmy evening in late 2019 in the courtyard of one of Dushanbe's bigger hotels a young man who had worked with a Chinese firm told us how he had started off as a university teacher, teaching Mandarin to other Tajiks. He had then been approached by a large Chinese firm which he declined to identify to try to find them some interpreters. Underwhelmed by what he had offered, they instead said they would give him a substantial pay increase to come and work for them. He was initially enthused by the idea, but soon discovered that they largely wanted him to go around and act as a go-between for them with corrupt local officials. He also could not understand what work the company was actually doing, beyond receiving and consuming large state-backed loans which he suspected were being siphoned off to pay off local officials and fill the Chinese businesspeople's pockets.

This particular firm may remain anonymous, but similar rumors exist around other projects. Key pieces of infrastructure investment have clearly been done with a view to curry favor with the regime in Dushanbe, like the roads linking the president's village to the capital; or the one toll road in the country that was Chinese-built and managed by a mysterious British Virgin Islands firm that is believed to be controlled by regime family members. Numerous negative rumors float around about China's long-term intentions, suggesting that any sort of soft power effort has so far fallen on fallow ground. But at the same time, go out to some of Tajikistan's more remote regions where Chinese infrastructure has been built and you can also hear a different story. While in these parts of the country it is almost impossible to find people who speak Mandarin, you do find locals who are complimentary of Chinese projects and workmanship. They may wonder about what their government agreed to in order to get the investment to build a road, but they point out that in contrast to when local contractors are hired to build something, when the Chinese win the contract it actually happens quickly. This tangible reality is an often-overlooked bolster to China's image in the region.

The soft power push in Kyrgyzstan is very different and far more visible. Quite aside from the far more numerous CIs, other efforts are focused on more traditional aid projects. Precise totals are unpublished, but the various projects announced in the media or through firms paint a picture. The Chinese government has donated Yaxing buses and tractors for Kyrgyz farmers to use.[7] In June 2011, the Chinese ambassador announced a donation of some $14.3 million to Kyrgyzstan to fix roads, power stations, and to support the construction of the railroad in the country.[8] In April 2013, the Chinese Red Cross signed a bilateral agreement with its Kyrgyz counterpart and handed over $200,000 in aid (described made up of medicines, yurts, blankets, tents).[9] Following on from senior level statements on agriculture support and cooperation from Xi Jinping and Wang Yi after visits to Kyrgyzstan, the two countries focused on improving connections between their agriculture industries. China provided training and technical assistance, including innovative techniques, to their Kyrgyz counterparts. In a direct link back to Xinjiang, Deputy Zhanybek

Kerimaliev spoke in 2016 about the fact that they were receiving assistance in greenhouse use and construction from agriculture firms in Xinjiang.[10] And like in Dushanbe, China Aid branded buses appeared on Bishkek's dusty roads.

But there are other aspects to China's cultural influence in Kyrgyzstan. In early 2009, the Kyrgyz government accepted a Chinese offer of 20,000 television receivers for individual homes in the Batken Oblast in southern Kyrgyzstan. A strip of land surrounded by Tajikistan, Uzbekistan, and mountains, locals were only able to receive news from neighboring countries using antiquated television receivers. This isolation meant that official messages largely failed to get through, and people got their news from Uzbek television reports, which painted the Bishkek leadership in a bad light. According to a senior foreign ministry official we spoke to in Bishkek, part of the exchange that the Chinese government extracted in return for the receivers was to allow Chinese national broadcaster CCTV (China Central Television) Russian to be broadcast directly into the country. Our translator repeatedly interjected to say that he had long before then received CCTV on his television cable package, but the point was that the channel was broadcast in the country to be received by antenna. The Chinese ambassador at the time was quite open about the soft power potential of CCTV in reaching Kyrgyzstan. As he put it, "now Kyrgyz viewers can get information about international events, including from China. They can also become more familiar with our culture."[11]

In addition to this, however, locals in Osh reported that they were able to receive Xinjiang television on their receivers without cable packages and are often surprised to find Kyrgyz language broadcasts included in the daily programming. This is not completely surprising: Xinjiang boasts a small but substantial Kyrgyz minority (about 1 percent of 22 million), who likely have some personalized broadcasts on Xinjiang's multilingual channels. But to the Kyrgyz we spoke to, it was a bit of a shock to discover a Chinese channel in their language, suggesting that this was something tailored specifically to them.[12] According to the US embassy, there was already a regular broadcast show in Chinese on Kyrgyz television, an hour-long broadcast focusing on the lives of ethnic Kyrgyz in China.[13]

But China is fighting an uphill struggle in soft power terms in Kyrgyzstan. It was never clear to us that anybody was particularly watching these Chinese channels. Whenever we asked people, they would say they preferred to watch Russian channels. The local press regularly talk about conspiracies involving the Chinese, and innuendo plagues Chinese efforts around the country. Sometimes with good reason, like after a power plant that was being refurbished by Chinese contractors in Bishkek broke down in the middle of winter, leaving thousands freezing cold in their houses. The subsequent investigation into the disaster revealed massive corruption and incompetence around the project. All of this had only served to reinforce people's perceptions of Chinese products being of low quality and Chinese firms as exacerbating corruption and governance problems within the country.

Other stories were more fanciful. In Bishkek one university professor jokingly told us as we sat in his office that the rumor going around was that the Chinese had built roads specifically designed to be able to take the weight of Chinese designed tanks. During the 2009 riots in Urumqi, Kyrgyz were provided with a regular digest of updates from businesspeople and students who had been trapped in the city, all of whom painted a grim picture of what was going on. As stories of the Xinjiang camps emerged from 2016 onward, including stories that ethnic Kyrgyz were getting caught up in them, people's concerns about China started to increase. On visits to Central Asia, more generally after the story became more public, people would articulate concerns about relations having potentially been caught up in the camps, but also about their fears that their own governments might start to emulate China's behavior.

Across the country, Chinese businesspeople and products are often held in relatively low esteem and Chinese-owned mines are regularly attacked. The reasons behind these attacks are opaque at best, though most seem to agree they tend to be due to a combination of accusations of environmental despoiling and local power-brokers leveraging angry locals to extract payoffs from Chinese firms. As discussed in earlier chapters, there are also concerns around the degree to which Chinese firms—correctly or incorrectly[14]—are offering locals jobs, or paying reasonable rates. All of which would point to a soft power push that has yet to find solid ground to stand on. The foundations of this local skepticism are equally easy to find among the Chinese community, however. At one market in southern Kyrgyzstan a Chinese girl running a stall selling cleaning products waved us away from purchasing her shampoo, "don't buy it here," she told us in Mandarin, highlighting her own sense of selling an inferior product.

Across the border in Kazakhstan, Chinese soft power expresses itself on a different scale and seems to be guided by state-owned enterprises. Kazakhs are generally quite skeptical about China and worry about its excessive influence, so much so that former prime minister, Karim Massimov, tends to play down his Mandarin ability in public. Already cast under a shadow due to his Uyghur ethnicity (the Uyghur community in Kazakhstan is estimated to be around 1.5 percent of the overall population, mostly resident in the border regions near China[15]), Massimov has been considered one of the more competent officials in the Kazakh cabinet for some time and has been one of the architects of China's relationship with Kazakhstan. Having studied in Beijing and Wuhan, his Mandarin is fluent, so much so that officials report being unable to keep up with what he has agreed when they attend meetings with him and Chinese officials.[16] Nevertheless, Kazakhs knowledgeable about this skill highlight the limited number of times he uses it publicly, a reflection of local paranoia about China. Kazakh officials openly admit that they face political backlash in overtly engaging with China. A public poll run by George Washington University in early 2020 pointed to a public in Kazakhstan which was as negative about China as it was about the United States, highlighting the uphill battle that both countries face. Russia was the preferred country, though not very much.[17]

So it is something of a surprise to arrive in Astana (now Nursultan) and find the overtly Chinese Beijing Hotel smack in the middle of the city. Designed with a Chinese-style roof, the skyscraper was erected by CNPC as part of an effort to win favor with the local government. Nursultan aspires to be an international hub, and consequently needs a five-star hotel (by the time we visited in 2019, Western brands like the Hilton and Ritz-Carlton had also set up shop). Chinese imagery runs adjacent to a softened version of the CNPC logo that adorns everything in the hotel. The restaurant offers excellent Chinese cuisine at elevated prices in a room that gently rotates, offering diners a panoramic view of the city.

Further along the Caspian coast CNPC has found similar ways of deploying its own soft power in Turkmenistan, paying an undisclosed amount to fly in international singing sensation Jennifer Lopez to sing to President Gurbanguly Berdimuhamedow on his birthday in 2013. The Chinese company reportedly relayed a last minute request to the singer that she serenade the leader with a special "birthday greeting." The singer reportedly graciously acquiesced, no doubt further strengthening CNPC's already strong relationship with Turkmenistan.[18]

But the firm also recognizes the need for discretion in response to a general tension toward China in the country. Visit Aktobe, home to China's large energy investments in Kazakhstan, and evidence of China is hard to find. Asking at our hotel reception for any local Chinese restaurants we were told there were none around and instead directed us to an overpriced Korean one as an alternative. Walking around the block, however, we were surprised to find a whitewashed building with a CNPC logo and no name above it, adjacent to a Bank of China branch. Inside the empty restaurant, a Chinese waitress from Hubei offered us a food menu exclusively in Chinese, while the Kazakh bank teller was able to tell us in good Mandarin that we could not access our Bank of China bank account from the branch.

The rationale for this concealed presence became clearer after we had spoken to locals who had worked for some of the other foreign energy firms in the city. The Chinese firms were reported to pay late and badly, offering only lowly positions to Kazakh workers. We could not confirm the accuracy of these stories, though they resonated with a general dislike of China that was visible whenever we asked. Rather than undertake some major soft power push, CNPC has instead elected to simply side-step local concerns and conceal itself. The Chinese staff live in an old sanatorium outside the city, and the Chinese community keeps largely to itself: aware of local antipathies, the firm chooses to simply disappear into the background. CNPC staff who are deployed in Kazakhstan are given special training to prepare them for the country whereby they are told to always go around in groups, make sure they have their documents on them at all times, and to expect to face regular requests for payoffs by local officials.

In Turkmenistan, we met a group staying in Turkmenbashi who were doing some unspecified work in the country. The company did not allow them to leave the hotel and they spent the evening drinking and playing cards noisily with their doors open. We heard about a separate group who had been deployed in Turkmenabat who after some awkward encounters with local women, had also been consigned to be locked in at their compound with no interaction allowed with locals. While CNPC has faced repeated problems in the region (including having to change banks in Turkmenistan after the bank they were using to pay staff quadrupled its service charges overnight), they have also managed to corner a lucrative part of the market and are able to command strong leverage with local authorities.

★ ★ ★

As noted earlier, in 2014 a decision was made to formally expand the CI footprint in Tajikistan with the opening of a second campus in Khujand at the Mining-Metallurgical Institute of Tajikistan. Signed into existence when President Xi Jinping visited Tajikistan on a visit built around an SCO leaders' summit, the visit was overshadowed by the initiation of two other bigger projects in Tajikistan. Presidents Xi and Rahmon oversaw the ground-breaking ceremonies of a thermal power plant (number two) in Dushanbe and of the Tajik portion of Line D of the Turkmenistan–China gas pipeline.[19] The visit came a year after CNPC had announced it was entering into what could be the biggest gas project ever seen in Tajikistan (described by some as having the potential to transform the country into a Gulf-style economy) at the Bokhtar field, in conjunction with French supermajor Total and smaller prospector firm Tethys. Mining and minerals were clearly going to be a major and growing feature of China's relationship with Tajikistan going forward. Consequently, the decision to establish a CI with Tajikistan's premier institute for higher studies of mining was especially strategic and forward looking.

In establishing the CI with the Tajik institute, the China University of Petroleum was quite open about the goal. Its aim was to "train Chinese-speaking talents for local mining and metallurgical companies" and to ensure that it was continually providing "Chinese-speaking human resource support for Tazhong Mining Co., Ltd."[20] While we never encountered any Tajiks who had studied Mandarin at the institute, we did encounter a number of Tajiks who had been recruited by companies directly from their language classes or who had chosen to learn the language to get jobs with Chinese companies or business-people, suggesting that the door the CI was seeking to push open had already been very much ajar.

Joseph Nye specifically identifies "multinational corporations" as "sometimes more relevant to achieving a country's goals than are other states":[21] a case made easily for China in Central Asia, where it is frequently the SOEs that are a major part of China's footprint in the region. As has been shown in other chapters, China's giant SOEs are reshaping the region's physical infrastructure, and in part they are playing a significant role in supporting the soft power push. Huawei in Uzbekistan (and presumably in the other countries where it is active as well) offers training based in China for its local middle managers.[22] In Kabul we were told that MCC had set aside a building on the site of their massive Mes Aynak project to teach locals Chinese. When it would open, however, was an entirely different question. In Turkmenistan, beyond sending Jennifer Lopez, CNPC was one of the companies that was providing support for the new International Oil and Gas University in the country. In Kazakhstan, we met local academics who told us about writing projects they had been commissioned to produce by CNPC which sounded like they were lucrative puff pieces about China's role and influence in the region.

But companies are represented by their staff, and some Chinese firms tried to find managers who spoke some Russian to be able to interact with their local counterparts. In Uzbekistan, over dinner, we met a trio from a telecoms firm who had been sent to the country as a result of their linguistic abilities. Adopting Russian names like Sergei, the two men and one woman had been in the country for almost a year and were relatively ambivalent about their experience. Sergei had studied Russian at university and had been sent by the company, it was his second foreign posting, though it was the first in which he had been able to use his Russian. The experience was made all the more bearable by the fact that he was able to bring his young wife along. Wearing the latest fashions that we had seen a few weeks before in China, she was utterly reliant on her husband and his friend.

The three of them formed a white-collar triumvirate helping Chinese industry slowly penetrate the closed Uzbek market. These quiet young people were in contrast to Misha, the Chinese businessman who joined us for dinner on a different night, at the invitation of some Uzbek friends. Chain-smoking and barely touching his food, he told us he had no need for translators as he spoke Russian and had picked up a bit of Uzbek. When he did need translators, he said, he would certainly not use students from the CI—much better to use those from the Oriental Studies University. He was far more interested, however, in having his children learn English, and spent most of dinner asking about how difficult and expensive it was to get into Oxford or Cambridge.

This contrasting pair of interactions summarizes in many ways the different faces of Chinese soft power in Central Asia. On the one hand there was the quiet institutional approach driven by Beijing—directed through CI and traditional media forms that pay careful attention to local sensitivities although they make little overall impression. In contrast to this there is the hard charging approach seen in Misha and other businesspeople like him, savvy entrepreneurs able to see market opportunity and pounce on it without a sense of or interest in the bigger picture. It is fundamentally these two forces that drive and shape the impression locals have of Beijing: quiescent workers diligently working long hours in a foreign land, or fast-talking salesmen undercutting the competition and focusing on extracting as much value as possible from the land. Both are fundamentally market driven, something that is a reflection of the underlying priority of economic development in China's investments in Central Asia. A reality that will continue to make it very difficult to forge any other image in Central Asia, no matter how many students are lured by the appeal of taking on Mandarin language classes.

6

Spreading the "Shanghai Spirit"

Tiananmen Square, Beijing

Getting into the Regional Anti-Terrorism Structure (RATS) in Tashkent was a lot easier than we had expected. A friend back in Europe with deep contacts into the world of multilateral counter-terrorism in Central Asia had helped us find the right phone number and email address to reach out to, and RATS had been surprisingly welcoming when we had requested a meeting. We were met at the gate by a Chinese official of uncertain age on secondment from the

Public Security Bureau in the regulation semi-formal attire that Chinese men go for, bland, striped polo shirt and black trousers with keys clipped on the side, who only wanted to speak using his limited English. He took us to meet our host, a Tajik general who was serving as the current deputy head of the organization. With an evocative Soviet-style handlebar moustache he proudly told us he had walked the length of his country's border with Afghanistan. Over coffee in their main conference room with numerous burly men in ill-fitting suits taking notes (one of whom fell prominently asleep during the meeting), he explained to us what the infamous RATS Centre does. "We have less staff than the UN," he told us, "but more than the Italian Embassy and less than the American," a nod to our respective nationalities as he laughed uproariously at his own joke.

The RATS Centre, like its mother organization the Shanghai Cooperation Organization (SCO), has a negative reputation. Bearing an unfortunate acronym, the organization is considered "responsible for the implementation of the SCO's counter-terrorism strategies."[1] A much discussed and little understood international organization, the SCO gets a lot of bad press in the West. According to the International Federation for Human Rights (FIDH), the SCO is "a vehicle for human rights violations."[2] Others, like Peter Brookes of the Heritage Foundation, call the SCO a "Club for Dictators" and see it "as a tool to eliminate US influence in the Eurasian heartland."[3] Alexander Cooley, the eminent Central Asianologist elegantly called the SCO the "League of Authoritarian Gentlemen" describing how autocrats grouped within the organization and across Eurasia, had "been working hard to forge an international front of anti-democrats, developing a new set of counter-strategies and regional legal tools."[4] Ambitious goals suggesting a coherence that seemed distinctly at odds with our encounters.

A case in point was the meeting at the RATS headquarters in which the grizzled Tajik officer told us in detail, through a translator we had brought, how his organization's major task was the management of a database of the names of "terrorists" and "terrorist organizations" from across member states. When pushed to tell us how this was deployed operationally, we were repeatedly told that they simply maintained the database, ensuring information was translated and the information was kept securely. He further told us that they were exploring doing things in the cyber realm. This was something that had been first brought up back in 2007 during the seventh SCO heads of state summit, and then mentioned every year since, in one way or another. But there is little tangible evidence that any "cyber police," as was proposed by the Kazakhs in 2012, has been established.[5] The RATS Centre, it seemed, was still seeking a role.

A month or so later in Beijing, we had an opportunity to ask at the SCO Secretariat about their particular duties and goals. We were there just when the annual SCO heads of state summit was in town and Beijing's main Chang An Jie was festooned with SCO flags and symbols. In the middle of Tiananmen Square, somewhat close to where the June 4, 1989, Statue of Liberty would have been, sat a giant triangular stand surrounded by flowers with the SCO logo in giant format. Families from out of town were having their pictures taken next to it. They did not appear to have much of an idea of what it signified when we asked, and were more intrigued by foreigners who spoke Mandarin, wanting pictures with us. The talk of the town was the fact that President Hamid Karzai had come to represent his country, a sign that serious agreements with Afghanistan were afoot. There to formally join the organization as an "Observer" state, President Karzai hedged his bets by also signing a bilateral agreement with China establishing a bilateral mechanism for engagement between the two countries. At the SCO Secretariat we were greeted by a friendly Kazakh diplomat and his Russian aide. The two spoke a mix of Chinese and English, but were quite clear when asked what this new proximity of Afghanistan to the organization meant: "we have no idea."

★   ★   ★

It was not initially meant to be like this. Born out of the embers of the Cold War, the SCO was initially known as the Shanghai Five, made up of China and its bordering states with the former Soviet Union: Kazakhstan, Kyrgyzstan, Tajikistan, and Russia. The grouping was first informally mooted when Premier Li Peng visited Central Asia in 1994, stopping in Kazakhstan, Kyrgyzstan, Turkmenistan, Uzbekistan, and Mongolia. Delayed by a year due to Premier Li's sickness, the tour avoided war-torn Tajikistan. In Tashkent he gave a speech in which he laid out an ambitious role for China in the region,

> For a bright future of China and the world at large, China will make every effort to manage its own affairs well, unswervingly pursue an independent foreign policy of peace, develop friendly relations and cooperation with all countries, especially the neighboring nations on the basis of the five principles of peaceful coexistence, and make a new contribution to peace, stability and development in Asia and the world as a whole.[6]

This first step toward Central Asia reflected a general Chinese acceptance of needing to reach out to at least the world around it, and the culmination of Deng Xiaoping's ground-breaking 1992 "Southern Tour," which sought to show how the country was open for business and had put the destruction of the 1989 Tiananmen Square massacre behind it. What Deng's trip did for China's south and coast, Li Peng's visit to Central Asia was meant to do for Eurasia.

By 1996, things were going so well that on April 26, Jiang Zemin hosted Boris Yeltsin of Russia, Nursultan Nazarbayev of Kazakhstan, Askar Akayev of Kyrgyzstan, and Emomali Rakhmon of Tajikistan in Shanghai for the signing of an "unprecedented five-nation border agreement on demilitarizing the nearly 8,000 km-long former Sino-Soviet border."[7] This historic agreement, coined the "Shanghai Five" grouping, was followed a month later by an international conference on the "New Silk Road" in Beijing hosted by Li Peng where he spoke of the central role that Eurasian rail links would play in promoting economic links and development between China and Europe.[8] A prelude to the discussions about a "new Eurasian landbridge" discussed during Wen Jiaobao's speech to Urumqi in 2012 and the later

Silk Road Economic Belt that is the foundational route of President Xi Jinping's Belt and Road Initiative (BRI).

In 1997, the heads of state meeting was held in Moscow, during which they confirmed the organizing principles of the organization, with a focus on the demilitarization of their respective border zones. Subsequent meetings were held in Almaty (1998), Bishkek (1999), and Dushanbe (2000), during which time they signed documents that "made an important contribution to the maintenance of peace, security and stability in the region and throughout the world, significantly enriched the practice of modern diplomacy and regional cooperation and had a broad and positive influence on the international community."[9]

These vacuous statements of positive intent masked tensions that existed from the beginning at the core of the organization. For the first two meetings in Shanghai and Moscow, in addition to the multilateral discussions involving the Central Asian powers, China and Russia held bilateral discussions during which they reaffirmed their bilateral "strategic partnership"—something that was crucial to establish in the wake of the chaos of the immediate post–Cold War and the lowering of tensions between China and Russia. For the Russians, the "Shanghai Five" meetings were something of an afterthought. In 1998, Russian head of state Boris Yeltsin failed to go to the summit dispatching Foreign Minister Yevgeny Primakov instead.[10] In 1999, according to Russian press reports, President Yeltsin again had not felt the necessity to attend and had his "arm twisted" in a phone call from President Jiang Zemin to come to Bishkek. As it was put in a digest of the Russian press from the time, "the 'Shanghai Five' or, as Yeltsin likes to call it, the 'Border Five' isn't any sort of political alliance or bloc: It has no organizational structures and no administrative apparatus. For that reason, it doesn't necessarily require the head of state's presence at its meetings."[11] From its early stages, Russia did not particularly take the grouping seriously, seeing it largely as one prominent Western watcher later put it to us, as a way "to contain China" by staying involved in an organization which it was using to grow its influence and links in Central Asia.[12]

In the pre-September 2001 world, however, the outside world had a different interpretation of the organization. In an article for *Newsweek*, astute American sinologist and Brookings Institution scholar Dr Bates Gill spoke of the Shanghai Five being "indicative of efforts elsewhere in the world which are seeking security-related mechanisms without the participation of the United States."[13] The Shanghai Five's gradual development from border delineating entity to potential regional security organization suggested that some greater geopolitical shift was afoot. Chinese willingness in particular to be the driving force behind a multilateral security organization that was not the UN was seen as significant, demonstrating the potential for a new pole in international affairs to develop. For China, this was an expression of the "New Security Concept" whereby non-interference in others' affairs was central. At this stage China was in the early phases of its "Peaceful Rise," whereby it aimed to slowly ascend to a position of influence and power in international affairs without raising people's concerns unduly.

Domestically, it is not clear what purpose the "Shanghai Five" grouping would have served beyond helping define China's western borders. For Jiang Zemin, it helped with his broader vision of the Great Western Development, which was aimed at pushing to develop China's historically underdeveloped western regions. Building strong links with neighbors in Central Asia helped not only with managing ill-defined borders but also in dealing with the constant concern in Beijing about Uyghur militancy. In May 2000, gunmen opened fire on a delegation of Chinese officials visiting Kyrgyzstan from Xinjiang. In the wave of arrests that followed, Kyrgyz authorities pointed to Uyghur dissidents. At around the same time, stories started circulating in the Russian press about how Uyghurs were joining Chechen run training camps in Afghanistan. Concerned Chinese authorities issued alerts to their bases in Hong Kong and to diplomatic posts about the possibility of being targeted. They also reached out to the Taliban authorities seeking to understand what was happening and gain assurances that these groups would not pose a threat to them.

By the June 2001 summit it was clear that something more was in the air, and when the leaders gathered once again in Shanghai for their annual meeting they had a new member at the head table, one who was sitting with the leaders rather than participating as an observer as he had in Dushanbe: Uzbek leader Islam Karimov. One Russian report from the time spoke of his addition "diluting" the grouping, and how Karimov's aim was to strengthen Uzbekistan's hand in its interregional struggle to beat budding regional power-house Kazakhstan.[14] But the overall regional response was positive. The perception was that this new entity would give all of the powers greater leverage in international affairs and highlight the importance of the alliances that it brought together. There was a sense that this was a new sort of multilateral organization, and given that its combined population was equal to about a fifth of the world's (though most of that was Chinese), it would be able to stand up to the world's only superpower, the United States. Given both China and Russia were in a period during which relations with Washington were frosty, this alliance was a good thing that would strengthen their hand in other ways as well.

Seen from Beijing, this was a momentous victory for Chinese diplomacy headed by leader Jiang Zemin. Commentaries lauded his notions of the "Shanghai Spirit" as the unifying vision that held this new entity together.[15] A new way was being forged in international relations, one that "speaks for mutual respect and seeking common points while reserving differences, which has been proved to be the only realistic choice for countries of different civilization backgrounds and cultural traditions to attain a peaceful co-existence":[16] a very Chinese formulation that focuses on the mutual win–win and harmonious benefits.

The reality, of course, was very different. While it was true that it was a Chinese formulation that lay at the heart of the new entity, it was not the multilateral dream vision that these public diplomacy statements suggested. Rather it was the Chinese phrasing of the SCO being focused on countering the "three evils" of "terrorism, separatism and extremism," that preoccupied Beijing. This ultimately provided the glue that held the organization together. The Russian press of the time saw the importance of this aspect, and how the "Shanghai Six" had been "turned into an antiterrorist coalition."[17]

Ultimately, countering radical groups, terrorist networks, and anti-state organizations was something that all six countries faced in common. Russia was in the midst of the Second Chechen War and had endured a series of brutal terrorist incidents at home as well as an ongoing bloody conflict on the ground in the North Caucasus. Uzbekistan was facing a domestic insurgency from the Ferghana Valley that was threatening Kyrgyzstan as well. Bombs had gone off in downtown Tashkent, showing the nature of the problem that the country was facing. Tajikistan had managed to conclude its brutal civil war, but tensions remained and its Gorno-Badakhshan region continued to cause problems for Dushanbe. Kazakhstan worried that these issues could express themselves violently at home, while China had seen its officials killed in Bishkek by militant Uyghurs and in 1997 faced the latest bout of violent rioting in Yinning, Xinjiang. Kyrgyzstan had faced the most dramatic problems, with invasions of militants in the south in the summers of 1999 and 2000. They had managed to push the problems back, but it was clear that there were threats to their stability from terrorist groups that used Afghanistan as a base.

Many of the SCO members bordered Afghanistan, a country that had proven itself to be a home for radical networks and continued to be a major source of narcotics. In his comments at the inaugural event in Shanghai in 2001, President Nazarbayev of Kazakhstan described Afghanistan as "the cradle of terrorism, separatism and extremism," highlighting collective concern in the organization. But in addition to these concerns, all of the members took quite expansive views of what constituted anti-state activity, unwilling to brook much political dissent and treating it as a small stepping stone away from militancy. Countering terrorism, in other words, was a unifying banner that they could all agree on and could all get behind. It is consequently unsurprising that looking at the output from the first session, beyond the good atmospherics, counter-terrorism and transnational threats score very high on the reported success scale, including the announcement of the establishment of the RATS, initially planned for Bishkek, but ultimately opened in Tashkent in 2004. This focus on counter-terrorism was only strengthened by the post-9/11 American and Western focus on international terrorism with links to Central Asia.

However, the US's return to Central Asia in such force in the wake of the September 11, 2001 attacks presented a dilemma for the SCO. As was laid out half a decade later by one of China's pre-eminent scholars on the organization, Professor Zhao Huasheng, the US's return called into question the SCO's capability to deal with issues in its own back-yard. The fact that a number of SCO members welcomed—against their institutional charter—American military forces into their countries to establish bases showed in what low regard they held the organization's rules. It highlighted a prioritization of respective bilateral relations with America over regional cooperation, and the overarching question became, were "the principles and views put forward by the SCO still relevant?"[18]

In other words, from its very birth, the SCO was a deeply conflicted and incoherent organization. Founded to counter terrorism, it had failed to react much to a large-scale terrorist incident that had emanated from its own backyard. And rather than rally together, its members had scattered and moved to establish close bilateral relationships with the United States, potentially bringing an antagonistic power back into the region. The organization, born to such promise and imbued with such optimism by its members, seemed to stumble at the first hurdle.

Chinese officials and academics love to talk about history. Most conversations with Chinese experts will result in at least one reference to history and the fact that China is no novice to whatever discussion is being undertaken. The purpose of these sorts of allusions is twofold: to confirm that China has a long connection and ownership over the issue being discussed, and to affirm that China has a long memory. Events from the Chinese perspective are seen with a more patient timeline: the Chinese are willing to wait and see how things develop. Seen through this lens, these initial problems with the SCO can be viewed as temporary hiccups that will eventually iron themselves out. The vision at the end of the day is to develop a permanent Chinese connection with the Eurasian heartland, one that will be able to withstand temporary political problems and reflects the fact that China is physically bound to this territory *ad infinitum*. The SCO in many ways was an early articulation of what later became the BRI.

★   ★   ★

Since its birth in 2001, the SCO has done both a great deal and very little. The initial infrastructure of the organization has been strengthened and developed considerably: ministers from across the respective cabinets meet for summits at which they discuss the coordination of respective policies. On the security side, ministries of the interior and of defense meet annually with each other to plan large-scale training exercises in which they will use heavy equipment like airplanes, tanks, and massed formations of soldiers to conduct "counter-terrorism" operations. Large multilateral operations are held regularly, calling themselves "Peace Missions." They mostly give China and Russia an opportunity to try out new equipment—even, as one cynical Russian observer once pointed out regarding the early sessions of these exercises, merely as opportunities for the Russians to show off their new equipment to some of their biggest consumers.[19]

At the same time, China in particular holds regular, smaller bilateral or trilateral training exercises under the SCO with neighbors, Tajikistan and Kyrgyzstan. Taking their name from the nearby mountains, these are called Tian Shan ("Heavenly Mountains") and involve smaller scale "counter-terrorism" operations focused on border security and issues related to the sparse badlands that the three countries share. China undertook its first big military exercises with the Russians under the auspices of the SCO focusing on large-scale scenarios the Chinese were worried about, and giving the Russians the opportunity to showcase relevant equipment that they were keen to sell to the

Chinese. Reflecting another of China's concerns, Beijing was at the forefront of pushing to establish an Afghanistan Contact Group which aimed to get the SCO to play a bigger role in managing the security problems emanating from its difficult neighbor, something that has been largely ignored except rhetorically by the others.

Beyond the security realm, the organization has further developed its profile in a number of other directions. In economics, relevant ministers meet regularly and discuss "coordination." Projects have been undertaken through the SCO, including some cooperative road-building projects and (thanks to Chinese money) some infrastructure projects in Kyrgyzstan and Tajikistan. When we visited Osh, we kept hearing about a "micro-rayon" ("district") that was supposedly being redeveloped under the auspices of the SCO, but no-one was able to point it out to us or tell us where exactly it was. China is regularly seen as the keenest player to push the organization toward greater economic cooperation: Chinese strategists talk eagerly about an SCO development bank and an SCO free trade area (FTA). During the May 2003 summit, Hu Jintao outlined how "economic cooperation is the basis for and a priority of the SCO."[20]

Talk to anyone outside Beijing and these ideas seem far-fetched. The SCO FTA seems wildly optimistic, and China's attempt to jump-start the development bank by putting $10 billion on the table when it hosted the SCO summit in Beijing in 2012 was met with a resounding silence. Sitting at an SCO conference in Shanghai in mid-2013, we heard a prominent Chinese economist give a presentation on the development bank that was based on information from years previously.[21] There had been little to no movement forward on the idea, which had floundered around in a limbo. Unsurprisingly, it was the Tajiks and Kyrgyz who were most pro the idea of establishing an SCO development bank—with Kyrgyz leaders consistently saying what a great idea it was and offering to host the Secretariat in Bishkek. The closest the institution has gotten to creating something along these lines has been an Interbank consortium which was established in 2005 and brings the development bank institutions from all the countries together.

Perhaps reflecting China's persistent desire to push forward the idea of the SCO as a tool for economic harmonization, and to demonstrate the multilateral nature of the SCO, in the wake of the Qingdao Summit in June 2018, China announced the establishment of a China-SCO "demonstration zone" which was focused on developing industries across the region. In reality it seemed mostly an opportunity to showcase Chinese firms. The project was opened in November 2020 with reportedly $8.6 billion worth of projects.[22] Heavily focused on Chinese tech firms, it remains to be seen how much of this will materialize other than as a Chinese economic project.

The problem, as it was put by a diplomat in the SCO Secretariat, was that "all the members of the SCO have different economic policies and economic situations."[23] Or as a prominent Chinese expert put it more candidly: the region "is concerned about Chinese economic dominance."[24] As has been repeatedly seen in earlier chapters, the Central Asian countries both fear and seek out Chinese economic might. On the one hand, it provides them with investment and affluence, but on the other it has the risk of enveloping them and transforming them into provinces that become utterly reliant on Chinese wealth and generosity. Currently, with the possible exception of parts of Uzbekistan (and trading in goods which are ubiquitous across the region), the SCO members are economies dependent on extractive industries. This is an economic strategy that ends when there are no more raw minerals to dig up. The longer-term solution for such countries is to develop an economic infrastructure that is able to produce refined goods and innovate up the value chain, which China is currently working on and the Central Asians would also like to do. But it is also something that the Central Asians will find challenging to achieve when planted adjacent to the world's factory in China whose economies of scale make it a fearsome competitor.

In this context, the SCO provides China with a less menacing umbrella through which to undertake investments, engage, and work on development in Central Asia. When things are flagged under an SCO banner they immediately become multilateral and therefore something that has been agreed by consensus (or are suggestive of this). In reality, of course, the grand plans for the SCO economic vision are largely underdeveloped, both held up by the practicalities behind China's overambitious plans and undermined by the simple reality that not everyone within the SCO agrees that they are a good idea. The SCO development bank, for example, was initially suggested with the offer of a $10 billion pot, which could be used to kick things off. But the money remains unused as it had all come from China. For the development bank to work, it would require a board that made decisions about where the money was to be invested. However, with only one investor, China would have to be willing to agree for others to be on an equal footing in decision-making despite their not having put any money in—and, at the moment, China seems unwilling to do that. Instead, China has established bilateral investment vehicles with Russia that are focused on projects of mutual interest, while with Kazakhstan and Uzbekistan it has provided soft loans through its policy banks. China has separately also created the Asian Infrastructure Investment Bank (AIIB) and the Silk Road Fund, a national fund focused on BRI investments. Both of these entities have been used to undertake projects in Central Asia. China has also invested in the creation of the New Development Bank, also known as the BRICS (Brazil, Russia, India, China, and South Africa) Bank, which is jointly supported by all of the BRICS members (at least three of whom are also SCO members). China at least seems to have lost interest at this point in an SCO development bank, with its establishment now mostly mentioned during annual summits, where usually the Kyrgyz leadership will posit it as a good idea and offer to host its Secretariat.

The country with the greatest fear of Chinese economic dominance, however, is not Central Asian. Russia has increasingly seen in the economic aspect of the SCO the seeds of Chinese dominance of a region that it continues to consider its own strategic backyard. Russia fears started in relation to the strategic consequences of loss of control, but over time they have become more focused on concerns about how the region could become a springboard for uncontrolled economic

and strategic penetration into Russia as well. Initially, as was explained
to us, Russia saw the SCO as a vehicle through which they would
control Chinese activity in Central Asia. With collective decision-
making processes, and over a space where Moscow felt confident in
its leadership, Russia assumed that by staying engaged it would be able
to act as a brake on Chinese efforts. As we saw earlier in this chapter,
Moscow was largely dismissive of the organization, with President
Yeltsin not bothering even to show up to some meetings. Over time
this view has shifted as they realized that it was not the only vector
China was using with the region, and China's constant activity was in
fact starting to transform Beijing's influence in Russia's backyard. The
response from Russia has been to remain engaged with the SCO, but
increasingly to try to add elements into the equation that complicate
the Chinese strategy of using the SCO as a vehicle for economic
expansion. Moscow has also pushed back with its own range of post-
Soviet tools to engage with the region and reassert its dominance, or
at the very least to keep its hand in play.

For example, Russia resurrected an idea first advanced by President
Nazarbayev of Kazakhstan, to create a Eurasian Economic Union
(EAEU). Essentially, a return to the Soviet Union, the principle behind
the EAEU is to create a community of countries that are all intertwined economically, which would act as a good parallel for the
Russian-led Collective Security Treaty Organization (CSTO), a security
alliance closer to a NATO model than the SCO. Having sat fallow as
a concept for years, in 2014 Moscow achieved its goal of pushing the
institution forward and reasserting some economic control over parts
of the former Soviet Union with the signing of a treaty with Kazakhstan
and Belarus, in the first instance giving Moscow a level of control and
deeper connection with Nursultan and Minsk. Initially composed of
Belarus, Kazakhstan, and Russia, the EAEU later expanded to include
Armenia and Kyrgyzstan (with discussions about Uzbekistan and
Tajikistan joining continually coming up). Bringing together their collective markets for goods, free movement, capital, and services, the
intention was to give everyone greater access to each other's markets

replicating a model that had been created by the European Union. In practice, however, it has given a great deal of control to Moscow, and greater leverage to Russian companies to operate in EAEU economies.

For China this is a potential spanner in the works for the ambitions of an SCO FTA. Grander plans for an economic space in which China can dominate and develop trade within its own agenda could become blocked at a border that is controlled by Russia. The EAEU could also damage bilateral trade between China and the member states. An interesting debate that was presented to us in Beijing was that there were two factions within the Chinese government on this matter: there were those within the Ministry of Commerce who saw the advantage to having a single space to trade with that reached all the way to Europe, whilst those in the Ministry of Foreign Affairs were concerned about what this meant for Chinese trade with Central Asia specifically.[25] The argument went that if the EAEU worked well, it could facilitate trade with the entire region, while others worried about its impact on bilateral trade. Diplomats on the ground in Kyrgyzstan downplayed these concerns as we saw in an earlier chapter, while when looking at numbers it was not entirely clear what the economic effect of joining the EAEU had been to the Kyrgyz and Kazakh economies.

Seen from the larger picture of Beijing's international trade, China's trade with Central Asia is a small fraction of the overall. But the risk to Beijing is that impediments to its bilateral trading with Central Asian countries will be directly damaging to Xinjiang. This may then have a negative impact on one of China's key goals in its economic relationship with Central Asia, which is to help Xinjiang's development. So it is understandable that China would want to foster greater economic connectivity through the SCO as an attempt to retain control, but it is equally understandable that Moscow would fear a complete loss of the region while also potentially opening itself up even more directly to Chinese economic power.

But the SCO, as we were repeatedly told across the region, is a new kind of organization and not one that fits previous molds. Beyond the economic and security aspects, the organization has further developed a cultural aspect, which President Putin in particular has championed through the development of an SCO University. With fifty-four affiliated universities, the idea is that students should be able to spend a year in one of the other countries in the group—with students encouraged to study topics that would be of use and interest for the organization or for regional integration. This is a model which in many ways replicates the European Erasmus program which offers a similar exchange between European universities. In Urumqi we had the pleasure of a visit to Xinjiang University where we were hosted by the drunken educator introduced earlier in this chapter who had an eye for travel to England, as they were hosting one of the pedagogical conferences associated with the SCO university.[26] On a trip to Tashkent many years later during the Chinese mid-autumn festival we came across an exhibit in a public square sponsored by the SCO which highlighted major cities within the organization's member states, encouraging people to visit. The SCO has now sponsored marathons, a film festival, cultural tours for journalists, has a youth organization (SCOLAR), and more.

Seen from the perspective of Western capitals, all of this points to an organization that lacks coherence. But this is not a view shared by other regional powers who have instead lined up to be allowed to become members or partners. Having prevaricated for years, the SCO now has a process for letting new members join. Obvious potential members like Mongolia or Turkmenistan either are not interested or get caught up in larger regional or global politics and continue to simply observe. Other countries in the area are not particularly wanted. Iran under President Mahmoud Ahmedinejad saw the SCO as a way of binding his country into an alternative international organization that seemed hostile to the United States, which he could then use to strengthen Iran's hand against Washington. Supported by Russia, the Iranian regime sought membership, but Beijing saw this as a bad idea given the inevitable tensions this would cause with the United States (China's principal foreign policy concern). President

Ahmedinejad's naked hostility toward the US and desire to turn the organization more aggressively against the US made Iran an unpopular candidate. Tehran nevertheless rushed in for membership only to be told that it could never become a member, being under UN sanctions, a status listed as being in contravention to membership requirements. President Ahmedinejad, en route to the summit in 2010, was disappointed to learn this and instead redirected himself to attend the World Expo being held in Shanghai at the time. There was an almost palpable sigh of relief from Beijing once this diplomatic issue had been resolved in a manner that allowed everyone to save face. However, the door was never closed and while Iran remains an observer member (alongside Mongolia, Afghanistan, and Belarus) it is now on the path to membership.

Some are not wanted for other reasons. During the 2005 Astana Summit, the leaders explicitly rejected US membership of the organization. At the time, relations between Central Asia and the West were complicated by the growing wave of so-called Color Revolutions that were sweeping through the former Soviet space (the Orange Revolution in Ukraine, the Rose Revolution in Georgia, and the Tulip Revolution in Kyrgyzstan), all of which were believed to be supported surreptitiously by the US government. Alongside the Andijan unrest in Uzbekistan in May 2005, which had been violently suppressed by the Uzbek government to loud condemnation in most Western capitals, this all suggested the wind of disruptive democratization might be sweeping through the region, something anathema to SCO members' thinking and leaderships. When we asked US diplomats, they dismissed the idea of membership anyway, and pointed out that the way the organization was structured would have meant that the US president would likely have had to attend meetings in the first instance in an "observer" status of some sort—something that was a complete non-starter for American diplomacy.

But the SCO has found ways of bringing others in. After much back and forth discussion, both Pakistan and India were formally shepherded into the family in 2017. Respectively supported for membership by China and Russia, the concern around their joint membership was that their intractable bilateral conflicts—such as in Kashmir—would get dragged into the SCO and tear the organization apart. However, this has not happened, and instead the two countries have proven willing to take part in joint counter-terrorism training exercises together under the auspices of the SCO, reflecting the organization's positive potential. India has not completely backed away from its anger with Pakistan, however, and at a summit in 2019, the foreign minister arrived with a single message focused on Pakistani perfidy at supporting terrorist groups in the region. More recent tensions between China and India do not appear to have impacted the SCO, with Indian participants still staying active within the organization and Prime Minister Modi telling the 2020 heads of state summit that he looked forward to doing more with the organization in the future.

Afghanistan would be another obvious candidate for inclusion in the SCO, but its domestic turmoil make it difficult to bring in. At time of writing, the US and NATO withdrawal was being completed, and once done it was unclear that the SCO members see eye-to-eye about what should be done and how the SCO might be able to help resolve Afghanistan's long-term problems in practical terms. China has long sought to get the SCO to engage more on Afghanistan to no avail, repeatedly seeking to get the Afghanistan Contact Group more engaged or get the topic of Afghanistan onto the agenda of the organization. Beijing in fact appears to have started to give up on the SCO as a useful vehicle for practical action in Afghanistan to the point that it has created a new and separate mini-lateral institution called the Quadrilateral Cooperation and Coordination Mechanism (QCCM) that brings together the chiefs of army staff of Afghanistan, China, Tajikistan, and Pakistan to coordinate and discuss border security questions around the Wakhan Corridor. While the organization (and Afghanistan) will be explored in greater detail later, the key point that is relevant for the SCO discussion here is that the creation of this grouping is a clear reflection of Beijing's exasperation at the SCO's failure to tackle Afghanistan. While clearly not giving up pushing to get the SCO to do more in Afghanistan (President Xi, for example, made it one of his key points during his speech at the 2020 heads of summit meeting), China has through the QCCM established another more direct mechanism to engage on security questions in Afghanistan.

Membership of any international organization like this is always inherently political. With joint decision-making, more actors around the table means more votes, and everyone will angle to ensure they control a bigger portion of these votes. Chinese analysts would tell us that letting new members into the organization is about Russia trying to find ways of diluting the coherence of the organization. This, they say, is similar to the UK's approach with the European Union, where London pushed for expansion to ensure that the core would not be able to retain its dominance. With more voices at the table, less can be achieved.[27] We have yet to find out what a Brexit moment would look like for the SCO.

Of course, there is a much less conspiratorial answer to all of this, as was put to us by a Beijing-based diplomat:

> no-one is against new members. But imagine, six friends get together. One says, I want to invite my friend. Another will say, no need we already have enough at six of us. Another will say, I don't know your friend. Whatever, the final decision will be taken by all the friends together.

Whilst intended to highlight how the decision-making process was complicated, the story does capture one reality in the SCO: everyone has a say and therefore everyone can hold up the process. By adopting the EU's unanimous agreement approach to decision-making, the organization remains hostage to whichever member has a problem with any given decision, and when one of the two biggest players at the table is fundamentally skeptical about the organization it is hard to see how it is going to advance quickly toward coherence.

★   ★   ★

But it is possible that our frame of reference regarding the SCO is all wrong. Go to Washington and you will find largely dismissive attitudes toward the organization. During one visit which included a stop at the Pentagon we found analysts mostly amused at the stories of spats between SCO members and eager to hear new ones (during that visit everyone was still talking about the appearance of Chinese forces in Tajikistan which had reportedly left the Russian defense community in Dushanbe apoplectic since they had not been informed in advance). In Beijing, foreign diplomats we spoke to were intrigued by the organization, but they did not see much to fear from its action. Focused on the fundamental incoherence and clash between China and Russia who sit at its center, most Washington analysts look at it as a largely empty institution. Measuring the limited deliverables the SCO can point to, they see it as an organization formed among authoritarians to enhance their own prestige. The addition of Pakistan and India somewhat confuses the authoritarian side of this analysis, but at the same time the continual bilateral clash merely serves to emphasize the fundamental incoherence at the heart of the SCO. At a conference in Beijing in 2019, we asked a panel of experts from across the newly enlarged organization what it was that the SCO had actually achieved during its almost two-decade history and they laughed, saying that it was a Western conception to seek outcomes in this way. From their perspective, the SCO's very continued existence was in some ways its greatest outcome. As a Chinese expert at one of the more influential foreign policy think tanks in Beijing told us when we asked him for indications of what the SCO had achieved in tangible terms, he smiled and told us "to not do anything is to do everything."

And this could possibly be the key lesson of the SCO. Rather than being an institution that was built to achieve things, it was an organization to incrementally develop relationships and proximity. It has, in practical terms, achieved little that can be pointed to beyond holding a lot of meetings and encounters. Even the initial impetus for the formation of its pre-SCO grouping, the Shanghai Five, was only relatively recently decided. The borders took many rounds of negotiation to determine, and for many in Central Asia they are still a point of contention. As late as 2019 people in Tajikistan were still darkly discussing what their country had given away in border delineation negotiations. Rumors were still flying around about what precious stones there might be in the territory that had been ceded to China and that the entire territorial deliberation was a source of great friction between the two countries. One well-informed insider in Dushanbe told us that, in fact, the negotiators had been celebrated and awarded medals for their hard work in the negotiations with the Chinese. Tajik officials we spoke to would continually emphasize that among the Shanghai Five countries to have had to negotiate border delineation agreements with the Chinese, they had ceded the smallest proportion of the total territorial sought by the Chinese. But the fact that this was still a point of discussion almost two decades after the Shanghai Five had evolved into the SCO reflected how unresolved and tense the issue still was.

The bigger point is that notwithstanding tensions (including Russia's early dismissal of the grouping), the SCO has continued to exist and grow. The addition of India and Pakistan now means that the organization can boast to include around half of the world's population under its auspices and three-fifths of the mighty Eurasian continent. The leaders of the member states and observers meet regularly notwithstanding other tensions and continue to plot a path forward. Their sessions may be full of overblown rhetoric and action might be limited, but in its short life, the organization has shown its resilience and strength. And in taking a gradualist approach, it is taking a very Chinese conception to its existence and policy. Not passing judgment on any of its members, the organization refuses to condemn any atrocities or abuses that might take place within each other's borders. This is appreciated by those of the members who are authoritarian, and those whose behavior at home is at odds with Western norms regarding human rights. But this reality is what illustrates the risk the grouping poses, it is a place where anti-democrats can thrive and show they have international support. And while all the members might in different ways appreciate the international support the organization provides, it is China which is really benefitting out of the SCO's long-term existence.

The year 2005 was pivotal for the SCO. It was the year in which the infection of color revolutions that were sweeping through the post-Soviet space reached Central Asia, leading to the chaotic overthrow of Kyrgyzstan's Askar Akayev. It was also in mid-2005 that Uzbekistan cracked down on protesters in Andijan by opening fire on a crowd, killing an unknown number of people. These two incidents and in particular the West's response to them crystallized for SCO members the reason why regional multilateral frameworks were important. The revolution in Kyrgyzstan was the product of economic problems, long-standing tribal and ethnic tensions, and Kyrgyzstan's generally fragile state. But coming in the wake of the color revolutions in Georgia and Ukraine that had quite decisively turned those countries away from the post-Soviet order that had existed since the dissolution of the Soviet Union, the interpretation of the global media was that the same thing was happening in Kyrgyzstan.

A pulse of concern went through the other Central Asian governments that the same might happen to them. Many were concerned about the influence of Western backed democracy promoting institutions in their territories and were increasingly worried about how long US forces were going to actually stay in their backyard after the initial invasion of Afghanistan. In fact, Kyrgyzstan's revolution was probably more *sui generis* and a product of local clashes than the other so-called Color Revolutions, but the fact that the West seemed to embrace what was going on in Kyrgyzstan as a signal of a changing world order merely heightened SCO member governments' concerns. When in May the West leapt to condemn Uzbekistan for its actions in Andijan, the result was predictable. Uzbekistan booted out the American forces based in Kashi-Khanabad and warmly embraced its SCO brothers, seeing them as offering a more comfortable partnership than the destabilizing West. The Central Asians may like the West as a place to study and visit, but their leaderships fear the chaos that Western democracy engenders.

However, just as 2005 crystallized why the region needed to support itself against a fickle West, 2008 highlighted how it was in fact China that had the upper hand in the region and in the SCO in particular. After months of provocations on both sides, on August 7, 2008, Georgia decided to move decisively against separatists in South Ossetia, a border region with Russia that had long been home to deep anti-Tbilisi feelings. Russia raced to protect the South Ossetians and used this as a pretext to invade Georgia. Again, Western anger flowed, with the European Union condemning Russia's actions while many in Washington called for the US to do something about protecting this NATO ally. Seeking international support, Russia went to the SCO requesting a statement of support, only to meet with rejection. China was appalled to see Russia's assertion of military supremacy in the former Soviet space, a sentiment echoed by the separatist concerned Central Asians. Not only did this set a dangerous precedent for separatist groups within their borders, but it further alarmed them that Russia would carry out such an invasion in their own territories. Kazakhstan in particular feared the precedent set in its relationship with Moscow. Having a long border with Russia, a population with a large ethnic Russian component in the north, and the impending leadership change with their aging President Nazarbayev, Astana (as it then was) saw the situation as presenting Moscow with a potentially analogous context. Should President Putin not like whoever ascended to the throne in President Nazarbayev's wake, Moscow might decide to intervene there too. The result of this incident was a further strengthening of China's hand within the SCO and the region, something it was able to build on further through its economic largess and other tools.

This dance was repeated six years later when Russia moved to claim Crimea and invade parts of eastern Ukraine in response to the collapse of the pro-Kremlin Yanukovich government. Again, Moscow sought support from the SCO powers and again they refused, though this time Beijing was more circumspect. It supported the majority view in the organization's Central Asian heart which largely reflected its earlier concerns about the Kremlin's assault on Georgia. But it also saw Moscow's side of the story more clearly, concerned about how Ukraine had been destabilized by democratic Western forces. The narrative around the incident in Beijing was closer to 2005 than 2008—more Color Revolution than separatist trouble. Seen in this light, it was more about bolstering allies in the Russian–Chinese sphere of influence who were standing up to a chaotic and democratizing West. Nevertheless, concern about Russian behavior played to Chinese advantage in Central Asia. Some whispered rumors we heard but could never verify went so far as to suggest President Nazarbayev visited Beijing with the explicit request that China step in should Moscow do the same in Kazakhstan.

The SCO is fundamentally a Chinese creation and one that is eager to make as few enemies as possible. Talk to Chinese strategists who believe in the organization (and not all of them do, one of them we met in Beijing was very proud of becoming a *persona non grata* at the Ministry of Public Security after he provided their newly appointed RATS representative with a largely negative assessment of the organization and its prospects[28]) and they will come up with a thousand and one stories about how the organization is purposely on a slow development path. As one of them put it when talking about the prospects for an FTA: "there are two ways to build an FTA: you can set a target and then run to it, or you can foster gradual integration. China prefers the second road."[29] Thinkers will tell you that the various Russian-led initiatives that seem to compete with the SCO's space are not important or relevant comparisons with the SCO as they are answering a different need. The SCO does not need to be a military organization, as the CSTO already has that role in Central Asia. The SCO is not a competitor to the EAEU, as its economic aspect is still developing and is nowhere near as structured. The SCO development bank is not necessary as there are numerous other development banks covering the region. China is bashful about its organization's ambitions and successes.

But more important is the fact that for Beijing, the point of the SCO is not to impose rule or control, but rather to bring concordance and coherence under China's guidance. While outsiders may look at the SCO as demonstrating the imposition of control by bigger powers on smaller ones, seen from inside there is a remarkable degree of genuine joint decision-making and agreement. The fact all members have veto power means that everyone has to agree for anything to move forward. And the fact that they get very little materially from the organization means the leverage is not that strong. But it does not need to be, from Beijing's perspective this is about creating a sense of unity and empowerment without actually giving anything away. President Xi's regular appearance at events and willingness to be respectful to countries whose size is a fraction of one of his provinces in China, shows a degree of humility the Central Asians in particular appreciate. Chinese strategists are always keen to emphasize how they see Central Asia very differently to Russia—as a group of senior People's Liberation Army (PLA) thinkers put it to us in mid-2018, Russians do not really see the Central Asians as independent, but rather as extensions of Russia. In contrast, China sees them as foreign countries with their own agency. And whatever might be said about China's overbearing influence, within the context of the SCO this is how China likes to be seen to act, something the face-obsessed Central Asians understand.

The game China is playing is consciously an incremental one. Visit the various institutions created around the SCO and China's contributions are the most visible, though kept subtle. For example, it is usually the case that China bankrolls the summits when they are held in poorer member states like Kyrgyzstan or Tajikistan. In the months running up to the visit, senior security officials will come to the region, and as part of the visit dole out money to cover the costs of the event. Until relatively recently this was not mentioned in reports, though in recent years it has started to be, perhaps with China gradually showing its hand in the organization a little more prominently.

Another way the approach is articulated is at an institution we visited in 2018 at the Shanghai University of Politics and Law. The China National Institute for SCO International Exchange and Judicial

Cooperation (CNISCO) was opened in 2014 at a ceremony co-hosted by then Kyrgyz president, Almazbek Atambayev, and then Chinese head of security, Meng Jianzhu.[30] Funded and developed by the Chinese Ministry of Public Security and aimed at border guard and interior ministry forces, the institution provided a variety of training courses to security forces from SCO member states and observers. Delivered by professors at the university and from around Shanghai, the courses lasted a few months and gave the officers sent there an experience in China as well as an understanding of its interpretation of international rules and norms regarding counter-terrorism legislation and practice. When we asked about which languages the classes were being taught in, we were told that it was mostly in English, as few professors could speak Russian to an adequate level. Not that many could actually do it in English either, so you had a situation of double translation sometimes—from Chinese to English, and then in some cases English to whichever local language was most suitable. It is hard to imagine much information being usefully imparted, and we were told that it was the Russian officers who attended who were the most professional. Most of the others treated it like a holiday of sorts, something China was clearly not averse to supporting as it would help strengthen her soft power influence in the country from which they had come. Unspoken of course was the obvious recruitment opportunity this also presented for China's intelligence services, as well as the soft security links it helped Beijing foster with key forces in neighboring countries.

In a shiny new set of buildings adjacent to the University's main compounds, the CNISCO's biggest problem we were told was that it was running out of people to train. Aimed not at junior officials, but rather mid-career captains and colonels in border and police forces, the idea was to focus on the professional cadre within each country's forces rather than each year's batch of new recruits. This meant you were creating within each system a growing cadre of officers who had some experience and connection with China. Having handled a growing proportion of those of the SCO members, the CNISCO was reportedly moving onto dialogue partners—including Belarusian and potentially even Turkish forces.

We visited at the moment when India and Pakistan had just joined the organization, meaning that an almost limitless pool of potential candidate officers for training was now opening up. From China's perspective, this was creating a deep and strong link to forces that were ultimately important to China, both in terms of being on the other side of China's borders, but also in defending borders (like Afghanistan's) that if handled badly could have repercussions for China. Who knows what links and information might flow from such programs, and how many of the individuals involved might ultimately ascend to more senior roles? This long-term approach of building up relations in the security field is something that will be explored in greater depth in a later chapter, but the point within the context of the SCO is to show the organization's longer-term planning in action and its potential impact.

During COVID-19 the SCO took another step forward in its march. In 2019, the organization took on a new leader, a former senior security official from Uzbekistan, Vladimir Norov, who had previously served as chief of the country's main strategic studies think tank (and before that in the Interior Ministry). Under his leadership, the organization seemed to take a more dynamic and creative turn. For example, in the middle of the year, Jack Ma (the founder of Alibaba, China's answer to Amazon) met with him and a number of SCO leaders to discuss how Alibaba could work with them to better connect up the broader SCO community of nations. As COVID-19 took hold the next year, Jack Ma pledged to send support to the SCO member states, and subsequently planeloads of medical aid arrived in the various capitals. In March, the SCO showed yet another aspect of itself when it signed an agreement with a Chinese e-learning platform called Weidong Cloud Education to help with e-learning during the virus-related lockdowns. Alibaba worked with the SCO to sponsor online webinars and health summits between Chinese and SCO member state doctors. Showing that the organization was not uniquely bonded to Alibaba, the secretary general also had public meetings with the senior leadership of JD.com, another Chinese online sales market, and JD.com was one of the early investors in the Qingdao China-SCO "demonstration park": a giant establishment in Qingdao which was to act as an incubator for companies that were going to undertake projects in the SCO space. The billions of dollars reported to have been allocated to the project mostly came from Chinese tech companies who had all been prominently meeting the SCO's leadership in the months before the opening of the institution. All of these activities took place alongside numerous other Chinese engagements with the region from sending vaccines to offering medical aid and support, to working with authorities to establish how to implement lockdowns.

The Alibaba relationship in particular might subsequently prove to be very significant. Alibaba was already responsible for the overwhelming majority of postage and package traffic between China, Russia, and the Central Asian members of the SCO. As more trade moves to online platforms like Alibaba, the longer-term economic link that China envisioned for the SCO and Central Asia may well be realized. The agreement signed in the middle of 2019 was followed later in the year by an agreement to establish a joint venture between Mail.ru and Alibaba which would create a new super-platform incorporating all of the companies linked to these two online behemoths, including e-commerce, social media, and payment platforms. The net result would be to closely bind China's new economy with Russia's, and likely to further tip things in China's favor, given the sheer weight of Alibaba in particular. The SCO spent much of 2019 and 2020 undertaking events with the company, as well as other Chinese e-commerce and e-payment providers, suggesting that the organization was becoming the new vehicle to enable Chinese penetration into Central Asia and beyond. The SCO may yet find a way to live up to the economic promise that Beijing has long seen within it. Li Peng's visions of new Silk Roads may still come to life through the SCO.

7

The New Great Wall

Border post at the Kunjerab Pass, Xinjiang, China

We had noticed the Chinese businessman in the queue for the plane. Having made many journeys on planes around the region, we had actually not seen that many Chinese flying between capitals, in contrast to the flights back and forth from China. Stuck in Bishkek's underwhelming waiting lounge with little else to do, we wandered over to strike up a conversation. Intrigued to find a foreigner who spoke some Mandarin, he engaged and told us about his work as a manager/engineer for the China Rail company. While he was vague about exactly what project he was working on, he was very keen to impress us with how well connected he was where we were going in Dushanbe. He did this by showing us pictures of a tall and severe looking Tajik security official in his full dress uniform whose pictures he had on his phone, and who he was pictured standing next to. As he reassured us about the importance of his connection, a young Kyrgyz man in army fatigues came over and started speaking Chinese, inquiring if that was in fact the language we were chatting in. Once confirmed he jumped right in, saying he appreciated the opportunity to practice. Somewhat confirming the importance of our new Chinese friend's Tajik contact, he recognized the severe looking officer in the pictures.

The Kyrgyz officer had learned his atonal but fluent Mandarin on a training course he had been sent on in Nanjing. During the eleven-month course, he had managed to learn some Chinese, but had much preferred the excitement and size of Nanjing's urban metropolis. He was particularly keen to tell us about the brothels and night markets he had found. The program was one he had been sent on along with a number of mid-ranking officers in his border guard unit, all of which was sponsored by the Chinese government. The Chinese businessman chuckled at this strange encounter with all these Mandarin-speaking foreigners and we separated to board the plane, though of course not before the obligatory selfie pictures were taken.

The encounter in late 2013 was an early insight into a depth and complexity of China's security relationship with Central Asia that we had not really considered when we started this project. When we started doing research on China in Central Asia, the abiding narrative (that has only recently started to change) around China's relations with Central Asia was that they were all about economics and trade. With the advent of the Belt and Road Initiative, this was redefined as being principally about infrastructure and extractives. But at no point did we find much of a sense that security was a part of the story. Rather, most analysis pointed to a bargain—unspoken or not—between Beijing and Moscow whereby China did the economics and

Russia the security. But when we started to dig into the relationship between China and Central Asia this seemed an odd conclusion. In the first instance, our entire sense of why China was interested in Central Asia was predicated on a domestic security concern. China wanted Central Asia to be secure, open, connected, and prosperous so that in turn its own part of Central Asia, Xinjiang, would also be prosperous and therefore stable. Ultimately, China's thinking about Central Asia was based on a goal for security at home.

There was also a very hard edge to this concern within Central Asia. As we have seen in previous chapters, China is concerned about militancy both within Xinjiang and across the border in Central Asia. Chinese diplomats, businesspeople, and visiting dignitaries had been targeted over the years in Kyrgyzstan by groups they assessed as being linked to groups of militant Uyghurs (and in some cases investigation subsequently revealed this to be the case). In the midst of doing research for this book, in 2016 the Chinese Embassy in Bishkek was targeted by a vehicle bomb. The subsequent investigation revealed a network with links to Uyghur groups in Syria. When we pressed Kyrgyz security officials for answers about the attack years later, they dismissed it as not having links to international terrorism, pointing to it as an instance of local "political" violence. When we asked what this meant they remained evasive, but suggested that the attack was one which the Kyrgyz saw as being linked to a specific grievance against the Chinese rather than anything else. The point was that China was specifically the target, rather than this being something linked to a broader international cause. Something that suggested a Uyghur return address. While there was little evidence of similar networks in other countries, China was nevertheless concerned about the possibility of such threats as well as about other groups that might emanate from Central Asia to threaten Xinjiang or China directly. In the wake of the attack, there was considerable concern from the security watching community in China around the potential for similar incidents in Tajikistan.

Second, as we uncovered the deep levels of distrust that existed between China and Russia in Central Asia in particular, it seemed very unlikely that Beijing would simply abrogate its security interests in Central Asia to Moscow. Chinese officials and experts we met repeatedly expressed their disdain for Russia, while at the same time maintaining a convivial public demeanor. Moscow's management of the post-Cold War collapse of the Soviet Union was treated as a textbook case in Beijing of how not to manage such a change in government. In Moscow we watched as, at a prominent event, one of China's top Russia watchers wowed an audience of cynical Muscovites with his fluent Russian, peppered with humor and Dostoyevsky quotes, as he talked about the relations between their two great powers. Over lunch afterwards, a Russian friend praised the Chinese academic's linguistic skills, joking it was better than theirs. Yet, a short year later we saw the same academic in Beijing before an audience of European experts in which he lambasted Russia and complained about how difficult they were to work with. He said China felt forced into a relationship with Russia because it was rejected by the West. Beijing would far prefer to be close to Europe. We heard the converse repeatedly in Moscow over the years from Russian experts as well. Both were clearly playing to their audiences, but it nevertheless highlighted a deep underlying mistrust.

The Sino-Russian relationship may be strategically important to both, and has grown closer in recent years through collective confrontation against the West, but they do not trust each other. The Sino-Soviet split in earlier times lays a heavy foundation. Frenemies is the best characterization we were able to come up with at the time, though it still feels unsatisfactory, where the two see themselves as important strategic allies, but fundamentally do not entirely trust each other and worry things may one day turn adversarial. This was repeatedly reflected in discussions we had where it did not take long in any bilateral engagement to find that the counterpart in front of us would complain about the other who was not present. Russians were always quick to complain about the Chinese, and after a little prodding the Chinese would reciprocate.

This tension was visible in our various engagements as well as publicly. Discussions around bilateral deals were always contentious and occasional spy dramas would play out in the press. In early 2020, a story emerged of the Russian FSB (internal security service) arresting prominent academic Professor Valery Mitko, president of St Petersburg Arctic Social Science Academy. A former navy captain, he was accused of selling secrets about Russia's submarine fleet to Beijing.[1] A year or so earlier, a similar story had played out in Kazakhstan, where a prominent academic sinologist who had advised the new President Kassym-Jomart Tokayev in his dealings with China was arrested for selling state secrets to China.[2] A former KGB (Committee for State Security) officer, Konstantin Syroyezhkin was given a ten-year sentence and stripped of his citizenship, meaning he faces deportation to Russia upon completion of his time in prison.[3] This conclusion merely serves to illustrate once again the close relationship that Russia has with the region, and how this competition can sometimes hit up against China.

The debate about Huawei and whether Russia should use the company in the construction of its own 5G network was a good articulation of the tension at the heart of the relationship for Moscow. On the one hand, Russia (and in particular its intelligence agencies) feared letting China into their digital and tech infrastructure, but on the other hand, they felt somewhat limited in their options. As we were told in Moscow, "look who is actually sanctioning us." They might not trust the Chinese, but they recognized at a strategic level that they are on the same page as Beijing rather than the Western capitals producing the alternatives to Huawei, meaning Moscow would have to go with the Chinese option.

With this as a backdrop, it seems illogical that Beijing would in turn rely on Moscow to guarantee the security of its growing assets and interests in Central Asia. Given Beijing's concerns around Xinjiang in particular and the importance of this to the Chinese Communist Party (CCP) and their control over China, this logic seems even more flawed, illustrating why the simplistic assumption that China does economics while Russia does security does not work. Nor is it visible on the ground in Central Asia. The reality was articulated perfectly to us during a visit to Bishkek where, as we were doing the rounds of the think tanks and ministries, we were repeatedly given the line that China did the economics while Russia did security, only for an official at the Ministry of Foreign Affairs to turn to us and say, "well, in fact, the Chinese did just build a new headquarters for our border guards."[4]

What was fascinating to watch was how Chinese assertiveness in the military domain in particular grew during the development of this project. From a power that was largely passive in security matters, it became a power increasingly flexing its muscles, developing a security footprint that not only served to advance China's direct and narrow interests but increasingly seemed to be aimed at embedding China within the region's security apparatus in the long run. What Moscow had assumed was solely theirs has over time been eroded. In Chapter 8 we will focus on Afghanistan, a security worry for Beijing which lurks like a menacing shadow in the background of their concerns about Central Asian stability. Here instead we will look at China's growing security footprint and relationships in Central Asia beyond the Shanghai Cooperation Organization (SCO). From providing border support and equipment, to language training and COVID-19 aid—China's military relationship with Central Asia is as ascendant as in every other area.

★   ★   ★

As was highlighted in Chapter 1, the stories of China's security footprint in Central Asia go back some time. The infamous Battle of Talas of 751 when an army of the Abbasid Caliphate met its counterpart from the Tang Dynasty is frequently people's historical starting point when looking at China's relations with Central Asia. The almighty clash was won by the Arab army, and it is the only time Arab and Chinese armies met each other on the field of battle. The reason for the conflict offers an interesting counterpoint for modern China's view of security threats from the region. Drawn in thanks to a princeling fleeing to rally an army in his support to fight the Tang, the clash was one that the Chinese dynasty was dragged into rather than sought. This habit of imperial borderland squabbles dragging in regional potentates and their armies has resonances today, where issues at China's borderlands are dragging Beijing into thinking more about regional security questions than it would care to, in some cases even going so far as having to deploy soldiers in response. While the end result is not the same sort of conflict that the Tang Dynasty found themselves facing against the Abbasid Caliphate, Beijing is finding itself having to build defensive barriers to protect China from violent threats that lurk on its fringes. Threats that this time have a direct potential link into China itself, and in some ways are a greater threat to the CCP than the warring potentates of the 8th century.

Tajikistan in particular lends itself as a useful lens through which to look at China's escalating security interests and efforts in the region. We sought to track this first-hand, but naturally struggled. Both the topic and the areas of Tajikistan where the Chinese forces were reportedly being deployed were complicated. In one of our early visits to Dushanbe in 2012, we heard rumors of Chinese soldiers being deployed along the Tajik border with Afghanistan. Hunched over a local interpretation of cheesy nachos and beer with an American expat who appeared to have spent too much time chasing conspiracy theories online in Central Asia, we heard how he knew categorically that there were Chinese soldiers manning guard posts along the Tajik-Afghan border in the sensitive Gorno-Badakhshan region. We would find them, he told us, by tracing the Chinese mining interests in the country. Look to where the mines were, and then see the nearest border post.

We registered his perspective skeptically and moved on, only to hear a similar story from our Tajik interpreter at a later meeting on the same trip. This time, however, the source seemed more reliable. She had seen the soldiers first hand, claiming to have been walking around near her village when she had seen Chinese men in military uniform. Doubtful, we pressed her, but she remained convinced of what she had seen, and the person we were interviewing at the time nodded agreement at what she was saying. None of this was verifiable of course, and anyone close to officialdom we met during this visit denied any such presence. When we went up to Murghab and Khorog, we also struggled to find anyone who could verify the story, though all were full of praise of Chinese construction and admiration for the Aga Khan. There is a large Ismaili community in the Pamirs, stretching across the border into Afghanistan, meaning the region and country is the focus of a lot of attention by the Aga Khan and his foundation. When we visited, there were messages of praise for the Aga Khan emblazoned into the sides of the mountains in white rocks. Few we met, however, had much good to say about the government in Dushanbe.

The story of Chinese soldiers in Tajikistan was one that went quiet for a few years after that, until in 2015 during a visit to Bishkek we heard stories once again about how Chinese soldiers were reportedly appearing in Tajikistan's remote regions along its border with Afghanistan. This time the story came from a well-connected foreigner who reported hearing the information reliably from Russian diplomatic sources who were furious that the Tajiks had let the Chinese deploy a security presence there. A year later, this story was officially confirmed when the Tajik government formally announced that they had invited the Chinese to help them build border posts. The report indicated that the government had instructed the State Security Council to work with the Chinese to build eleven border guard posts and a training base along Tajikistan's border with Afghanistan.[5] This came at around the time that the Tajiks were holding one of their first joint public training exercises bilaterally with the Chinese.

In mid-2017, we were in Washington talking to various officials on the topic of China in Central Asia and brought the story up again, only to hear it confirmed with great glee at the tension that this was stirring up between the Chinese and Russians. This confirmed what we had heard anecdotally on the ground. The report given to us was that the local embassy was furious when they had learned about the bases and training efforts, and were particularly perplexed by Tajikistan's decision to join the Quadrilateral Cooperation and Coordination Mechanism (QCCM) being run by China about Afghanistan without any consultation or discussion with their Collective Security Treaty Organization (CSTO) partners. But more about the QCCM in Chapter 8, on Afghanistan. By 2018, the narrative of China in Tajikistan had advanced further, and the International Crisis Group published a report in which its sources confirmed the presence of Chinese soldiers, where they were located in Gorno-Badakhshan, and described them as staying at a "joint counter-terrorism center."[6] In February of the next year, a *Washington Post* reporter actually visited the location, Shaimak, and met some of the soldiers.[7] Soon after that, the *Wall Street Journal* reported that Chinese soldiers were replacing Tajik soldiers along the border.[8]

When we asked Chinese experts in Beijing about these later stories, their response was fairly sanguine. Why would they not have a presence there? they asked us. China had concerns about security in Afghanistan, and they were not certain about Tajik capacity to deliver guarantees. This echoed what we heard from Chinese security watchers in the wake of the attack on the Chinese embassy in Bishkek in 2016. It was also the case that the threats that China had seen there had been ones which had potential direct links with China, and consequently were all the more important.

This level of concern helped explain the Chinese presence. The People's Armed Police (PAP) force that had been deployed was there to help their allies strengthen their border and ultimately to help address Chinese security interests—a joint endeavor. The Chinese experts we spoke to in Beijing would characterize the model of cooperation as a replica of what had been employed in the Mekong Delta, where Chinese forces had undertaken joint patrols with their Myanmar, Thai, and Lao counterparts to deal with criminal threats that were damaging China. In that context, criminals had murdered a group of Chinese fishermen, leading to an enhanced security response which ended up with the establishment of a platform for direct cooperation with neighboring countries to deal with cross-border security threats. The successful program in Southeast Asia had led to the detentions and death of criminals, and was maintained to ensure China's ongoing security was guaranteed. What was happening in Tajikistan was merely a local reiteration of this structure, whereby Chinese security forces worked closely with their neighbors ultimately to address a Chinese security concern.[9] None of this would seem unreasonable, and the explanation helped rationalize why it was that Chinese security forces were appearing in neighboring countries. The fact the story evolved over almost a decade from outright denial to open acceptance and admission highlights China's sensitivities around any issue until it has been resolved.

This drip-by-drip revelation of growing Chinese presence was emblematic of China's approach to security issues in Central Asia. This was not a subject many Chinese experts were keen to talk about in much detail (or necessarily even knew much about), and when we asked questions on the ground, there was little information offered. Chinese soldiers who were deployed were unlikely to want to talk to foreigners, even those who spoke a bit of bad Mandarin, and anyway they were usually only to be found in remote places. But what was noticeable was that there was a gradual increase in both presence and stories throughout the period that we were visiting the region. From a narrative of division of labor, it was very clear that China's security footprint was encroaching on Russia's traditional territory across the region. But Beijing was doing this in a way that was gently changing things on the ground, so that by the time the changes became an open secret they had been fully incorporated into the fabric of the region and had a reasonable logic of their own. By the time of writing, it was clear that as with almost every other aspect of life, China had penetrated fairly deeply into the security side of Central Asia.

★　★　★

In many ways, this was not very surprising. It does not take long to see that China has long had security concerns and ambitions in Central

Asia. The security concerns have been highlighted in earlier chapters around Uyghur militancy and cross-border links. Ambitions have been visible through the SCO. The SCO was the first non-United Nations international organization with a strong security aspect that China joined. Intimately involved in its creation, there was little mistaking the organization's security flavor and focus on Central Asia (notwithstanding a clear Chinese desire for it also to go in an economic direction). Additionally, the first bilateral military exercise that China undertook was with the Kyrgyz army in 2002 and it was held under the SCO's auspices. The Tian Shan exercise preceded the much larger (and Russian influenced) SCO "Peace Missions" which started years later, but highlighted China's early interest in building links with Central Asian security forces. The decision to start with Kyrgyzstan reflected the concern China had with the country, having watched repeated attacks on officials and businesspeople there and fearing cross-border links between Uyghurs, a threat picture that was compounded by a lack of faith in the local authorities' capability to manage the problems. Developing more direct relations through the SCO, an organization founded to tackle terrorist problems, seemed a natural route.

But over time China's attention and security efforts have grown in many different directions. And much like other areas where attention tends to focus on one aspect of Chinese engagement, this misses the fact that China works through bilateral and multilateral structures at the same time. The SCO has continued to develop as we saw in Chapter 6. Yet beyond the SCO, China has made inroads across the board into Central Asia's security apparatus. From providing aid and support, to increasingly moving into military sales, and finally moving into building the technological backbone for the region, China is not only developing and deepening security links across the region but also embedding itself deep into Central Asia's future.

Chinese military aid to the region has been limited (in particular in comparison to Moscow's), but it has been consistent over the past few years. While absolute numbers are hard to calculate due to a lack of information, flows appear to commence sometime in the late 1990s. Some reports suggest that China was providing military aid as early as 1993 to Tajikistan (in the midst of its civil war),[10] but it is hard to trace the specific details. Clear support to Kyrgyzstan starts to emerge in the 1990s with initial bilateral agreements and aid at around $750,000 per annum which included uniforms, communications equipment, radio stations, and night vision devices.[11] Tajikistan was reportedly receiving a similar level of support in the early years, with reports suggesting some $15 million was given between 1993 and 2008.[12]

There have been further reports of China providing aid in the 1990s to Kazakhstan and Turkmenistan. Between 1997 and 2003, Kazakhstan was given some RMB (renminbi) 30 million RMB ($4.5 million) of technological aid, communications equipment, and vehicles.[13] Much later, in 2015, China gave Kazakhstan thirty trucks and thirty large-load trailers worth $3.2 million.[14] Details with Turkmenistan are almost impossible to clarify, but experts and diplomats based in Ashgabat have reported that at various points China has been providing support for Turkmen security structures.[15] A report by the Jamestown Foundation identified a loan of $3 million by China for Turkmenistan in 2007 to acquire "precision equipment," with no clarity about what the terms of repayment might be.[16] Beyond this, while on the ground, we heard occasional reports of Chinese firms working near Turkmenistan's borders potentially providing some support for the soldiers guarding them. We were unable to verify these statements, and it was impossible to know if these were private security officers, the military, something else, or simply figments of our contacts' imagination. We did, however, see first-hand Chinese military equipment on national day parades in Ashgabat, the Turkmen capital.

Aid support is provided through Ministry of Defense grants usually agreed and signed during defense minister or chief of defense staff engagements, or through grants from the Chinese Ministry of Public Security (MPS) to its counterparts. There are news stories about uniforms, communications equipment, office furniture, and machinery,[17]

as well as more recent gifts of unspecified vehicles.[18] In 2014, this
escalated to the construction of officers' quarters and barracks in both
Tajikistan and Kyrgyzstan.[19] This push in 2014 followed a noticeable
up-tick in Chinese contributions to both countries, with Defense
Minister Chang Wanquan announcing that the country was to give
"hundreds of millions" to Tajikistan,[20] while announcing a further $16
million to Kyrgyzstan.[21] In 2017, a further large gift of $14.5 million
was announced by Chief of Staff Fang Fenghui on a visit to Bishkek.[22]
These numbers were likely overtaken by General Xu Qiliang's visit in
October 2018, though details were not released.[23] Earlier in 2018, the
China Ordinance Industry Group donated its VP11 patrol vehicles to
Tajikistan to help their border forces in Gorno-Badakhshan better
patrol the area.[24]

An interesting observation that might explain some of these
Chinese contributions was alluded to earlier in the text by a Chinese
interlocutor in Shanghai in 2013 who pointed out that when the
annual SCO summits had been held in Bishkek or Dushanbe, there
was almost always a visit shortly before by a senior Chinese official
during which time Beijing would dispense money to help cover the
costs of the event. The 2013 meeting was held particularly late, and
when we investigated, we were told that it was because the Kyrgyz
were waiting for China to come through with the funds. Ahead of the
June 2019 Bishkek SCO summit, Minister of Public Security Zhao
Kezhi visited Bishkek and provided funding of around RMB 30 million, which included monies to support summit security.[25]

But not all Chinese military support is free, and as time has gone
on, Beijing's defense contractors have seen opportunities in Central
Asia, in particular among the richer countries. Or the ones more eager
to project an image of power and strength rather than being seen as
aid recipients. In particular, Kazakhstan, Turkmenistan, and Uzbekistan
have all made purchases of higher end equipment which they might
have traditionally purchased from Russian contractors. In some cases,
they have purchased the weapons in a barter system using their hydro-
carbon resources. Turkmenistan and Uzbekistan are both reported to

have used natural gas to pay for FD-2000/HQ-9 long-range surface to air missile systems.[26]

One visible example of China's presence in the region's defense military industrial complex is at the biannual KADEX Defense Expo that is held in Kazakhstan. Initiated in 2010, KADEX is an opportunity for the burgeoning Kazakh defense industry to showcase its wares (which China has shown an interest in through signing a license agreement with KPE to potentially buy their armored vehicles[27]), while also providing an opportunity for key regional players to have a location to sell directly to a regional customer base. China has been a consistent presence at the Expo since its first iteration, but it is noticeable that its presence and reporting around it have increased as the years have gone by. On a tour of the 2018 Expo after his opening speech, President Nazarbayev made a particular point of visiting the Chinese and Russian pavilions after the national Kazakh ones.[28]

What is also noticeable is that the Chinese military sales that are reported tend to be for higher end platforms. Kazakhstan has purchased Chinese Wing Loong drone platforms,[29] as well as Y8F200W military transport aircraft from Shaanxi Aircraft Corp.[30] This latter purchase is likely to have been galling for Russia as the craft is an evolved version of the Soviet-made Antonov An-12 "Cub"—suggesting it was a sale that would once have gone to Russia. Turkmenistan has also purchased unmanned aerial vehicle (UAV) platforms,[31] the HQ-9 surface to air missile systems (SAMS),[32] and their portable equivalents MANPADS.[33] Finally, Uzbekistan has also bought higher end sniper rifles,[34] the FD-2000/HQ-9 SAMS,[35] and drones.[36] Tashkent has also reportedly even managed to broker a deal whereby it gets some local knowledge transfer through the development of a local factory to assemble and make drones.[37]

The approach of working with locals in such sensitive areas, or providing opportunities for investment there which will help develop Central Asia's industrial base is exactly what the Central Asian governments want, and it is something that is also evident in the technology space. Uzbekistan has long been the regional hub for Chinese tech companies Huawei and ZTE.[38] Both have long-established factories in the region and used it as a base from which to sell regionally. While this is mostly commercial software and hardware (ZTE established a modem factory in the region in 2011[39] and a handset phone factory in 2013,[40] while Huawei has been making handsets there since 2006[41]), they have also for a long time been among the main technology hardware providers around the region, building national telecoms infrastructure and providing technological solutions to school systems, hospitals, and rail and oil infrastructure.

More security specific is the development of "safe city" programs mostly by Huawei that have been delivered in Dushanbe,[42] reportedly in Astana (now Nursultan),[43] as well as long-standing discussions of such projects in Bishkek and Osh. In Kyrgyzstan, the company has encountered the same problems that innumerable other Chinese traders have found with a high degree of pushback from locals, leaving them having to suspend projects or at the very least delay them. However, in 2019 it was revealed that a Chinese surveillance tech provider, China National Electronics Import & Export Corporation (CEIEC) was providing equipment to the country to enable facial recognition technology on closed-circuit TV (CCTV) around the city.[44]

At the border between civilian and military, Huawei, Zhongxing Telecommunications Equipment (ZTE), and Hikvision (a surveillance camera provider) hardware are ubiquitous throughout the region, in terms of both the communications equipment armies use and the surveillance cameras used in official and private residences. As we have seen in other contexts, Chinese products are cheap and easily available, which makes them attractive to local security forces (and private citizens) at every level. The quality may be questionable, but oftentimes this is not important—as long as the product does something similar to what it is supposed to do, this is enough. And all of this is in addition to a growing use of Chinese tools like facial recognition technology, online applications, large data storage services offered by Chinese companies across the border in Xinjiang, as well as reports of Chinese artificial intelligence (AI) tools sold to the region, which all point to the various tools of the surveillance state that China has developed at home being offered to Central Asian governments. Whether the intent is to simply strengthen the Central Asians' capability or to provide Chinese security forces further leverage or access to intelligence databases in Central Asia is unclear, but it is another aspect of the region's security apparatus that China is developing a deep influence within.

Notwithstanding these widespread sales and influence, Russian legislation still underpins a lot of what happens in Central Asia in the security space. The SCO is slowly moving into this territory, but it is still dominated by Russia through its deep links and organizations like the CSTO which has long worked with its Central Asian members to help raise their legislation to Russian standards. China is still developing its footprint in this area, but is clearly starting to deepen its reach, in part through the growing adoption of its tools which necessitate accompanying deeper connections and new standards.

But the picture is dynamic, with tensions still occurring between China and the region. As was highlighted earlier, Huawei does not always get its way there. And there are other problems as well. During one visit in the region in late 2019, we spoke to security officials about problems they were facing in terms of managing security threats from terrorism and the spread of radical ideas online. In most capitals they saw the main problem in this regard coming from Western and Russian platforms, but in Turkmenistan they mentioned that the application they found most difficult was in fact the Chinese app IMO. It was used widely in the country (with Facebook, Twitter, WeChat, VKontact, and other more commonly used apps tending to be blocked), but they had struggled to make contact with the firm in China. When they reached out to Chinese counterparts for assistance, they were met with a wall of silence. It seems not all authoritarians get along all the time.

Notwithstanding all this activity from China, it is still always important to note Russia's significant role. In hard power military sales and links Russia remains the preeminent provider, with vestigial Soviet links still dominating military procurement structures and training. Soldiers and military buildings are often still adorned with Soviet imagery. However, Beijing is increasingly becoming the procurer for the future, providing the region with its communications technology, modern tech in the form of drones, and some bigger ticket items like missile systems (and oftentimes Chinese versions of weapons that were reverse engineered from Russian equipment, making them fairly straightforward to use for armies used to Russian kit). As with many other spaces, this is a market which is Russia's to lose. And in some ways, this entire debate is one that is reflective of the growing debate within Russia about Chinese technology and military sales.

★   ★   ★

In late 2012, we took a long drive from Dushanbe to Khorog in a shared taxi. Despite probably paying multiple times more than all the locals traveling with us in the Toyota Landcruiser, we had ended up using this method of transportation after we had realized that going by air was not an option. When we had asked, we had been told that flights were erratic thanks to challenging weather at both ends, and anyway even if we had bought tickets we might have been bumped off the list if someone more important (or better connected) had decided they wanted to go. We concluded a long car ride was a better option, also because this would enable us to get a better look at the country. Having got to Khorog after a twelve-or-so-hour journey we spent the night there before taking another long ride out to Murghab, heading ultimately to our final destination to see the Chinese border at Kulma Pass.

On the journey from Khorog to Murghab we found ourselves stuck sharing a taxi with two workers heading home who broke wind incessantly while asking us about Princess Diana in broken English and gestures. We decided to pay for a whole car to ourselves on the way back. This also gave us the opportunity to get our driver to stop more frequently, and allowed us to try to track down the small village

of Bash Gumbaz where our guidebooks told us there was a mausoleum to a dead Chinese officer. In grandiloquent phrasing, the book
told us that the tomb to the unknown officer "marked the high tide
of Chinese influence on the Pamir." The Kyrgyz farmer who took the
time to take us out to the site (after much effort trying to identify
someone who knew what we were looking for) enjoyed himself on
the way back telling us in broken Russian about how there were
Kyrgyz all over the Wakhan and how they had bravely fought the
Chinese off centuries before.

At the time we went, we had understood it to be a tomb of a fallen
officer. However, subsequent reports we were able to find suggested
it might instead have been a lost trader. Either way, the symbolism
was there in terms of showing China's confused security and trade
footprint in the region and the long shadow this had cast. While it
was always repeated to us, and clear when looking at the numbers (as
well as the language, uniforms, weapons, and doctrinal thinking), not
to mention the forces deployed around the region, that Russia was
still the dominant force, China was nevertheless making persistent
inroads in its own way, gradually increasing its footprint and
presence. The opaque cross-over between trade and security suggested
in the reports around the mausoleum in Bash Gumbaz captured
this well.

From Beijing's perspective, security and stability flow from prosperity.
This was true at home in Xinjiang, but also in Central Asia. It helps
explain the double focus on security and economics across the region.
But for economic prosperity to deliver security and stability, this
would take time and patience. This is the commonly discussed cliché
of Chinese strategic patience, but it is clearly visible in some aspects
of Chinese thinking and planning. When looking at China's security
presence in Central Asia and its long shadow, the reality is most clearly
illustrated in some of the individual-level security relationships that
are being cultivated across the region. These do not happen overnight,
but are the product of long-term relationship building and development whose fruits take years to develop.

This was articulated most clearly on a visit to a People's Liberation Army (PLA) linked think tank in Beijing in 2018 when we met with their preeminent experts looking at Central Asia and Russia. The meeting ran through the usual talking points (with a particular focus on Afghanistan and some questions about Halford Mackinder—including curiosity as to why British visitors were so fascinated with Central Asia), but as we were leaving, one of our hosts kindly offered to give us a lift to the nearest underground stop. As we walked out he started telling us stories about the Central Asian delegations they had hosted recently—mentioning how amused they had been on recent Tajik and Uzbek visits to discover that the deputy chiefs in both cases had received advanced training at the Chinese National Defense University. This anecdote fit with another we heard at a conference in Tashkent, where a senior Tajik security official mentioned he had done his PhD in China. When we visited Dushanbe on another visit, we heard stories about Chinese security think-tankers spending time with the local state security, with our interlocutor surprised at how many of them there were and how long they had spent in the building with officials apparently on an exchange and training mission. In Kazakhstan, the former prime minister and current National Security Council chief Karim Massimov is a man with deep China experience, while President Tokayev is fluent in Mandarin and Chinese trained. In Kyrgyzstan we met a senior adviser to the president who reported that there was a special senior level training program offered by the Chinese to Kyrgyz officials working in the highest ranks of government.

Looking beyond anecdote, China has been running training programs of one sort or another for Central Asian security forces for decades. These are not always easy to deliver, starting with a substantial language barrier that often needs to be overcome. Between 1990 and 2005, fifteen Kazakh officers were sent to China for training, with another sixty-five taking courses in China between 2003 and 2009.[45] In 2004, it was reported that some thirty Kyrgyz officers had received training,[46] while in 2008 it was reported that an agreement was signed by which ten officers a year would receive training in China.[47] In

2006, it was reported that Tajik border guards were to receive training in China, presumably the same course that our Kyrgyz officer had enjoyed in Nanjing.[48] While in 2008, it was reported that some thirty members of the Tajik army received training in Chinese military academies.[49] These numbers were quite limited, but reflected a general and consistent offer on the table to Central Asian security forces to train in China.

All of this is in addition to the training mentioned earlier taking place at the SCO's outpost in Shanghai, which by 2021 was planning to have provided training for around 2,000 officers from across the SCO space.[50] This is not exclusive to Central Asians, and when we visited in 2018 the Indian and Pakistani flags were already up alongside the founder member standards. Additionally, we were told that they were in discussions with Belarus and Turkey to train some of their forces too.[51] But nevertheless, when we spoke to some of the teachers, their abiding memories were of Central Asians and Russians, with an emphasis on the numbers of Central Asians they had seen (though admittedly this could have been influenced by their knowing where our interest lay). The cohorts were made up of mid-rank officers from borders and police forces, and the institute was funded by the MPS, a primarily domestic security agency. Chinese police organs associated with the MPS also provide the officers who staff the Chinese contribution to the SCO's Regional Anti-Terrorism Structure (RATS) in Tashkent, while the Public Security University developed links with its counterparts across the region. In Uzbekistan they funded a simulation center, as well as getting some of the Interior Ministry forces to come to Beijing to train Chinese police cadets about Uzbek culture and history.[52] During the COVID-19 pandemic, the MPS officer stationed at the embassy in Tashkent had a meeting with his local counterparts to discuss how they had managed to impose lockdowns in China.[53]

This link to domestic Chinese security agencies was also interesting to note, and reflected a further important detail in China's security relationship with Central Asia. China has a number of different security forces, but the one that has seen some of the most recent growth in activity in Central Asia is the PAP. A paramilitary organization that answers to the Central Military Commission (the central organ that directs all China's military apparatus), it is principally focused on domestic security questions. It is a form of *gendarmerie* force that is deployed to manage large protests, suppress rebellions, or provide heavier armed security within the country when required. It is PAP forces that are reported to be manning the border posts that China has been helping build in Tajikistan, PAP forces who were present across the border providing training and support in Afghanistan, and PAP forces that have undertaken joint exercises and patrols with their counterparts in Kazakhstan, Kyrgyzstan, and Uzbekistan. While the agreements with the Kazakhs were signed in 2014, leading to patrolling in 2016, joint exercises with Kyrgyzstan and Uzbekistan only took place in 2019.[54] This PAP activity helps tie China's security role in Central Asia more directly with China's domestic security response.

All of this is done in parallel with the SCO as direct bilateral engagements, reflecting once again China's habit of doing things through the SCO and then seeming to replicate them through adjacent structures. Another example of this can be found in the Lianyungang Forum, an annual event and forum hosted by the MPS which brings together law enforcement bodies from across the world—including Interpol, Europol, Afripol, Aseanapol, UNODC, and the Chinese-created SCO and Lancang-Mekong Law Enforcement and Cooperation Center. Focused on improving security and law enforcement connections along the New Eurasian Landbridge, the forum is a part of a broader constellation of activities that China is undertaking in security terms across Eurasia, with a particular link to Central Asia.[55] Through this, China engages with its regional partners, becomes their conduit to the international organizations, and strengthens its own institution (the SCO) by presenting it alongside widely recognized international bodies.

A final pillar to China's security presence in the region which we were never personally able to experience on the ground in Central

Asia but did meet in Beijing, was the burgeoning private security industry. Made up, from what we could tell, of former security officials, mid-level managers, and legions of analysts spotting an opportunity in the market for providing advice to Chinese state-owned enterprises moving into dangerous countries, the private security industry in China took off in the mid-2010s as more Chinese companies started to fall foul of security situations in foreign countries. A push developed from the central government in Beijing for companies to start to worry more about their security and to hire people to provide it. While previously they had largely relied on paying people off and hiring local security, a market now developed for domestic private security. Wealthier companies would opt for international partnerships, with Western companies like G4S or Control Risks dominating the market. In 2018, rules started to be imposed on companies to provide clearer evidence of planning for security problems, with Xi Jinping pushing for a greater proportion of the firms to be domestic, creating a huge opportunity for some of the many soldiers recently demobilized from the army in the wake of President Xi's other push to reform China's armed forces.

In Central Asia it was never certain exactly how these people would be deployed. But there was clear pressure from Beijing and its firms to let them in. We heard stories, which were later reported in the press, about how the Kazakh government had come under great pressure to allow Chinese private companies in.[56] In Kyrgyzstan, we heard reports they had been there since 2015. In Uzbekistan and Tajikistan, it was never entirely clear, but given the companies that had signed contracts with the Chinese companies in Kyrgyzstan (like Zijin mining or Huaxin construction) were operating in Tajikistan as well, it seemed likely there would have been some cross-border activity there as well. A detailed on-the-ground report done in 2020 by researchers in Kyrgyzstan provided some analysis of the companies engaged on the ground, and identified at least six that had a substantial footprint in Central Asia. Their activities covered providing bodyguards, security assessments, internal security within sites, and more.[57] There was very little evidence of any of these firms actively moving into Afghanistan.

But Central Asia, notwithstanding occasional problems, is largely stable internally. While there were undoubtedly tensions between Chinese companies and locals, given the nature of these tensions it seemed unlikely that the insertion of Chinese security personnel would have improved the situation. Rather, it seemed as though these companies were going to provide training for those working there to enable them to plan and defuse situations, as well as to plan for any occasional threats that would emerge. In 2015, we were involved in a roundtable in Beijing which a number of these firms attended, sitting alongside the managers at the Chinese companies they were going to be protecting. The company managers complained about the constraints the security officials placed on them, pointing out that they were simply there to deliver a project. This was a common refrain among the Chinese businesspeople and managers we met in Central Asia, who were often baffled by the anger they would encounter among some locals. They saw themselves as there to do a job; they lacked a sense of why they needed security to do this. The potential for threats to their interests were, however, vividly made clear in 2020 in the wake of the protests that shook Kyrgyzstan which included a number of instances of Chinese factories or mining sites being overrun by angry locals. These sorts of security threats were ones that Chinese private security firms should logically have been able to provide some form of deterrence against, and the failure reflects the still limited security available to Chinese firms on the ground.

Serious security threats do emerge both at an individual level to Chinese businesspeople, traders, or diplomats and at a strategic level from the unstable neighborhood to which Central Asia is adjacent. These require all levels of protections on the ground, but at a higher level, China requires a security shield within Central Asia that will help ultimately deliver security for it at home. In much the same way as Russia has always seen Central Asia as something of a buffer from the problems that have historically emanated from Afghanistan, China sees the benefit of this cushion too. But for Beijing, the security dimension spills once again into the economic space, with the region also being a key conduit for Xinjiang's long-term domestic stability. This complicated blend of hard security concerns spilling over and a need to enhance security and stability in order to deliver a security outcome at home was explicitly mentioned in speeches by Xi Jinping about Xinjiang delivered during his visit to the region in 2014.[58]

For Beijing, security in Central Asia is tied to a key domestic security outcome and one that will need to have a hard power component to it to guarantee its success. This is to protect specific Chinese interests, but also to help with longer-term goals. While a great deal of investment has gone into Central Asian security forces, they are still developing their capabilities and it is not always clear that they are able to deliver effective outcomes. The attack on the embassy in Bishkek in 2016 highlighted this, and Chinese concerns are clearly visible in their growing presence in Tajikistan. Even earlier than this, occasional attacks on Chinese diplomats and businesspeople had clearly illustrated the risks in the region.

One way to ensure the security and stability of neighbors is to strengthen the external and internal security forces of other countries that are next door. This helps potentially shed light on why Beijing is increasingly focused on growing the footprint of its traditionally domestically focused PAP—to help them strengthen their ability to respond to potential cross-border threats and gain some experience in the world, but also to enhance the capabilities of forces that will deliver stability within these countries. In other words, by extending its domestic security blanket into Central Asia, China is again helping its own security at home.

Notwithstanding all of this activity, at the time of writing, it was still not clear that Beijing had achieved the absolute upper hand in security terms that it might be seeking. Moscow was still the major provider of equipment and training, and Russian was still widely spoken. When military parades or events took place in Moscow, the Central Asian leaders could be relied upon to turn up. On the other hand,

China's gradual expansion into this area of Central Asian life is, like much of China's activity in the region, a slow process but nonetheless on a permanently upward trajectory. Beijing has little need ultimately to snub Moscow publicly about its activity in the region, as Russia has shown little ability to control it. Nor necessarily does Russia have contradictory long-term interests, beyond a fear of Chinese dominance and influence. But even this Moscow seems willing to tolerate in favor of ensuring China's geostrategic support in its confrontation with the United States. China continues its relentless march forwards, strengthening links, opening markets, and expanding its footprint to ultimately deliver the goals it is seeking to achieve. The world used to look to the United States to deliver security and stability, but as we heard a Kazakh expert declare somewhat presciently at a conference in Tashkent in 2018, "Pax Americana would be done by 2020." What we appeared to be seeing emerging was a growing *Pax Sinica*.

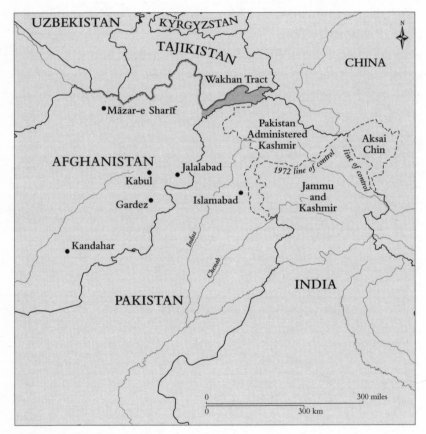

Afghanistan's eastern borders

8

Inheriting Afghanistan?

" I'm not really a guide," says Farid, "I have a degree in economics from Tajik State University." Without Farid, we would be utterly lost on our way from Faizabad to Sar-e-Pul province in northern Afghanistan. Despite his claim of amateur status, he has an uncanny ability to notice shifts in the dusty track aligned with the surrounding topography to divine our next turn. We're traveling low budget in what they call soft vehicles. It is imperative that we keep moving and know where we're going to lessen the likelihood of attack from the numerous militias that scour the scrub-brush desert and surrounding mountains.

Farid's academic credentials are emblematic of this part of the country. An ethnic Tajik from Afghanistan's remote Badakhshan region, he skipped over the northern border to Tajikistan to avoid the fighting of the 1990s, and after working various odd jobs and pulling numerous extended family connections was able to enroll in the Soviet-era Tajik State University. He is one of many ethnic Tajiks, Uzbeks, and Turkmen from the northern provinces of Afghanistan that hold strong ties with their brethren on the other side of the old Russian imperial line. It was these sorts of familial and clan connections that helped to sustain the Northern Alliance as it fended off the Taliban at the turn of the millennium.

These are the same links that facilitate drug trafficking north across the porous borders. When traveling a year earlier along the Panj River on the Tajik side we witnessed only one bedraggled border patrol of emaciated teenage guards trudging along the border during our twenty-hour journey. The boisterous Pamiri women in our shared taxi insisted that we stop to give them loaves of bread and encourage them to keep up their trekking. Before and after we came across them, we noticed several local villagers nonchalantly crossing the border. It would not have seemed out of the ordinary if a few of them carried large packages across.

During our travels, we were able to visit Afghanistan a number of times before the catastrophe in Kabul which tore our project apart. We were also able to travel close to the Afghan border in Tajikistan, Turkmenistan, and China—closer in Tajikistan than the other two where rigid restrictions kept us to a distance that meant we could only observe the border from afar. In Turkmenistan, our driver was game to take us to the border if we had the right permissions, but these were of course very difficult to get—especially for an American passport holder. Our driver told us that we would not want to cross anyway, laughing as he told us about some Polish adventurers whom he had brought to the border crossing who had called him the next day from Mazar e Sharif terrified and asking him to return to pick them up again. As we mentioned earlier, our driver in Xinjiang stopped along the road pretending his car was having troubles to point to the Wakhjir Pass which marks the China end of the Wakhan Corridor that links the two countries, but refused to take us much closer. This was one of the few transgressions he was unwilling to make—having been separately willing to take us all the way up to the Pakistani border without the requisite paperwork, sneak us into tourist sites in Tashkurgan, and take us off the road in parts of the Tajik Autonomous Region of Xinjiang to see local communities up close.

China's relationship with Afghanistan is a big subject in itself. But it is equally relevant vis-à-vis Central Asia alone. From Beijing's perspective, there is a strong connection between what happens in Kabul and what happens in Central Asia, something that most Central Asian powers increasingly acknowledge as they seek to incorporate

Afghanistan into their regional formats. Afghanistan is also intimately linked to what is going on within Xinjiang, providing in some ways the most menacing potential threat to China that it believes it faces outside the United States. In mid-2014, President Xi Jinping made a speech in which he outlined one of his core concerns around the region. "After the United States pulls troops out of Afghanistan, terrorist organizations positioned on the frontiers of Afghanistan and Pakistan may quickly infiltrate into Central Asia," Mr Xi said, "East Turkestan's terrorists who have received real-war training in Syria and Afghanistan could at any time launch terrorist attacks in Xinjiang."[1] Soon after this speech there was a suicide bomb and knife attack at Urumqi's main train station. While no clear link to Afghanistan has been shown and the incident was claimed by Uyghur jihadists, the attack illustrated once again to Beijing policymakers the danger of violent Islamist or separatist threats, which they saw were very active across the border in Afghanistan.

Security is China's key concern with Afghanistan. This includes direct security threats to China from the country (concerns that have a long history as we saw earlier), as well as damage to Central Asia (and Pakistan) where China has invested a growing amount. This investment is intended to ultimately help the security situation in Xinjiang. At the same time, it is a country which has had a major American military presence since the attacks of September 11, 2001. This means that China's principal adversary has set up military bases right on its border. These various dimensions highlight how Afghanistan ties together a lot of different strands for Beijing in a country which was repeatedly described to us as "a graveyard of Empires" (often with a smirk when they wanted to have a dig at America). The war that is going on there is one that they see as America's fault and America's responsibility. But it is a conflict that sits on China's border, which Beijing cannot completely ignore.

This should make Afghanistan a key country for Beijing's policy-makers, yet it is one that rarely makes any headlines in China or is ever likely to get to the top of Xi Jinping's inbox. In the two decades since the overthrow of the Taliban regime, China has hedged her bets in

Afghanistan, both leaning in and engaging and yet never actually committing. Beijing builds relationships across the board, offering investments and providing some security assistance, while at the same time ensuring to never be the one left holding the badge of responsibility. Chinese companies have committed to some of the biggest projects in the country that have failed to move forward, while they have gradually developed a firm control over the direct security threat that Afghanistan might pose to China. Yet, as with Central Asia, China's relationship with Afghanistan is a complicated one which has a web of individuals involved all connected in innumerable different ways. In our travels and during our research we met Chinese officials who had been involved in payoffs to the Taliban, experts who were passionate about Afghanistan and were deeply involved in its history, people who had met Mullah Omar pre-9/11, company executives struggling to deliver projects in the complicated country, and smooth-talking diplomats who were courteous and focused on delivering China's outcomes in Afghanistan no matter how messy it looked. Afghanistan was geographically part of the Belt and Road Initiative (BRI), yet it was also clearly, not when you looked at the many maps laid out of the BRI.

We were never quite able to pin down China's vision for Afghanistan, but instead observed a relationship important to both Beijing and Kabul where China felt it could simply coast, waiting for some natural resolution to come. At a meeting of an official Chinese think tank in Beijing in the autumn of 2011, we suggested that Afghanistan was like a broken tea pot. To the Chinese experts we were sat across the table from, it was a tea pot broken by the United States and it was therefore incumbent on Washington to put it back together again. But as we pointed out, the geographic realities of Central Asia meant that the broken tea pot was on China's side of the table. Even if China bears no responsibility for breaking it, Beijing will be obliged at some point to clean up the mess. As Afghanistan's richest neighbor, it seems hard to imagine that it will not have to take a leadership role at some point. The think-tankers smiled at the analogy but were uncompromising in their resolve that China will not clean up a mess created, in their opinion, by the United States.

★   ★   ★

China National Petroleum Corporation (CNPC) is the first company in history to pump oil out of Afghan soil. During the Soviet Union the Russians explored opportunities but they were mostly focused on the country's gas potential—exporting it at a substantial saving to Moscow, in a trick repeated across the Union. CNPC's wells were our destination in Sar-e-Pul, not far from the northern border with Turkmenistan, a project initially undertaken on the basis of prospecting reports developed by Soviet geologists. The Russians had done considerable surveying of the country's resources, though it is not clear how much they were actually able to profit from these surveys given the conflict they ended up becoming embroiled in.

CNPC's interest in the site stemmed from company geologists who had been involved in the firm's considerable operations in neighboring Turkmenistan. Having seen the rich supply on the Turkmen side of the Amu Darya river, they saw an opportunity on the Afghan side.[2] In fact, CNPC were more interested in the gas potential in the area, but knew that making their presence felt in the country early on would support their subsequent ambitions. Once they established a track record in Afghanistan they would be able to then bid for subsequent gas contracts that might be likely to emerge in the area.

The company was not naïve in the region. Aware of the fact they were entering Afghanistan, a country riven with conflict and factionalism, they elected to go into the project in partnership with the Watan Group—a firm run by Ratib Popal, a cousin of the ex-president, Hamid Karzai. They also offered to build an oil refinery, much like in Kyrgyzstan, which would ultimately help the country achieve greater energy independence. Signed in 2011, the project was seen with great optimism in Kabul and beyond, potentially signaling that government coffers could at last benefit from the country's reputed massive mineral wealth. CNPC's history in the region and willingness to operate in difficult environments suggested a company that was more likely than others to deliver.

But this optimism has seemingly failed to deliver much. Visiting the site in Sar-e-Pul in 2012 Farid spent a lot of his time lowering our expectations: "I have never seen it up close. I have a contact who can show us where they are. We will not be able to enter the complex." For him and other locals we questioned, the presence of a Chinese state-owned enterprise (SOE) in these parched, forbidding environs is a sort of mythical, ominous occurrence. An elderly Uzbek with a wispy beard informs us that the Chinese are here to build an airbase in preparation for driving the Americans out: first the Russians, then the Americans, then the Chinese, he says, counting with his fingers for emphasis.

We caught the project on a day where there was some activity on the site. For a relatively small drilling operation, CNPC's project seemed to have a large footprint. Several layers of fences and containers serving as blast walls surround the extraction site, which includes dormitories, an office complex, and various security structures. Throughout the day, trucks ferry in equipment and more containers. On the outside, the faces are all Afghan, but CNPC's unmistakable logo and three bright red Chinese slogans are easily distinguishable.

CNPC has faced difficulties there notwithstanding their use of the Watan Group to help provide them with local security and connections. In 2012, reports circulated of Chinese engineers being harassed on site. In Ashgabat we met an oil executive who described how the company site was being surrounded by armed locals on motorbikes who in a *Mad Max* style scenario were racing around the site and not letting the Chinese engineers leave. This was despite the generous terms of the deal for Afghanistan: CNPC is paying 15 percent royalties on oil, a 20 percent corporate tax rate, and is yielding 50–70 percent of its profits to the government in addition to building a new refinery to facilitate Afghan energy independence. Yet it is not clear that this was adequate to resolve the problems around the site, since the Watan Group was a Kabul company, with the wrong sorts of links for that part of the country.

The key figure they should likely have engaged with from the outset was Abdul Rashid Dostum, the legendary warlord of the north, and perennial on and off Kabul cabinet member. But once the Chinese figured out that his gunmen were looking for a payoff, CNPC apparently arranged a "protection" scheme with Dostum which not only stopped the attacks but also provided the Chinese company with a type of provincial "street-cred." This meant their security problems abated for some time. It is not clear, however, that this has resolved the larger issues around the project or that it is now actually in production. On subsequent visits to Kabul or China, or meeting with others who had knowledge of the project, we found little evidence of forward movement, on either the oil production or the refinery. In fact, as we shall see, reports now indicate that the project has been suspended.[3]

CNPC has reportedly considered major regional projects connecting pipelines through Afghanistan's north into its regional network and directly into China. Meeting Chinese pipeline executives in Beijing we asked about their plans for Afghanistan and were given a variety of stories, from quite detailed discussions to later stories of problems on the ground. At one point CNPC's pipeline subsidiary was reportedly planning to open an office in Kabul, but by 2019 it no longer appeared that this was the case.

It was almost impossible to get confirmation about much around the deal. Various reports from the ground confirmed that the project had started, and at one point that some oil was being produced, but it was not clear where the oil was being refined. There was considerable uncertainty about which of Afghanistan's northern neighbors would refine the oil, which according to CNPC and the Afghan Ministry of Mines is to be reimported in the form of various petroleum products, like gasoline and kerosene, for Afghan consumption. CNPC has said on numerous occasions that the crude is being trucked in convoys across the Turkmenistan border to be refined in sites managed by CNPC. Other reports suggested that it was in fact being sent to Uzbekistan, though disputes over border transit appear to have also

held up the progress of this route. Finally, in 2020, after years of hearing that the project was not moving, we received confirmation that in
fact the Afghan government had given up on the firm, and pulled it
from the contract. Reportedly, the central government was going to
take over the project, but we were also told that CNPC were contest-
ing some of the issues through legal avenues. Where any of this stood
with the new Taliban government is entirely unclear.

But while the relatively small CNPC project (the initial investment
was reported as being around $400 million) may have experienced a
stop-start process leading ultimately to shuttering, the far bigger and
more important copper project in Mes Aynak has been a catalog of
disasters and emblematic for many Afghans of China's lack of interest
in their future and progress. On every encounter with Afghans asking
about China, the topic would come up at some point, and the continued stalling by the Chinese firm was a source of unhappiness.
During events in which we would engage with senior Afghan officials
who were deeply involved in their country's economy and mining
sector, they would always express positive hopes that China might get
the project going, but as years passed the rumors we heard were
increasingly that the Ministry of Mines was eager to pull the contract.
In 2020, we were able to ascertain that the project was largely immo-
bile, with the lead Chinese firm reporting to its stockholders at the
Hong Kong Stock Exchange that it was going to reallocate funds that
had been raised for Mes Aynak to other projects the company was
undertaking.[4]

This was not how it was meant to be. The gargantuan but uncertain
mining project at Mes Aynak, 30 kilometers south of Kabul, is cen-
tered around the world's second largest copper mine. Two Chinese
SOEs, Metallurgical Corporation of China (MCC) and Jiangxi
Copper Corporation (JCC), won the tender in 2007. China bid high
for the contract, offering a total investment $2.9 billion (although
there are reports that the figure was in fact as high as $4 billion), $0.5
billion more than the next offer. There were generous provisions for
the Afghan government: a maximum royalty of 19.5 percent and a

bonus of $808 million to the government as a signing bonus (the next closest was $243 million).

On paper, the project was supposed to encompass a coal-fired power plant and a railroad. Speaking to officials in Kabul we heard how initially the project tender submitted by the Chinese firms did not actually include a railway line, which was included in a tender submitted by a Kazakh company that also bid for the project (the company was Kazakhmys, a firm we encountered earlier in this book). By the second round the Chinese bidders increased their offer to include a railway as well and won the contract. The point was made to us by experts that the train line was a bit of a luxury—a processing plant could be built adjacent to the site, with the copper processed there before being loaded onto trucks using the existing roads. Nevertheless, Afghanistan was a country with great needs, and more infrastructure like a railway system in Logar province (where Mes Aynak is located) would be a positive gain. At the time of the project's awarding the world was excited. Here at last was a good news story in Afghanistan, with the massive investment the country would need to get itself back on its feet finally flowing in. Some in Washington resented the fact that China appeared to be benefitting from American provided security. As long-time American Central Asia expert Frederick Starr put it, "we do the heavy lifting. And they pick the fruit," but at the same time no-one could deny the outcome sounded positive for Afghanistan.[5]

The company decision to undertake the project was reportedly a product of enthusiastic MCC engineers who were aware of the terrain and project and pushed their company to undertake it. According to reports from the Chinese press, an executive for MCC working in neighboring Pakistan saw the opportunity for the project in the immediate wake of the US-led invasion of Afghanistan. Sun Changsheng was working on a goldmining project in Balochistan as the US invaded Afghanistan post-9/11. Seeing the opportunity in Mes Aynak, he submitted a proposal to the interim Afghan government which caught Hamid Karzai's eye. He then organized a visit for the

Afghan minister of mines to visit an MCC project in Pakistan to show
them the company's capabilities. Unfortunately, the Cessna they were
all on crashed en route, killing all on board.[6] The company persisted
with the project nonetheless, as part of a bigger push driven by the
central government in Beijing's *diktat* that China's SOEs should
increasingly find ways of pushing themselves out into the world.

This cursed start to the project, however, might have been an indicator of what was to come. Having signed the contract, the company
moved very slowly.[7] Shortly before the announcement of the contract's awarding, the Afghan foreign minister visited Beijing with a
large delegation during which visit mining and security were discussed. The Chinese foreign minister expressed concerns which were
soothed by the Afghan officials who reassured their counterparts that
security for Chinese workers in the country would be a priority.
Security would remain a major concern throughout China's engagement with Afghanistan, though it was never clear from our conversations whether it was a problem the Chinese company (or government)
thought insurmountable.

The project subsequently stalled, with innumerable excuses produced to explain these delays. When we visited Kabul in 2012, we
were told that the site had lots of construction on it, with buildings
for workers, a school to help them learn Mandarin, and housing for
locals. This was in a part of Afghanistan which needed development.
But the main topic of conversation during the visit was the archaeo-
logical dig on top of the site. Having uncovered the site, the company
worked with the Afghan government to help bring in a specialist
team of archaeologists, in particular from the French government
supported DAFA (Délégation archéologique française en Afghanistan).
Established in 1922, DAFA has helped repeated Afghan governments
uncover and catalog the historical artifacts on their land. Closed in
1982 by the pro-Soviet government, it was able to reopen in 2002
following the Taliban's eviction.

At Mes Aynak, the international archaeologists worked with locals
to uncover the rich heritage of Buddhist statues and other artifacts.
The pool of material was reportedly almost limitless, with the biggest

problem being where to store it.[8] When we met with some of the archaeologists, they had lots to say about the Chinese firm and it was mostly positive: that the Chinese firm had been very supportive and accommodating to them. The CEO had reportedly visited at one point and highlighted his own personal interest in Buddhism, while his engineers onsite would reportedly regularly wander over to chat and watch the archaeologists do their work. The archaeologists were sanguine about having to clear the site to allow the Chinese company to undertake the project, but they reported not feeling too much pressure from the company to complete their work. In fact, they suspected that they served as "useful idiots" to the company, providing an excellent excuse for them to sit on their hands.

This narrative of China not being in much of a hurry with the project was one that we encountered repeatedly. In 2013, the story went even further when we heard reports that there had been rocket attacks on the site. While Afghan analysts later concluded that this had most likely been angry locals,[9] one conspiratorial version of events we were told at the time was that the attack had been specifically ordered from senior figures in the Taliban's leadership in Pakistan. They in turn were reacting to a prompt from their Pakistani paymasters who were acting at the behest of the Chinese to provide them with a reason to withdraw from the site.[10] In fact, however, the Taliban were supportive of the project, and in 2016 they made a statement about how they would not target the site or many of the other infrastructure projects going on around the country.[11] Trying to paint themselves as a government in waiting, they were eager to show China and other regional governments who they would have to eventually work with, that their views on Afghanistan's economy were sensible and compatible with their own. Chinese officials and their advisers were fairly sanguine about these promises, although we met with a few who had engaged with the Taliban, and we did not find many that had complete faith in such promises.

Less conspiratorial versions of the problems encountered on the site instead spoke of the government making a hash of the land compensation deals for locals. The latter's anger over this had led to problems at the site, with endless negotiations with local villagers. For a while the company complained about the lack of phosphate, a crucial ingredient in smelting copper. During one session in Beijing, we heard first-hand from MCC employees that the authorities had not met their ends of the bargain on a number of fronts. Local coal deposits, which were important, as they would provide fuel for the electricity plant also planned for the site which would help power the entire area around the site as well, were not as rich as expected. This led to the company demanding renegotiations and the removal of certain elements of the deal. All of this meant that the company had started to kick out some of the key elements of the project that the Chinese firms had promised to deliver and that had made the Chinese company's bid attractive to the Afghan government.

Most galling to the Afghans, however, was the company's hesitance over the construction of a train line. Always the most ambitious part of the project, it was hugely important for the Afghan government, the locals, and the project for a variety of reasons. Not only would it enable the Mes Aynak mine, but it was a key component for another nearby mineral project which China had been unable to win, the Hajigak iron ore mine. This concession was won by Indian firm SAIL AFISCO, and it is worth more than double the money of the Mes Aynak project. Part of the logic of the Hajigak project's being worthwhile was its provision of a functional railway in the country. In 2015, in Beijing we were told that the railway was never actually a part of the deal, but rather that the company had committed to doing a feasibility study about whether the railway was even viable.[12] This approach of getting a deal signed and then having the project stall, with the Chinese contractor coming back to renegotiate was characteristic of many projects we saw across Central Asia (and beyond)—it seemed that for Chinese companies the contract signature was the start of the negotiation rather than the conclusion.

The project which started with such promise has fallen into chaos. The problems were admittedly not simply within Afghanistan. For

MCC and Jiangxi Copper, the project had been acquired when copper prices were high. They had slumped soon afterwards. On top of this, MCC proved to have made a few bad decisions as it pushed itself out into the world at Beijing's behest, leaving a series of ill-judged projects on its books. One report suggested that MCC's plan all along had been to simply buy the site and then sit on it, blocking others, while the firm waited for the best moment to exploit it.[13] By the end of the decade, it was getting to the stage of being the butt of humor among Afghans. Talking to Afghan officials in 2019 the narrative was that the company was going to withdraw the concession from the Chinese consortium. However, it was unclear who else would step in. Kazakhmys, the Kazakh company which had reportedly made the next most promising bid (and one that we were told the Afghan government had actively solicited[14]) was not as clearly interested as it had been before. As was touched on in a previous chapter, in the mid-2010s amidst stories of scandals and stolen wealth, the company was broken in two—with some of the more dubious projects moved into a private company while the cleaner assets were put in a new company called Kaz Minerals. It was unclear at this stage whether they would be interested in engaging in such a challenging project with such an unfortunate history.

In 2015, Mes Aynak came up during President Ghani's side-bar bilateral with President Xi Jinping during the Shanghai Cooperation Organization (SCO) heads of state summit in Ufa, Russia. The two men discussed the establishment of an intergovernmental committee which would help move the project forward. When we asked Afghanistan watchers in Beijing at around the time, they had no knowledge of the committee and were largely dismissive.[15] There was little evidence of any progress after that, and as the years ticked by, Mes Aynak became a byword for Chinese hedging in Afghanistan. By 2016, the company told stockholders,

> As the Company is currently negotiating with the Afghanistan government for amending the Aynak project mining contract in aspects of contract scope, product plan, economical efficiency of the project,

security measures and conditions for commencing construction, it is estimated that the Aynak Project temporarily may not need a lot of funds.[16]

A holding pattern statement that has now been issued on an annual basis every year since.

Mes Aynak and Amu Darya are not, however, the only projects that Chinese companies have been involved with in Afghanistan. Chinese construction firms like Xinjiang Beixing or China Railway Shisiju Group won contracts from international financial institutions to rebuild Afghanistan's roads. Both companies were willing to work in quite dangerous environments and suffered as a result. In June 2004, a group of gunmen attacked a Shisiju site near Kunduz killing eleven workers, in an attack that the Taliban denied carrying out and which was blamed on Gulbuddin Hekmatyar's forces.[17] Chinese companies are hardy enterprises though. One story we were told from someone close to Xinjiang Beixing was that the firm had been involved in a road building project near Kabul. As they worked on the road, they could hear fighting across the mountain near them. They continued operations. The firm also suffered attacks on its encampments a number of times, though it seems as though no Chinese staff were hurt. Nevertheless, progress on building the road was slow, leading to complaints by the local Afghan authorities.[18]

These infrastructure projects faced numerous issues, with Chinese companies often complaining that the security situation was the biggest problem they encountered. Though it was sometimes surprising how shocked or underprepared the Chinese firms were over security issues in the country. In one conversation in Beijing with some experts who had consulted MCC before it had gone into Afghanistan we were told that the firm had not factored in security costs prior to going into the country.[19] This was surprising for a company heading off to work in a country which was an active warzone.

Most interesting, however, was the work undertaken by telecommunications companies Zhongxing Telecommunications Equipment (ZTE) and Huawei, which both started to work on projects in Afghanistan even before the fall of the Taliban. According to Andrew Small's excellent book on China-Pakistan, at Pakistan's instigation, China sought a *rapprochement* with the Taliban government in Afghanistan in the late 1990s, with ZTE and Huawei each tasked with providing phone systems for Kabul and Kandahar.[20] The companies were of course obliged to suspend work in the wake of the September 11, 2001 attacks, and Huawei in particular made adamant denials about their involvement in Afghanistan, despite evidence to the contrary.[21]

Both ZTE and Huawei were quick to reappear in Kabul. In August 2003, Huawei signed a contract with the new Afghan Ministry of Communications to install 87,000 digital telephone lines. Most were in Kabul, but a certain number were allocated for other regions as well.[22] In August 2007, the company signed a further $10 million deal with the government to deliver a code-division multiple access (CDMA) network around the country to enable Afghan Telecom to deliver national mobile telephony access.[23] In 2012, ZTE signed a $32 million deal in conjunction with Afghan Telecom with the Afghan Ministry of Communications and Information Technology to supply the infrastructure for 3G and The Global System for Mobile Communications (GSM) in Kabul.[24] By the time we had started visiting the country, mobile phones were easy to obtain and reasonably fast Internet was an accessible commodity.

Beyond these large firms, there has also been a sporadic push by enterprising Chinese traders into the country. In the wake of the collapse of the Taliban government, brothels started to appear masquerading as Chinese restaurants. On one visit to Kabul when we were seeking to explore every aspect of Chinese life in the city, we sought out a Chinese restaurant. Asking at our hotel reception we were given directions. Upon arrival, we found Chinese people, red-lit rooms, scantily clad women, but discovered no kitchen in sight and confusion when we asked for food. We rapidly called a car and left to find a restaurant with a kitchen.

Various Chinese traders headed to Afghanistan seeking opportunities. In Beijing we met Chinese businesspeople who were somehow exporting precious stones and gems from Afghanistan's dangerous regions. While they were vague about their sourcing, it seemed likely they were getting them from so-called artisanal mines and smuggling them out of the country. Gemstones were a big source of Chinese interest more generally, given the large market for such jewels in China. We heard stories of bribes needing to be paid to various Taliban groups to get stones out of the country on the one hand, while the Chinese government officials we spoke to raised ideas of helping the country develop its gemstone processing capability.

Chinese goods filled markets in Afghanistan, while Afghan traders are regular features at markets in Yiwu, Shanghai, Beijing, and Urumqi. However, a lack of regular flights and difficult visa regimes has made it easier for Chinese traders to come to Afghanistan than the reverse. The issue regularly came up in most conversations with Afghans, in particular in any discussion in which we were trying to understand the extent of cooperation that was possible between China and Afghanistan. While Chinese officials spoke regularly about their country's desire to support Afghan development, the narrative was almost immediately undermined by this practical reality. One great success that was pointed to was the development of an air corridor that would enable the sale of pine nuts from Afghanistan. While undoubtedly an important industry for a few Afghans, it was certainly not the scale of opportunity that the Afghan government was hoping to see from China.

This highlighted one of the fundamental problems in relations between the two countries. While China has talked a lot about cooperation with Afghanistan, it has not actually delivered much. The clearest articulation of this was the absence of Afghanistan from any of the early maps that were issued laying out the BRI. In fact, close examination of many of the routes showed a V shape emanating out from Xinjiang—on the one hand turning Pakistan into a corridor for China to the Gulf, while on the other there was a route through Central Asia to ultimately reach over to Europe. Afghanistan sat at the crux of that V, clearly adjacent to either route. In later years, a narrative started to emerge that China was keen to connect Afghanistan to the infrastructure projects associated with the BRI that were in Pakistan or Central Asia, but it was difficult to find much evidence of this on the ground and it was not clear that the Pakistanis or Central Asians were all that keen either. While Tashkent did a lot to try to develop its infrastructure links with Afghanistan, Turkmenistan and Tajikistan seemed less likely prospects. And while there is a huge natural connection and cross-border trade already between Pakistan and Afghanistan, it was not clear the grand and vague visions associated with BRI would necessarily help them much more on the ground.

★   ★   ★

As we discovered to our misfortune, China's concerns with regard to Afghanistan's security situation have not been misplaced. Since long before we embarked on our project and continuing up to this day, Afghans have suffered in a conflict that has claimed many thousands of lives. Seen in this light, it is understandable why Chinese investment and projects have repeatedly highlighted security concerns as an issue. Chinese workers have been killed and kidnapped, while the country shares an admittedly remote, though direct, border with Afghanistan. During the Taliban's time in power, China's concerns were focused on the possibility of Uyghur militants using camps in Afghanistan as a base to launch attacks against China. This concern persists and has been expanded to Chinese interests in the region, with attacks against Chinese nationals and diplomatic missions in both Kyrgyzstan and Pakistan. While the Pakistani attacks are for the most part the product of Baluchi groups angry at Chinese support for Islamabad in their home province of Baluchistan, these groups have bases in Afghanistan, and some of the other targeting of Chinese nationals in Pakistan is the product of groups which have networks and bases across the border. To those of a conspiratorial inclination, India's dark hand is often seen behind these networks, reflecting historical tensions between Beijing, Delhi, and Islamabad. As time passed, we found that voices highlighting possible American involvement as well started to grow, with senior Afghans and Chinese telling us, first *sotto voce* and then increasingly publicly, that the United States might be manipulating Uyghur groups in Afghanistan to create instability in Xinjiang.

China's concerns about Afghanistan have been based around four pillars whose importance and prioritization has shifted over time. First is the direct threat that is posed by groups exporting violence and dangerous ideologies from Afghanistan into China (mostly assessed by Beijing as being Uyghur). Second, is the threat of instability from Afghanistan impacting the region around Afghanistan and China's interests there. Third, there is the concern of other problems like narcotics flowing from Afghanistan into China. And, fourth, there is the fear of US bases and presence in a country on China's borders—this blends with a concern that the US or India might use Afghanistan as a base to target China using proxies like militant groups.

The first three in some ways are all articulations of the same problem—security threats from the country having some impact on China through different corridors. And Beijing also sees how the fourth pillar, the United States, is in fact potentially an answer to the problem as well. The dilemma comes from a dissonance, in that, on the one hand, China realizes that it needs America to stay in Afghanistan to deal with the problems there; but, on the other, they fear a long-term American presence on their border. In Central Asia the issue was dealt with quite effectively through the SCO by Uzbekistan which reacted negatively to American condemnation of the deaths of protestors in Andijan in 2005, that led to a discussion within the SCO that member states should eject US bases, though the one in Manas, Kyrgyzstan only grew after the Uzbek bases were closed.[25] In Afghanistan, however, it was more complicated.

When we first visited Kabul in 2012 the focus was the impending American withdrawal. At the time President Obama had signaled that he wanted to get the United States out of the conflict he had inherited, and placed a timeline on this departure. It was not really a new message however, and it took a while for the message to sink in with Beijing. It was only by 2012 that China started to really take it seriously and there was a clear, yet gradual, shift from cultivated disinterest to growing engagement. As the potential security vacuum left by Western withdrawal came into sharper relief, Beijing realized that it would have to play a role in encouraging a more stable and developed future for Afghanistan. Until that moment, China's approach had been characterized by prominent Central Asia observer Zhao Huasheng as a watching brief, leaving security issues to the United States and its allies.[26]

The most visible and significant element of China's renewed focus on Afghanistan was the visit in late September 2012 of Politburo member and security supremo Zhou Yongkang to Kabul. This was the first visit by a Politburo-level Chinese official to Afghanistan since 1966 when President Liu Shaoqi had visited the country just prior to being purged during the Cultural Revolution. In an interesting instance of history's rhyming, it was also Zhou Yongkang's last formal trip abroad as a Politburo member. Soon afterwards he attended his last party congress, after which he was investigated for corruption and ultimately incarcerated. It seems that visits to Kabul are bad omens for Chinese Politburo members.

But this was all in the future. When we visited earlier in 2012, the focus of discussion was the diplomatic push between Afghanistan and Pakistan that China was advancing. On February 28, 2012, Beijing hosted the first Afghanistan-China-Pakistan trilateral dialogue. Held at the level of foreign ministry director-general positions (or rough equivalents), the meeting was given a senior stamp of approval when the group was met by Chinese foreign minister, Yang Jiechi, a day after the discussions. Showing that China was keen to engage with all of those playing a role in Afghanistan, in May the Chinese Ministry of Foreign Affairs and the US State Department initiated a joint training program for Afghan diplomats. The group of a dozen young diplomats would get a fifteen-day experience in both Beijing and Washington in a program that was inaugurated by Secretary of State Hillary Clinton and her Chinese counterpart Yang. Then in June, as China was hosting the regional SCO summit in Beijing, President Hu Jintao signed a bilateral "strategic and cooperative partnership" agreement with President Karzai and welcomed the country to becoming an official SCO observer state.

President Karzai thanked President Hu for helping facilitate the SCO upgrading, saying "without your support, we cannot do this." Just over a month later on July 27, this was followed by a further high-level meeting between China's Central Military Commission, Vice Chairman General Guo Boxiong and Afghan Defense Minister Abdul Rahim Wardak. The focus of the meetings was to "enhance strategic communication and strengthen pragmatic cooperation in order to contribute to bilateral strategic cooperation." Again, history seems to rhyme in the wake of this encounter, with Wardak resigning a week later after a no-confidence vote back in Kabul.

But the overall signaling was nonetheless clear. As Washington approached 2014 and drawdown was likely, China was going to have to step in to take more of a role, though how forward leaning it would be was unclear. There were clearly dissenters in the system, and many of the security focused Chinese officials and experts we met were quite clear that this was a problem of Washington's making which China wanted little to do with. The recurring phrase about Afghanistan being a "graveyard of Empires" still echoes.

All of this change in Chinese activity was however undermined by the fact that a year later the US did not leave. Notwithstanding President Obama's repeated assertions, in the end he did not withdraw US forces from Afghanistan. While the presence was shrunk considerably, the US retained a capability to launch attacks and kept bases in the country. But what we had also not considered was the fact that within China things would sharpen as well. In April 2014, President Xi Jinping visited Xinjiang. This came after a tumultuous period for the region in which the country had seen incidents linked to Xinjiang spread around the country—including a car and incendiary device attack on Tiananmen Square and a mass stabbing incident in Kunming, as well as escalating violence in Xinjiang itself. Just as

President Xi was leaving on a visit to the region, attackers launched a knife and bomb attack on Urumqi's train station.

In his speeches about the threat in 2014, President Xi made a clear link between what was going on in both Afghanistan and Xinjiang. Beijing's answer to this concern with Afghanistan appears to have been to produce a two-pronged strategy. On the one hand, they escalated their levels of engagement, building on what was already going on to create a wave of bilateral and multilateral formats to be used with other partners in Afghanistan. It seemed as though China was going to take on a more active role in the country than it had before, aware of the fact that no matter whether the US stayed or left, the latter country was likely to be an erratic partner they could not rely on.

In July 2014 China created its first Special Envoy for Afghanistan appointing a prominent and popular former ambassador to Kabul, Sun Yuxi to the role.[27] His role was to serve as a point of contact and coordinator for China's engagement with the Taliban, and subsequent to his arrival there was a noticeable uptick in public engagement between China, the Taliban, and the government in Kabul. With the election of President Ghani in October 2014, he immediately signaled the importance he placed on the relationship with China by making Beijing the first capital he visited in his first formal trip.[28] During this visit he not only attended the "Heart of Asia" process meeting hosted by China but also laid the groundwork for the formal peace talk negotiations with the Taliban at a behind-closed-doors meeting hosted by the Chinese government.

By early the next year stories emerged that China was playing a more forward role in brokering peace talks; and, in conversations in Beijing, officials we spoke to said how they were willing to act as hosts for any future peace talks.[29] By May 2015, senior Taliban figures were meeting with representatives from the Afghan High Peace Council in Urumqi.[30] In July another round of talks was held in Pakistan at which Chinese participants also played a role.[31] A further multilateral track-two engagement took place in Norway which both Afghan government representatives and their Taliban counterparts attended.[32] One of the Chinese participants told us how strange it was to be sitting at a table across from Taliban interlocutors in such a format.

The Chinese-supported peace track seemed to be bearing fruit, until abruptly in late July 2015 the news was leaked that the Taliban leader Mullah Omar had in fact died back in 2013. This declaration scuppered the discussions, setting the Taliban in disarray as an internal leadership struggle took place as to who would be Mullah Omar's successor. It also complicated China's contribution as it suddenly meant it was not clear who exactly the relevant partner to engage with on the Taliban side would be or where China could play a role. Talking to Chinese experts at the time, they seemed baffled, even hinting that they might have known this was the case (to be fair, some of them had suggested in discussions earlier that something might be afoot given how long it had been since Mullah Omar had been seen—something a number of Afghan watchers had speculated for some time).

Accusations of blame were passed between Islamabad and Kabul, but the net result was an uptick in violence that made it harder for the Afghan official side to negotiate with full confidence. Chinese officials we spoke to at the time almost immediately fell back into stating that it was up to the United States to step up and play a stronger role in supporting the Afghan government and national security forces.[33] They further noted that until there was greater clarity on the Taliban side about who the main negotiator was, talks were unlikely to bear much fruit.

But it seemed that China maintained its contacts. In fact, Beijing has had a long history of maintaining contacts within the Taliban, dating to when the group was last in power in Kabul. They were one of the few countries that did engage with them, though for the most part this was through their contacts in Islamabad. In the early days, the focus of discussion seemed to be in ensuring that any trouble in Afghanistan did not spill into China, and a desire that the Taliban should maintain control over the Uyghur groups that were there. Meeting with some Chinese experts who visited Afghanistan-ruled

Taliban in the late 1990s, they told us that they were surprised during their visit to learn of large numbers of Uyghur militants in the country.[34] The Taliban authorities reportedly sought to reassure the Chinese that they would stop these individuals from launching attacks from their territory against China.[35] It was never clear whether the Uyghur groups did adhere to this, in much the same way that Osama bin Laden had failed to keep his promise to the Taliban about not attacking the United States. Certainly, Uyghurs did not leave the training camps in Afghanistan. We later met individuals who had been to Taliban-controlled Afghanistan and been to al Qaeda-managed camps who told us stories (that were corroborated by others) of seeing Uyghurs in the camps in large numbers.

Once the United States started to agitate about leaving, it seems as though China decided to lean forward and start to use its contacts to develop direct links to help protect its longer-term interests in the country. Aside from seeking to broker greater discussions between the Taliban, Pakistan, and the government in Kabul, China also sought to bring the United States into the discussions. In 2012, the United States and China established their joint training program. In December 2015, on the fringes of a Heart of Asia Conference in Islamabad, representatives from the United States, China, Afghanistan, and Pakistan all met to start a process of creating a new diplomatic discussion grouping called the Quadrilateral Coordination Group (QCG). This group started a process of again trying to bring all the sides together and appears to again have come close.

It did not work, however, but the opportunity and concept of multilateral engagement with all sorts of partners in Afghanistan seems to have taken off in Beijing. By the mid-2010s, Beijing was engaged in numerous bilateral, multilateral, and mini-lateral engagements around Afghanistan. One senior Afghan diplomat told us during a session in Tashkent how exhausted he was running between all these different events.[36] It was not clear to him how much utility they actually provided, but it seemed important to their Chinese counterparts so they had to be involved. They also held out hope that it might result in something. Other Afghans we spoke to were far more scathing about Beijing's engagements behind closed doors. One former senior defense official told us over breakfast in Delhi that they had been forced to dispose of most of the equipment that China had handed over, claiming "it was full of bugs." They had been particularly unimpressed by the Nuctech airport security devices that had been handed over, which reportedly did not work, a reality that was made awkward by the fact that the company was owned by Hu Jintao's son.[37] Others claimed that they had evidence that the Chinese were paying off and providing military equipment to the Taliban, something that was partially confirmed to us by a Chinese contact who reported being involved in the physical hand over of money to the Taliban.[38]

We were never able to independently confirm this, but it did speak to a greater sense of confidence in Beijing about what it was doing in Afghanistan. In November 2015, Vice President Li Yuanchao visited Kabul to celebrate sixty years of diplomatic relations, followed in March 2016 by People's Liberation Army (PLA) chief of staff, General Fang Fenghui. The latter visit appears to have been far more significant as it seems to have been the start of a new mini-lateral regional organization that met for the first time in August 2016 in Urumqi. The Quadrilateral Cooperation and Coordination Mechanism (QCCM) brought together the chiefs of army staff of Afghanistan, China, Pakistan, and Tajikistan "to coordinate with and support each other in a range of areas, including study and judgment of the counter terrorism situation, confirmation of clues, intelligence sharing, anti-terrorist capability building, joint anti-terrorist training and personnel training," adding that "the coordination and cooperation will be exclusive to the four countries."[39]

The question we repeatedly asked, but never received an answer to, was what was the need to create this institution when many of its responsibilities were theoretically things that the SCO would have done? While Afghanistan was not a full member, it had been made into an observer by China, and logically the institution offered a locus for such a gathering. Our sense was that the QCCM was a signal of

China's lack of faith in the SCO and its willingness or ability to do anything useful in Afghanistan. As a result, Beijing felt the need to create a new regional grouping to deal with its direct security concerns with Afghanistan. By bringing together senior security officials with all of the countries which had a presence around the Wakhan Corridor, China was helping secure its own border and creating a format through which it could monitor it. The structure also formalized the PLA's responsibilities and roles in Afghanistan. Until then, our understanding was that the relationship from Beijing's perspective with Afghanistan was one that was dominated by intelligence channels.

Alongside the creation of the QCCM, China also started to make its own security contributions to the other members of the grouping more public. In Pakistan this was largely unsurprising and an extension of what had long been going on before, though it was noticeable that Beijing started to make a particular focus of providing aid and support to forces in Gilgit Baltistan—a controversial move given the territory is under dispute with India. But far more dramatic were the revelations of China's contributions to Afghanistan and Tajikistan. In Afghanistan, China revealed that it had built a base and was providing direct funding for a mountain security force in Badakhshan, and locals reported seeing Chinese soldiers patrolling the region.

In Tajikistan, China was reported to have built around a dozen border posts for Tajik border guards, as well as a base for its own forces in the country's Gorno-Badakhshan region. The Tajik effort was the most controversial in many ways. As mentioned earlier, when we visited Central Asia in 2015, foreigners we spoke to reported how the local Russian Embassy had been livid as Moscow had not been informed of the creation of the QCCM or the deployment of Chinese forces.[40] When we asked in Moscow, people were circumspect and more respectful, but mostly focused on the fact that the Chinese would consult with them on anything they did in the region.[41] When we spoke to people in Beijing, they were dismissive, saying of course they had a presence in Tajikistan given its proximity to their borders.[42] This atop the lack of faith that they had in the Tajik authorities' ability to deliver effective security outcomes highlighted how China was increasingly moving to guarantee its own security interests in the region, and specifically protecting its border regions with Afghanistan. China was in essence creating a clear security buffer to seal itself off from direct threats from Afghanistan into China.

★   ★   ★

Afghanistan in many ways serves as a perfect example of our central concept. The country is one in which China is doomed to play a significant role, but it is a role that it is studiously avoiding taking. None of Afghanistan's other direct neighbors has the global clout, financial might, and security interests to do something. And yet, China is untested in such a scenario and is unlikely to decide that Afghanistan is the place where it will start testing itself in this way. While China has spoken of Afghanistan as part of its ambitious BRI, linked to both the China Pakistan Economic Corridor (CPEC) on one side and the Silk Road Economic Belt (SREB) that dominates this book on the other, in reality the tangible economic links between China and Afghanistan amount to the export of Afghan pine nuts to China and the construction of a fiber-optic cable down the Wakhan Corridor to help Afghanistan get on the Internet. The bigger commodities extraction projects have failed to deliver any of their promised wealth. Talk about BRI in Kabul and people will constantly say good things and hope for greater engagement, but they are still waiting for this to materialize.

China is concerned about its security interests in Afghanistan and can see the situation could deteriorate further, but its answer has been to largely seal itself off, hardening its own border and strengthening the next closest borders along which there could be a threat. Afghan businesspeople still find it difficult to get visas into China, and flights are irregular. Through a web of multilateral engagements, China has offered itself as a peacebroker, host, discussant, but never moderator. No-one can say China is not doing anything, and it is certainly doing more than it did before. At the same time, it is clear that notwithstanding its significant interests and role, it is not going to step into a leadership role. Beijing has all the trappings and potential to be a dominant player, but it has made a strategic decision to continue to watch from the side lines. There is little evidence this has changed so far early into a Taliban-led government, and it remains to be seen if in fact this gradualist approach might actually be the solution that Afghanistan needs.

9

Tying up the world

The Silk Road Economic Belt

Perhaps arrogantly, we felt a strong sense of validation when we saw it reported that President Xi Jinping had given a speech in Nursultan (then Astana, the capital of Kazakhstan) at the Nazarbayev University in which he inaugurated a new vision for China's foreign policy in that region. Calling it the Silk Road Economic Belt (SREB), it felt like both clarification and affirmation at the same time. It helped explain why we had heard such resistance to the American New Silk Road vision that then Secretary of State Hillary Clinton had articulated in Chennai in October 2011. It also felt like there was something grander to our research on Central Asia and China than just another of China's international relations partnerships. President Xi's decision to start his series of speeches that outlined the Belt and Road Initiative (BRI) in Astana seemed a clear signal that the region was an important one for his broader foreign policy vision and thinking. As we said grandly to skeptical-looking foreign diplomats in Beijing in the weeks after the BRI speeches, "this is going to be President Xi's big foreign policy idea."

While admittedly hubristic, our thinking was shaped by the fact that we had just spent the previous year or so traveling around China's borderlands in Central Asia and talked to numerous Chinese experts and officials focused on the region. While we could never pin down a clear strategic vision, what was happening felt clear. China was trying to develop Xinjiang, but in order to do this, it would need to encourage greater development in Xinjiang's neighborhood. This was a positive foreign policy projection, and one that fit with the levers of power that China had at its disposal. Eager not to be seen to be using hard coercive power, China was instead using the economic tools at its disposal: its policy banks, deep pockets, large domestic market and production base, and infrastructure companies. These powerful tools could be game-changers in poorer countries, and they were levers that Beijing could more easily control and deploy discreetly than large tank formations. And they would be more likely to encourage the change in environment that would suit China's end goals.

This thinking was what shaped our sense that this was going to be the outline for China's broader foreign policy vision going forward. Beijing's thinkers, we thought, had realized that what had been going on in Central Asia for the past decade or more was a model which could be transposed elsewhere with relative ease given the tools required to advance it. It gave China a foreign policy concept which was essentially built around the uncontroversial rhetoric of opening markets and making money. A positive perspective few could reject.

This was affirmed by what we saw then happen. The decision to start the roll-out of the BRI in Astana, followed up with a further speech in Jakarta in which President Xi spoke of the 21st-century Maritime Silk Road (together with the Astana speech, this gives you the "Belt" and "Road," though paradoxically the "road" is in the sea), highlighted the significance of what was going on in Central Asia within this broader vision. President Xi was stamping his brand on what was happening in Central Asia, and then transposing it as the model for China's engagement everywhere else.

The path to the BRI concept, insomuch as it is possible to trace, has a number of different roots. Among the most important is the work of the much-cited Professor Wang Jisi, then dean of the School of International Studies at Peking University (China's equivalent of Oxford or Harvard). In October 2012, he wrote an article in which he

called for China to "march westwards."[1] The thrust of the article was
that China had long overfocused on its relations with the United
States and China's eastern seaboard, to the detriment not only of
China's interior regions but also of the rich opportunities that lay
over China's western borders. Sketching out what in retrospect can
read like an early outline for the subsequent BRI, Professor Wang wrote:

> Firstly, China needs to make an overall plan and cooperate with many
> other countries, with a view to ensuring that the supply channels for
> oil and other bulk commodities to the west of China's borders remain
> open. These can be divided into three routes—southern, central and
> northern—and we can quickly build a "new Silk Road", led by China.
> This "new Silk Road" would extend from China's eastern ports,
> through the center of Asia and Europe, to the eastern banks of the
> Atlantic Ocean and the Mediterranean coastal countries in the west.
> A major route from China's western regions through the Indian Ocean
> should also be constructed as quickly as possible.[2]

Developed in 2012 during a period in which Professor Wang was
reported as having spent a lot of time visiting countries on China's
borders rather than in the US, this concept would have been circulating in Beijing's body politic during the year in which President Xi
was ascending to power. While the concept of the BRI is widely associated with Professor Wang's article, it is unclear whether this was the
exact trigger. A story that emerged in early 2019 suggested that the
father of the concept was in fact Le Yucheng, a former Chinese ambassador to Kazakhstan and India who went on to become deputy foreign minister. When we hosted Professor Wang at a conference that
we had co-organized with the Shanghai Academy of Social Sciences
(SASS) in Shanghai in 2015 we found him modest in terms of talking
about his role in the conception of the BRI. However, he did say he
liked the headline of the conference, "China's Eurasian Pivot," telling
us that this was the reason why he had accepted the invitation in the
first place:[3] it fitted with his view that China's "March Westwards" was
in part a response to Washington's "Asia Pivot" which President
Obama's administration had championed.[4]

But while it is highly likely that Professor Wang's thinking had played some role in the birth of the concept, the actual idea is one that has deep roots in Chinese strategic thinking. As we saw earlier in the book, Premier Li Peng in many ways started the contemporary Silk Roads conversation on his 1994 tour of Central Asia that started in Xinjiang. During his tour of the region, which covered all of the countries except war-stricken Tajikistan, he met with business delegations and leaders, and in a speech before President Karimov in Tashkent, spoke of how "China attaches great importance to its relations with the Central Asian countries and with them, we are willing to work to build a new silk road, with a perspective toward the future and the next century."[5] At a speech in Almaty (then known as Alma-Ata), before the Kazakh business community, Russian news agency ITAR TASS reported him as having said that:

> transport facilities and means of communication will be needed to build a new "Silk Road". Li Peng noted in this connection the importance of the agreement concluded for this purpose during the current visit. In his opinion, China and Kazakhstan must exert every effort to ensure the efficient work of this transport "bridge" between Europe and Asia.[6]

The visit was reported as being focused on economic opportunities, many of which would later become very familiar, like the discussion in Ashgabat about building a pipeline from Turkmenistan to China. It was also about China ensuring that the Central Asian countries would do their bit to ensure that Uyghur separatists could not use the region as a space in which to foment trouble in Xinjiang. During the stop in Tashkent, President Karimov was reported as saying "We cannot over-emphasize the role China plays in this region, in preventing separatist feeling and establishing peace and stability in the region."[7] While playing out against the backdrop of a civil war in neighboring Tajikistan, it is quite clear from reports at the time that Premier Li was pushing Beijing's line on Uyghur dissidents at every stop. Some reports suggest that this harder line followed an earlier failed attempt brokered by then Russian intelligence chief (and later prime minister),

Yevgeny Primakov, for China to try to negotiate with Uyghur leaders in Central Asia. Having failed to get this confirmed, Premier Li's visit was in part an attempt to ensure the leaderships in Central Asia were on board to help China manage its separatist concerns.

The broader conceptual vision that Premier Li was articulating during his visit was echoed in other visits he undertook either side of the tour of the region in Europe and meetings he subsequently held in Beijing. In 1992, as leader Deng Xiaoping was doing his famous "southern tour" which led to the unleashing of China's economy, the local government in Xinjiang was seeking to do something similar, establishing the Urumqi Trade Fair to help the region's trade with its neighborhood (similar to the later China Eurasia Expo mentioned in earlier chapters). Premier Li visited the first session in 1992 at around the same time that the first border market between China and Kazakhstan opened at Khorgos. In the two years between Premier Li's visit to Xinjiang and his subsequent tour of Central Asia in 1994, most of the Central Asian leaders visited Beijing to start to build relations with China after their liberation from the Soviet yoke.

Later in 1994, Premier Li visited Europe—with stops in Germany, Austria, and Romania. Bringing with him a large delegation of businesspeople, the narrative was focused on economic opportunities and the fact that China was now opening up. This was, however, five short years since the massacre at Tiananmen Square, and while the financial press was keen to emphasize the opportunities posed by China's opening, Premier Li was publicly berated at many of his stops.

Perhaps this helps explain why initially much of the narrative around the "new Silk Road" that China wanted to construct with the Central Asians at the time focused on how China and Xinjiang could be a thoroughfare for Central Asian goods and commodities to get to Chinese coastal cities, with the ultimate goal of reaching booming Asian economies like Japan. When discussing the pipeline from Turkmenistan during Premier Li's visit in 1994, the focus was on Xinjiang becoming a point of access to China and beyond. He had already discussed the idea with Japanese officials when they visited

Beijing in 1993, meeting with then Mitsubishi head, Minoru Makihara, to talk about doing a joint feasibility study regarding building a pipeline to bring Turkmen gas across China and then across the seas to Japan.[8] This idea appears to have continued to circulate, though it is not clear that Japan has remained the target destination. When President Jiang Zemin visited Ashgabat in 2000 and signed a bilateral agreement between the two countries, the agreement specifically referred to "The two sides" who "agreed to conduct feasibility study on the project of laying a natural gas pipeline linking Turkmenistan and China on the basis of the actual progress of China's project to transmit natural gas from the western part of the country to the east."[9]

And the vision included more than simply gas. In October 1994, Premier Li followed up on this conceptual vision of a "new Silk Road" hosting the transportation ministers from Russia and the five Central Asian powers to discuss regional connectivity ideas and new silk roads. During this session, he also announced a cessation of the previous custom of China trading on barter terms with the Central Asian powers, shifting instead to cash. Central Asian officials and traders were reported as visiting China's coastal cities, exploring what opportunities might exist for them to transport their goods using these cities as access points to the world. President Nazarbayev was particularly bullish about this vision, having signed agreements with China to open up the Alataw Pass for rail transport between China and Kazakhstan in 1990, with goods starting to flow through in December 1992. In July 1996, Jiang Zemin went on his first state visit to Kazakhstan where President Nazarbayev highlighted how "we can work together to solve a lot of problems, including reviving and developing the Silk Road." Within Xinjiang, there was a push to improve rail connectivity, with Premier Li and President Jiang Zemin both placing their personal *imprimatur* on the famous Nanjiang rail route across Xinjiang, connecting Kashgar in the south to Turpan.

But in many ways, during this period of history, the more significant outward-looking transport corridors could be found on the other side of "western" China looking from Yunnan southwards. Here, the scenario looked different. Rather than a seeing a collapsing superpower with which China had fought conflicts and still had to define borders, Beijing instead found itself looking at a series of poorer nations that had deep economic and ethnic links back and forth across China's equally poor borderlands. While there are certainly similarities between Central Asia and Xinjiang, the densely packed border region between southeast and south Asia that this part of China butted up against was far more complicated in some ways. The region was rich in population and natural resources, and it was connected to some of the most fertile parts of Asia. Recognizing the need for something structural to help link China to this region and help Yunnan develop, in August 1999 over one hundred academics and experts from China, India, Burma, and Bangladesh were brought together in Kunming for a conference at the Yunnan Academy of Social Sciences (YASS). At the conclusion of this session an outline was laid out for what would become known as the Bangladesh-China-India-Myanmar Economic Corridor (BCIM-EC). Six key themes were laid out:

- Practical and strategic significance for the regional cooperation among China, India, Bangladesh, and Burma;
- Feasibility of cooperation in the economic, trade, and technological cooperation among China (Yunnan), India, Bangladesh, and Burma (including industry, agriculture, tourism, and finance);
- Study of the construction of communication channels and networks between China, India, Bangladesh, and Burma (including the opening and reconstructing of roads, airlines, water routes, and railways);
- Prospect of and basis for economic cooperation between China, India, Bangladesh, and Burma;
- Open-door policies, and a trade and investment environment for China, India, Bangladesh, and Burma;
- Construction of a framework for regional cooperation between China, India, Bangladesh, and Burma.[10]

The "Kunming Initiative," or BCIM-EC as it became colloquially known, was focused on improving infrastructure and opening markets, and was dreamed up as a way of developing China through cooperation with its border nations. A refrain that echoes the BRI narrative that subsequently emerged. The broader vision was one that was actually suggested a few months earlier in March 1999 at the 9th National Party Congress in Beijing by President Jiang Zemin. Crystallized in speeches delivered later in the year and put on the front page of the *People's Daily* on June 19, 1999, the "Great Western Development Strategy" was a vision that suggested the "time was ripe" to speed up the development of the central and western regions, and that this "should become a major strategic task for the party."[11]

All of this is again very reminiscent of the BRI as articulated through Wang Jisi's thinking, though he added the spin to it that China needed to end its fixation with the United States and its Pacific seaboard. Talking to some of Professor Wang's colleagues at Peking University in the wake of the announcement of the BRI, a number mentioned how he had been surprised at how his article had been received. We were told his point was much more about reminding Beijing that they had an entire western area of the country that they needed to worry about as well, which needed investment but at the same time it also represented a significant geopolitically strategic opportunity. From Professor Wang's perspective, it was a moment when the world was looking East to China and "China should not limit its sights to its own coasts and borders, or to traditional competitors and partners, but should make strategic plans to 'look westwards' and 'march westwards.'"[12]

★   ★   ★

By 2010, it seemed as though the world had remembered its Mackinder. When we went to Xinjiang University in 2012 to talk to the students, their interest was in trying to understand how their region and Central Asia fitted into the bigger sweep of history. Years later when we had a similar discussion at one of China's military academies, we were asked a different set of questions around Mackinder, specifically why it was that European experts were so interested in this territory; and what it was about the great British geographer's ideas that so appealed to us in London today. The implication was that there was a British obsession with "Great Games," something armchair geostrategists the world over enjoy discussing. But what was striking was the degree to which this thinking had started to permeate across into the broader geopolitical discussion. People's reasons for this were varied and different, but many regional and global powers started to focus their attention on the heart of Eurasia, bringing Mackinder back into relevance. Professor Peter Frankopan's masterful *The Silk Roads: A New History of the World* perhaps best captured this mood in the literature, offering a historical sweep that refocused attention on the Eurasian heartland that Mackinder had identified as key to controlling "the World Island."[13]

Professor Wang has also identified this trend in his writing. As a serious academic, he analyzed the various powers through history that had recognized the geostrategic importance of China's Eurasian hinterland, seeing it as a territory requiring investment and control. He methodically identified each power's interest in Central Asia in particular, most often centering his analysis on the region's natural resources. He also concluded that by focusing on the "west Asian" region, as he defines it, China will be involved in an area where it is less likely to have a conflict with the United States, and could even offer opportunities for cooperation with them. He noted that Washington had stolen a march on Beijing in this regard, with then Secretary of State Hillary Clinton's speech in 2011 at Chennai (and another series of meetings that year), in which she spoke of creating a new silk road which would in essence tie together Central Asian energy resources with energy-poor South Asia.[14]

The vision laid out by Secretary Clinton was an ambitious one, and did indeed articulate a new silk road concept before President Xi got to it (though after Premier Li Peng had done so, as mentioned earlier). In her Chennai speech, she spoke of creating "not a single thoroughfare like its namesake, but an international web and network of economic and transit connections. That means building more rail lines, highways, energy infrastructure."[15] But the core of the vision was in many ways a parochial one, and based around creating a north–south corridor between Central Asia and South Asia which would ultimately tie Afghanistan back into its region. At this point, the United States had been fighting in Afghanistan for just under a decade and President Obama had made a commitment on his campaign trail to get out of this conflict he had inherited. Washington's approach to achieving this was to defeat this adversary, while reaching out to the regions around Afghanistan to urge them to take on a greater role there. These neighbors would ultimately have to live with whatever was left behind once the US withdrew. This plan even extended to finding ways to engage with China in Afghanistan, as seen in Chapter 8.

But while it was clear that Washington's vision for getting out of Afghanistan was a major part of the push to advance the New Silk Road concept, it was not entirely clear what resources the United States was going to deploy to realize this. While a number of projects were flagged as being part of it—for example, the Turkmenistan-Afghanistan-Pakistan-India (TAPI) pipeline or the Central Asia-South Asia electricity connectivity projects (CASA 1000)—both of these were ideas that had been maturing for some time. The concept of connecting Central and South Asia was one that had grown out of longstanding international discussions and thinking around the region, and the idea of connectivity across greater Central Asia was something that the Asian Development Bank (among others) had been talking about for years prior.

Central Asians we spoke to about the American New Silk Road vision would always ask what it actually entailed, and then largely dismissed it. Their discussion and interest was focused much more on what the United States was going to do for their nations in particular, with little interest in big visions which they saw through the lens of a sporadic American interest in the region. The fact Secretary Clinton had made the announcement in India and then followed it up with a series of discussions around Afghanistan, reflected from the Central Asian perspective, Washington's focus.

Meeting with officials in Washington, or at US embassies across the region, we never got a sense of a strong vision or strategy for Central Asia. There was a lot of engagement, and given the sheer size of America's institutions and budgets, this meant that even a limited effort was substantial as compared to others. But it never seemed like Central Asia was a priority. From Washington's perspective, it always seemed to us that, for the first few years, the relationship was seen as simply an add-on to their engagement with Afghanistan, and then latterly in terms of opposition to China. Once Beijing had announced its SREB and subsequently the grander BRI, the Silk Road terminology was defined in China's terms and left little room for others to try to adopt it for their own visions. The American New Silk Road, however, continues to percolate in the State Department with officials occasionally giving speeches in which they seek to revive an American focus on the New Silk Road in their own terms. But the larger structure through which the United States engages with the region is: 5 (Central Asia) + 1 (the United States)—a format that China (and others) have emulated, creating their own Central Asia 5 + 1 discussion formats. America's answer to the BRI remains inchoate, articulated through the Blue Dot strategy of President Trump, a vision to help develop key infrastructure and push specific development objectives around the world to counter BRI. Under President Biden, this has been pushed heavily within a Group of Seven (G7) context, with the Build Back Better World (B3W) initiative that was announced during the 2021 Cornwall summit. The idea seemed to be to suggest a new infrastructure to the world, though the details were still to be worked out.

The other power which had a greater claim to providing a grand geostrategy in the region is Russia, which has responded to China's strategic enveloping of Central Asia with a growing degree of concern. As we saw in the earlier chapter on the Shanghai Cooperation Organization (SCO), Moscow's view of the organization initially was that it provided a way to control Chinese activity in their backyard, a penetration that Moscow ultimately saw as reaching deep into Russia itself. Shortly before the creation of the SCO in 2000, President Putin visited Russia's far east. During a speech at Blagoveschensk he made the point that Moscow was going to lose the region unless something was done quickly. As he put it, "if we don't make a real effort to develop Russia's far east, then in the next few decades, the Russian population will be speaking mainly Japanese, Chinese and Korean . . . we are talking about a fundamental issue—the very existence of this region."[16] This was more of a domestic than external concern, but it reflected a fear from Moscow that its eastern regions were slipping away from control. Given Russia's sense of ownership of its immediate neighborhood, this was a feeling that by extension also applied to post-Soviet Central Asia. By the time President Putin was getting ready to end his brief interregnum as prime minister in 2011, he realized that Russia's neighborhood was drifting out of Moscow's control. His plan to secure it was to announce that he endorsed the creation of a Eurasian Economic Union (EAEU).[17]

The foundations of what President Putin wanted to build already existed. In the wake of the collapse of the Soviet Union in 1994, during a speech at Moscow State University, President Nazarbayev of Kazakhstan had called for the creation of a Eurasian Union. A former Soviet *apparatchik* who, like most of his Central Asian peers, had not really wanted the Soviet Union to collapse, President Nazarbayev's call was in essence to recreate the USSR once again under a different name. The idea was one that had bumped along for some time, gradually picking up steam over the years as different constellations of former Soviet powers were bound together around Russia on some new common economic agreement. The whole thing played alongside other former Soviet Union-driven structures like the Commonwealth of Independent States (CIS) or the Collective Security Treaty Organization (CSTO) which sought to retain some of the connections between countries that had existed under the Soviet Union.

The EAEU (so named to distinguish it from the European Economic Union; EEU), gave a more solid foundation to these various forms of alternative union. It also placed Moscow firmly in the driver's seat on most issues, as things were determined on the basis of national economic size. The vision was very much along the lines of the European Union (EU), focusing not only on border and tariff harmonization but also on the free movement of people, goods, and services. When we visited the EAEU's Secretariat in 2015 (the Eurasian Economic Commission) we were overwhelmed with information about the plans that Moscow had for the organization, from common currency to harmonization of digital tools, tariffs, taxes, railway standards, and infrastructure, all with an undertone of politics seeping through the discussion. It felt clear to us, though our interlocutors repeatedly denied this, that much like the EU itself, the architects of the EAEU had political harmonization in mind as the end goal.[18]

And this was one of the many reasons why the Russian vision encountered its own problems. In his article on China's "March Westwards," Professor Wang identified Moscow's vision of "the Caspian Sea region and the Central Asia Union states as its backyard," and pointed to Moscow's determination "to hold on to its traditional position in this region."[19] Everyone, including the other members of the EAEU, clearly had a sense of this. Within Central Asia in the first instance it was just Kazakhstan that agreed to join the EAEU (somewhat unsurprising given the idea had first been articulated by President Nazarbayev), but by the time of writing Kyrgyzstan had joined and there was discussion about Tajikistan and Uzbekistan coming in as well. But whenever we spoke to Kazakh experts and officials they had little that was positive to say about EAEU membership, pointing out that rather than opening their companies to opportunities in Russia, it seemed to largely favor Russian companies coming into their economic space. Furthermore, when Kyrgyzstan joined, it feared the decimation of its trade with China. And while the evidence seemed to point this way in the first year, trade volume seems to have stabilized with a higher level of concern in the end about the volumes of illicit goods and contraband that might now be flooding into the broader EAEU space through Kyrgyzstan. In sum, it was not clear how negative EAEU membership was for the Central Asians' relationship with China, but it was equally not clear that they had benefitted as much economically as Russia had.

Russia's challenge was that the EAEU was in part an attempt to retain some level of control over Central Asia (and the rest of the former Soviet Union) and to keep China out. At the same time, President Putin was clearly eager to try to catch some of the opportunities that China presented. When in March 2013 President Xi followed a longstanding Chinese tradition of making Moscow the first foreign stop for each new Chinese leader, President Putin made a big show of emphasizing his desire to strengthen their relationship and "catch the Chinese wind in our economic sail."[20] This paradox meant that any vision Moscow had for the region needed to somehow strike a balance between blocking Chinese expansion (or at the very least controlling it), while also ensuring that Moscow could still have some access.

And of course, none of these Russian ideas ultimately took into account what the Central Asians wanted. While at a political and public level, people in Central Asia still tended to be more Russophiles than Sinophiles (or more positive toward the United States[21]), at a government level there was a similar natural inclination toward the Russians, but there was also a keen awareness of the importance of the economic opportunities presented by China. Furthermore, as relatively young countries who over time grew to appreciate the benefits of independence and started to push for greater expressions of their individual nationhoods, they feared the EAEU's political embrace. While this political aspect was continually downplayed by Moscow, it seemed inevitably written in the sands of the EAEU's future.

The apex of contact between the EAEU and China came in May 2015 during President Xi's visit to Moscow as part of the celebrations around the seventieth anniversary of the "Great Patriotic War." While attended by all of the leaders of the EAEU, we were told that President

Putin still signed an agreement with President Xi by himself, linking the EAEU with China's BRI without informing the other delegations that were in town.[22] This reflected a general approach we consistently found with Russian behavior under the EAEU: one focused on Russia's own interests without necessarily undertaking the (tiresome) consultations to bring the other members on board that one might expect. Moscow led, leaving the others to follow whether they liked it or not. Admittedly, Russia was a major economic partner for all of the other members of the EAEU. This suggested that there was a logic to harmonization in a number of fields. At the same time, all of the members were in their different ways concerned about the degree to which Moscow was going to start determining their external choices. There was also a certain lack of coherent logic to the idea of linking the BRI with the EAEU—the two were very different constructs. The BRI was Xi Jinping's foreign policy vision, while the EAEU was a quite specific economic structure with a secretariat and rules. The idea that two such structures could sign an agreement as peers made little sense, but it reflected how from Beijing's and Moscow's perspective the two structures were in fact simply grand geostrategic concepts.

Others also articulated varying visions of how they would engage with the Eurasian heartland. South Korea and Japan offered a very similar perspective, which was largely focused on developing their links to the region through a Eurasian landbridge—this drew on the grander concept of the New Eurasian Landbridge that the Chinese leadership would speak of in a vision that stretched across Central Asia. In 1997, Japanese Prime Minister Ryutaro Hashimoto made a speech in which he laid out his country's conception of the new world order he saw emerging from the ashes of the Cold War, with a particular focus on the "Silk Road region" of the Central Asian and Caucasian states.[23] The discussion is an echo of the vision of the silk roads that was emanating from Beijing at the time and was about reconnecting these countries up to the world via the Pacific Ocean. China was to be the thoroughfare in this vision of the world, rather than the leaping-off point.

South Korea had a similar approach, focused on developing its booming economy and connecting it to the rich mineral reserves in Central Asia. Korean efforts were further enhanced by the presence of a residual ethnic Korean community in Central Asia, creating a natural connection with Seoul that the Central Asians have often sought to capitalize on. While a miniscule number compared to the workers who head to Russia, a couple of tens of thousands of Uzbeks regularly head to Korea to work as migrant labor. The Uzbek government has also always looked at the Korean development model (from an authoritarian government to a mixed economic system that includes a variety of private freedom, combined with centralized economic planning and government regulation) as one they would like to follow, giving Seoul an interesting role as potential partner for the region.

For Japan and Korea, the impediment of having China in between them and the Central Asian powers meant they needed to have good relations with Beijing for the corridor to function. While in the 1990s this was not a problem, and Japan in particular was instrumental in helping China come out into the world, from the 2000s onward there were periods of heightened tensions, complicating their efforts. In his prescient speech from 1997, Prime Minister Hashimoto identified this as: "Japan has certain issues in its foreign policy toward China which arise due to its location as a neighbouring country,"[24] words which take on considerably stronger meaning in the wake of the repeated clashes and confrontations that China and Japan have had in the subsequent decades.

The EU also merits some mention in this context. As Europeans we always sought EU experts and officials when we traveled through the region, and did some work with EU officials who were focused on Central Asia. Europe has long looked at Central Asia as a region with which it could connect, but the complexities of EU politics has meant that it has sometimes become hostage to the rotating six-month presidencies (meaning varying levels of interest across the EU in Central Asia, resulting in sporadic bursts of attention in six-month increments), even though a substantial and growing cadre of officials and businesspeople advance a massive program of investment and aid across the region. Collectively, the EU was by some counts Central Asia's biggest economic partner, and logically should be a bigger strategic player in the region. Unfortunately, the EU's Central Asia policy seemed to oscillate between a desire to engage with the region on an individual basis and that of engaging with it as a cluster of five countries. The broader strategic vision has never been articulated. Rather, many in the EU remain uninterested, and those who do engage with Central Asia tend to focus on their own narrow interests rather than seeking to make a collective effort. In 2015, the EU created in cooperation with China an EU-China Connectivity Platform, which was intended to facilitate potential cooperation between the BRI and the EU. Officials we spoke to would often mention Central Asia as an interesting space to advance the discussion of cooperation with China in practical terms through the Platform, but we saw little evidence of material progress.

Iran has also explored ways of engaging with Central Asia, with varying degrees of success. Iran has largely focused on Tajikistan, drawing on their common Persian ethnicity, but has floundered as Iran has fallen out with the Tajik government and as President Rahmon has grown closer to Saudi Arabia. Whether this is something Riyadh or Dushanbe has encouraged is not entirely clear, but the result has been growing animosity between the two capitals and a distinct shift from the supportive role that Tehran had played in the immediate wake of Tajikistan's brutal civil war. Elsewhere in the region, Iran is seen with great skepticism, with the secular Central Asian leaders being wary of the theocratic revolutionary state. Turkey has similarly made a number of approaches, but these have largely faltered outside the cultural domain and some economic links. The most natural partner to the region outside Russia in many ways, Turkey has never been able to punch at the same level as any other regional power.

India is also consistently spoken about as a potential player in the region, and Prime Minister Modi (like his predecessors Atal Bihari Vajpayee and Manmohan Singh) went on a grand tour of Central Asia during which he spoke of initiating greater connectivity between the region and India. But the impediments were substantial. The presence of war-torn Afghanistan and hostile Pakistan in between meant direct transport links would be complicated. Not to be deterred, Delhi has long championed instead opening up the port of Chahbahar in Iran which would provide unfettered access for Indian goods to reach Central Asia, with Iran being a friendly neighbor. But notwithstanding agreements signed years ago, it is not clear that the project has advanced at all. Iranian experts we met would shrug, although Chinese executives would simply confirm that Tehran had been approaching them for help to get the port set up.

Nevertheless, we would constantly be met with good feeling and Bollywood films whenever we traveled around Central Asia, as well as often seeing large British Indian tour groups whenever we flew through Ashgabat. Turkmenistan Airlines has established a route connecting Birmingham in the UK (home to a large and wealthy Indian diaspora) to Amritsar, home to the largest and holiest *Gurdwara* of the Sikh faith. This led to some strange encounters in the early hours of the morning at Ashgabat airport.

The most strategic aspect of India's play in the region was for the use of military bases in Tajikistan, which were forward deployments to get equipment and aid into Afghanistan. Through bilateral agreements with Tajikistan that appear to have been guaranteed by Delhi's close ally Moscow, India was given access and provided aid to expand two bases in Tajikistan—the Ayni and Farkhor airbases. Ayni sits just outside Dushanbe, while Farkhor is near the border with Afghanistan. This set of locations provided Delhi with a convenient way to access Afghanistan without having to go through Pakistan. But while much was made of this deployment, very little seems to have followed. Delhi appears to be still using this route, but has never managed to turn it into the bigger strategic play that had been touted in India when the news had first emerged that India would use the bases. India's attempted strategic engagements with the region consistently fail to live up to expectation. We had a pleasant lunch with the Indian defense attaché in Dushanbe in 2013 where we heard about military hospitals the Indians were helping with, and we got a strong sense that this was where Indian military engagement stopped. We subsequently paid visits to his colleagues in other capitals, as well as their officials and experts in Delhi who enjoyed the vigorous Great Game style discussion with a particular focus on China, but we found little evidence of a considered and calculated approach being followed through, notwithstanding the appetite in the region for more options. India is a consistent underachiever in Central Asia, creating another space in which it appears to be losing out, in this case to China.

★   ★   ★

During the Hu Jintao era (2002–12), relations with Central Asia were largely dominated by the SCO, the Color Revolutions, and the war in Afghanistan. The post-2009 riots in Xinjiang transformed China's perception of what needed to be done in Central Asia to support Xinjiang's development, and its vision of how to achieve that. Until then, the region had largely been left on its own under the dominance of strongman Wang Lequan. His defenestration in 2010 and the subsequent reorientation of efforts in the region were at the heart of the domestic interest underpinning the SREB. By the time Xi Jinping ascended to power in 2012, Xinjiang continued to be a problem for Beijing and the effort that had gone into direct security support and economic investment had not yet delivered the outcome that was desired.

In fact, as we saw in earlier chapters, the situation seemed to worsen, with incidents linked to Xinjiang increasingly taking place around the country and violence in the region itself worsening. Taking a cue from Wang Jisi's thinking, President Xi decided that his foreign policy was going to be about China standing up in the world, but he would take a staggered approach to this, starting with China's immediate periphery. He marked this shift in foreign policy by hosting the Peripheral Diplomacy Work Conference in October 2013. It was the first time since 2006 that a major work conference involving the most

senior Chinese leadership had been held on foreign policy; and
(according to some experts) it was the first time since 1949 that a
conference on "periphery diplomacy" had been held.[25] In part this
was doubtless a way of marking early on how President Xi was going
to treat foreign policy differently to his predecessor, but it also clearly
laid out some of the key principles that he saw as driving his foreign policy.

Central to Xi Jinping's vision was the concept of "rejuvenating" the
great Chinese nation, which touched on another big idea that
President Xi advanced: the "China Dream" (an articulation that consciously draws on the concept of an "American Dream"). This comparison with the United States reflects China's ambition to mirror
America's position in the world. Xi's goal is to achieve what he
describes as a two-century long plan to restore China to its former
greatness. This is a vision that will require time and work, with the
country's focus in the first instance being on China's periphery, with
the view that these areas must be helped to develop so that China in
turn can grow.[26] President Xi is somewhat opaque about where he is
referring to in terms of this "periphery," but others have pointed out
that China's "periphery" has in fact already been defined by other
prominent Chinese voices, such as that of thinker and now head of
one of Beijing's most prestigious think tanks, Yuan Peng. In his writing, he defines this area as having an "inside ring" of the fourteen
countries China directly shares borders with; a "middle ring" made up
of China's maritime borders, including those in the Indian Ocean, as
well as the parts of Central Asia and Russia which do not border
China; and finally an "outer ring" which extends to much of the rest
of the world.[27] As head of the China Institutes for Contemporary
International Relations (CICIR), the think tank linked to China's
external intelligence agency the Ministry of State Security (MSS),
Yuan Peng is in a highly influential position within China's foreign
policy thinking apparatus.

The idea of China being at the center of a global order accords
with China's larger conception of itself as one of the preeminent

powers on the planet. However, before Xi Jinping's reign, articulating this perspective publicly was not China's way. China had been living under a maxim offered by Deng Xiaoping to "observe calmly, secure our position, cope with affairs calmly, hide our capacities and bide our time, be good at maintaining a low profile, and never claim leadership." During Hu Jintao's time, this had been refined to reflect how they saw China's role gradually changing, with experts talking about China's "peaceful rise." China was moving up the ranks of world powers in terms of international affairs, but it was not taking its place at the top table quite yet, eager to hide behind a screen of nascent development as a still ascending power.

In fact, during the Hu Jintao years the push from the West was increasingly to get China to step forwards. This was most clearly articulated by then Deputy Secretary of State Robert Zoellick who memorably called on China in September 2005 "to become a responsible stakeholder in that system...that has enabled its success."[28] His point was that Beijing was profiting from the world as it was currently constructed, but that it was doing little to contribute to the global commons that everyone relied on. By 2009, this call had developed into anger with analysts like Stephanie Kleine-Ahlbrandt talking of China as a "global free-rider."[29] China was an economic behemoth at this point, and was clearly on a continually upward trajectory, but whenever others pushed for China to assume some responsibility, Beijing would demur saying that it was a developing power that had too many problems at home to tackle anything outside. When pressed, Chinese officials and experts would endlessly refer to the volume of poor people who still existed in China, saying that Beijing's priority remained in sorting itself out at home before it could take on any responsibility in the wider world.

By the time Xi Jinping came to power, China had established itself as a major power on the world stage. Yet, it was still stuck in the "peaceful rise" narrative, which suggested a timid power. When we spoke to experts in China at around that time, we found them considering how to move the discourse on from "peaceful rise" and its accompanying "non-interference" foreign policy principle. They recognized that China was no longer the ascendant power that Deng Xiaoping had spoken of, and that it was instead a global power with strength, prestige, and influence. They concurred that it was indeed time to start to use this on the world stage as was befitting the great power China envisioned itself to be. As one prominent expert told us, chuckling over dinner in Beijing, the "peaceful rise" framing no longer worked, as "we have risen" now and the country needs to maybe look at talking about "constructive interference."[30] China needed a new rhetorical framing to explain its engagement with the world.

It was decided that this new framing and vision should start on China's periphery and go out from there. Beijing needed to have a new expression of its power in its own neighborhood, and then use that as a springboard to go out into the world. The different spheres of relationships that Beijing needed to foster to ultimately help support domestic growth required a thread tying them all together, and everything needed to be articulated in a more positive way, as suggested by phrases like "constructive interference." China was seeking a new foreign policy identity and vision.

This, finally, is where the BRI vision comes in. Laid out in a pair of speeches in Astana and Jakarta in 2013, it was teed up by a visit in May 2013 by Premier Li Keqiang to Islamabad during which he signed a memorandum of understanding talking about the establishment of an "economic corridor." It was formalized in the China-Pakistan Economic Corridor (CPEC) when Prime Minister Nawaz Sharif visited Beijing in July that year.[31] Just over a year later in September 2014, President Xi visited India and signed various agreements with Prime Minister Modi, including an agreement that the two would work closely on reviving the BCIM-EC,[32] with all of these corridors emanating out from China laying the foundations for the BRI.

In addition to these various ancillary "corridor" discussions, while President Xi was in Jakarta he also announced the creation of the Asian Infrastructure Investment Bank (AIIB). This would be an institution that would answer a number of needs, from a desire by Beijing to be seen as a net contributor to the international common goods to a feeling among developing countries that Western capitals had dominated the international lender space for too long. By suggesting the creation of a new multilateral lender along the lines of the many other development banks in existence, but as one not controlled from a Western capital, Beijing was stepping into the role of leader of the developing world. This was a role that it has long felt it should hold.

The AIIB did not come alone, for in late 2014 China announced the creation of the Silk Road Fund, a further financing vehicle that was meant to take advantage of the commercial opportunities offered under the BRI. Its aim was to "promote common development and prosperity of China and the other countries and regions involved in the Belt and Road Initiative."[33] AIIB and the Silk Road Fund are intended to create a complementary pair, with one on the aid side and the other commercial, respectively, thus reflecting the two sides of the BRI vision that China was advancing. As a diplomat involved in the establishment of both put it to us, they were intended as "sisters" that would help the BRI come to life.[34] While they presented an appealing outward face in terms of the BRI, the truth was that the volume of investment they were offering was dwarfed by the vast amounts that were also being spent bilaterally by Chinese banks like Export–Import and China Development Bank.

All of this—the various development corridors, the two new financial institutions—gets wrapped up together under the BRI banner. This transforms the idea of economic corridors emanating out from China, first in its immediate neighborhood, and then, ultimately, reaching across the continent and oceans to Europe, into China's grand foreign policy vision. Beijing's concept of how it will engage with the world has become entirely defined through the lens of connectivity and trade corridors, which will help goods and prosperity flow both ways in the sort of harmonious "win-win" vision that Chinese leaders love to talk about. This requires building infrastructure to help facilitate the hoped-for trade and connectivity, which

China had long been developing at home and had also been exploring building in the regional context for some time. Ultimately, the goal was to create a web of connections and links emanating out from China, tying it more intimately to its immediate periphery, and in the longer term restoring China to what it sees as its rightful place at the center of a new global order. And the key to all of this is Central Asia.

*   *   *

However, while everyone talked about the new vision as a great big and wonderful idea, few could talk specifics about what it meant. Often the vision didn't hang together in anything but a rhetorical sense. In July 2014, we had a meeting at the SCO Secretariat in Beijing. They told us that the SREB was "still an idea...still not worked out"; they could not tell if it was "a new philosophy that had grown from the Shanghai Spirit or something else." China needed to clarify what it meant before everyone else was likely to leap on board, and anyway (in a comment that might have reflected our interlocutor's Russian heritage) "the Silk Road does not always have a good historical reputation in Central Asia, it was as much about conflict as trade—the route was a route for wars."[35]

That same year, we had a conversation in Bishkek at a meeting with a Kyrgyz think tank close to the government. When we asked them what discussions they had had with their Chinese counterparts about the SREB, their response was that the Chinese had replied, "you tell us how you want it." Beijing appeared to be telling Central Asians that they should come back with their counter-proposals and this would be the foundation of the initiative in the region.

And significantly some did—most prominently the Kazakhs, who in November 2014 announced their own Nurly Zhol (or "Bright Path"), a massive program for economic development which quite openly spoke of connecting with China's BRI. While not quite as explicitly laid out, Tajikistan and Uzbekistan have subsequently also spoken in similar terms about how their longer-term economic development strategies are linked to China. And there is little surprise in this, as the Central Asians are still developing economies that sit adjacent to the biggest economic boom story of our times. It would be unnatural for them not to seek to find ways of connecting with this opportunity.

Notwithstanding the deep tensions that could be found in some quarters of Central Asia toward China, Beijing was still able to offer a vision which the region liked and reached back to connect with. There was some reticence and concern, but the opportunity was clear. For them, being more bound to China was logical and sensible—and unlike the Russians, who wanted to envelop them with concepts like "Greater Eurasia" or projects like the EAEU, China seemed to be offering a more transactional concept.

Only time will tell whether this is indeed all Beijing wants. But at this stage, the ties that are being offered and are captured under the BRI banner are those that would provide the region with the economic opportunities that they want and need. What the longer-term consequence will be is unclear, but given the economic disparity between China and her Central Asian neighbors, it seems clear to the Central Asians that China's economic powerhouse is something which they should take advantage of. And while the West is increasingly skeptical and pushing back against China, there is a logic to the vision that China articulated for Central Asians. A logic that holds in many other parts of the world as well, parts that the BRI would affect, where there is little interest in worrying about whether they like or dislike China's ideological outlook (or feel like they are in a position to do anything about how China might be treating its people at home). There are problems in some cases and projects, and when governments change issues often emerge, but the BRI is seen in most of the world as a relatively neutral concept.

This is in some ways the simple genius of the BRI concept. Created out of a model that had been implemented in Central Asia for some time, its fundamental concept of offering infrastructure development, trade, and investment in exchange for an expansion of the Chinese presence is something that most countries will find themselves willing to accept. Coming to power, Xi Jinping inherited an already extant model in Central Asia, and he used his rhetorical firepower and podium to globalize the idea. And while there are undoubtedly problems in the region, the bigger fears that are often highlighted—like the myth of debt trap diplomacy—are not always clearly visible. Moreover, it is not clear that China has forced nations to give up infrastructure in exchange for investment as is sometimes alleged. In some cases, mining rights have been sought as collateral, and there is an incalculable volume of corrupt money probably sloshing through many projects, but these are choices made by *local* governments. A case exists that China is incentivizing them to behave in this way, but this is not at all a clear-cut case nor is it clear that this was part of the Chinese goal from the outset.

The impact of the SREB is, however, potentially more far-reaching than all this granular detail might imply. The longer-term effect is to rewire a region to bind it more closely to China, reorienting its future from being determined by Moscow and the West to being pulled into China's orbit instead. The web of links that we have outlined in this book show that it is not a simple economic transaction, but a much deeper binding and penetration. This is the centrifugal force that Beijing offers through the BRI, a way of slowly bringing countries closer to them through the many different branches of influence, investment, and connectivity offered through BRI. There are clear benefits and potential risks to this, but the overarching push from Beijing is clear. China is being restored to its rightful place at the center of international affairs.

Conclusion

The inadvertent empire to the west

On paper, the Karakoram Highway stretches from Kashgar in China's far western province of Xinjiang to Islamabad. In reality, it unfolds like a ribbon across China's westernmost moonscape-like border regions before its tarmac comes to an abrupt halt at the Khunjerab Pass on Pakistan's border. As with most countries, China's foreign relations are heavily determined by domestic considerations. The many stops and diverse communities along the Karakoram reveal the sheer complexity of this reality. China's domestic concerns are anything but uniform and are deeply intertwined with their neighbors. Making the trip along this road in 2012, it provided us with a snapshot of how interconnected China was to its Central Asian neighborhood.

Our journey started in Urumqi, a grubby metropolis of more than 3.5 million people that looks like many other second- or third-tier Chinese cities. Large boulevards cluttered with imposing buildings are filled with frenetic construction as the city rushes to erect more shopping malls to feed insatiable local consumers. Dashes of Uyghur culture are still visible, but are increasingly subsumed by the more commercialist vision that defines China's modern urban metropolis. As the capital of an autonomous region which is China's largest political subdivision, and home to a substantial portion of China's natural wealth, it is also a draw for poor fortune-seekers from neighboring provinces. A taxi driver from the adjacent province of Gansu boasted how opportunities in Urumqi are plentiful and he had girlfriends to match this bounty. One for each day of the week, he told us.

The driver who picked us up in Kashgar, about 1,000 kilometers south of Urumqi, had a very different story to tell. A local Uyghur who had developed a tourism business in which he managed to employ a number of his family members, he complained about the ineptitude of the local police as he pointed to the visibly heavy security around the airport. Kashgar distinguishes itself as majority Uyghur with traditional Uyghur culture and history perceivable at every turn. The Id Kah Mosque, the largest in China, sits on the edge of what is left of Kashgar's old town, a warren of mud-brick houses reminiscent of Kabul or the dusty trading centers of Central Asia, which has for the most part been completely rebuilt and modernized.

When we visited in 2012, the most visible aspect of this push could be found on the first part of the Karakoram Highway on the way out of Kashgar. Immense construction sites with names of Guangzhou companies filled either side of the road with large billboards advertising the modern wonders to come. One high-class establishment advertised a luxury experience complete with an English butler service. Another artful rendering of a shopping mecca under construction was surrounded by a list of the famous Western brands soon to be on offer. We later realized that these were likely similar or the same developers we would meet at the Xinjiang-Uzbekistan Expo a year or so later.

Our Uyghur driver on this longer journey was a younger chap still trying to find his way in the world, preoccupied with the demographic shift likely to come with the construction. Related to the man who had picked us up at the airport, he was an angry young man. According to his figures, some 600,000 Han were expected to flood in, overwhelming the Uyghur population and changing the face of Kashgar. He worried about the competition and what this would mean. Already feeling increasingly shut out of his own land, he could only see this getting worse with an influx of more Han. Whatever the actual numbers, watching carts pulled by donkeys hauling farmers and their wares to and from the city in front of these billboards, there was a sense of the rapid, monumental change underway. For Han moving out here to escape poverty in China's interior or the crowded southern provinces, this change represents a new beginning. For our Uyghur driver, it was an ominous symbol of cultural erasure.

According to Chinese officials in Xinjiang that we spoke to, the end goal of this construction is far less menacing. The current policy, they said (and still say), is directed at connecting one of China's less developed regions to the country's regional neighbors—the hope being that trade would bring prosperity and soothe some of the tensions so often on display between the communities in the province. This means revitalizing Kashgar's historical role as a key trading hub on the old Silk Road, thirty-five years after the Karakoram Highway had opened up a direct route to Pakistan. Developing Xinjiang and Central Asia is an interlinked project in their minds, although ultimately their end goal is stability in Xinjiang.

As we continued along the highway, the presence of China's regional neighbors became more visible. Opal, a small hamlet about 60 kilometers southwest of Kashgar, is a dusty crossroads with fruit-sellers and donkey carts whose main claim to fame is the mausoleum of Mahmud al-Kashgari, the Turkic languages' own Samuel Johnson. Born in Kashgar in 1005 AD, al-Kashgari studied in Baghdad and drew up not only the first Turkic dictionary but also the first known map of the areas inhabited by Turkic peoples. Today he rests down a beaten track off Opal's main thoroughfare. His statue stands in front of a weather-beaten museum. A grim-faced Uyghur guard looked up from her knitting to tell us not to take pictures as we enjoyed its limited pleasures. Al-Kashgari's mausoleum is a whitewashed 1980s renovation watching over a vast mud cemetery with the Kunlun Mountains barely visible in the distance, veiled by a sudden dust storm.

Along the side of the road leaving Opal, set apart from the desolate landscape of scrub and red-clay mountains and near one of the occasional open-pit mines that reveal the natural wealth of the province, a group of coalminers watched as one of them packed up to leave. Their faces were haggard and stained with soot. One burly Qinghai native complained about the bad working conditions as a Yunnanese family gathered their belongings for a bus ride to Kashgar and then on to Urumqi, where they hoped better times awaited them. Our Uyghur driver, too, had thoughts of leaving. He had been trying to find a way to move to Turkey, he told us, where he hoped that a common ethnicity would help open doors for him. He was struggling, however, to get a passport. Grasping at straws, he wondered if there was anything we could do to help him, mentioning that some earlier American clients had suggested they might be able to do something. We had to demur.

About halfway between Kashgar and the Pakistan border, we came across spectacular Lake Karakul. On its banks, a hut owned by local Kyrgyz herders provided some refuge from the howling wind. Our driver had heard stories that the Kyrgyz in this area were known to have helped authorities find a group of wanted Uyghurs who sought to cross the mountainous borders that surround the lake.

Further down the road in Tashkurgan, he told us a similar story about the local Tajik community, highlighting how tense relations can be between the various ethnic groups in this part of China. On the Chinese side nearer the country's border with Tajikistan, this Persian-Tajik community speaks a different language to their ethnic brethren across the border. Notwithstanding his concerns, he took us to see one of their villages as they were gathered and in the midst of a famous eagle dance celebration. Communicating with them in a mix of languages he explained vaguely who we were as they gathered around our car chattering, eager to show us their hamlet.

Our driver became tenser the closer we got to the border regions. The area is very ethnically diverse, and the languages used are neither Mandarin nor his native Uyghur. Security is also a more visible concern, with regular army posts visibly stamping Beijing's dominance. The notably empty town of Karasu marks the Chinese side of the Kulma Pass, the way into Tajikistan. A brand new customs post sat awaiting business with plastic still covering most of the furniture inside the building. The roads here had arches going over them at regular intervals with cameras atop—reportedly to track vehicles as they were going along to watch if someone abruptly disappeared or took too long between arches.

At Daptar, our driver was hesitant to stop. Another Pamir village, it is home to the last civilian inhabitants on the Chinese side of the border with Afghanistan. Off in the distance, a "V" in the mountains denotes where the Wakjir Pass leads to the Wakhan Corridor which runs into Afghanistan. Locals were clearly on high alert given both their location and that the road that leads to the border with Afghanistan is a poor brother to the spotless and new Karakoram Highway. Here the highway is festooned with cameras, tracking the progress of all non-military vehicles. In the vicinity and visible from the road, large stone writing on the sides of hills instructs in Mandarin, "Protect the border; protect the country; protect the people." The only way our driver could think to let us stop and stare at this was by pulling over and lifting the bonnet to his car, in a pretense that there was some issue inside.

The Chinese side of the Karakoram Highway came to an abrupt halt at the Khunjerab Pass, at the top of a hillock, leading to a more dilapidated path on the Pakistani side. White markers define the border and an imposing arch emblazoned with the Communist Party of China symbol straddles the road. On a visit a year or so earlier, a gaggle of Chinese domestic tourists exploring China's farthest reaches eagerly took photographs of one another. One middle-aged woman decided she wanted to explore Pakistan for herself and meet a Pakistani. This agitated the young soldier from Hubei in distant central China whom we had been chatting with, who dropped our conversation to frantically order her back. But she waved him off with *mei guanxi* ("no worries)" as she trotted across the border, curious to explore for herself. Having noted disappointedly that the Pakistani guards were not leaving their hut that day, she returned to Chinese soil.

The locals tell stories of those who try to cross the border by themselves often losing their way in the snow between isolated peaks. At more than 4,000 meters, the border itself seems more porous than it likely is. Long empty valleys lead to rugged, snow-capped mountains with no clear fence to demarcate one side from the other. Our driver became quieter and more visibly tense during this part of the journey, only really calming down when we got back to Tashkurgan and sat down to dinner. Back here at a strategic peak in the middle of a valley leading to Pakistan, it was easier to objectively consider our journey along the Karakoram Highway, through the patchwork of peoples along the route binding the two close allies together. The nations it brings together may be "higher than the mountains" as Chinese and Pakistani diplomats will say in reference to their nation's close bond, but for those living in the valleys, the differences remain strong.

The gap between eastern and western China is wide, but it is narrowing day by day. Xinjiang lives up to its name: it is a frontier and it is the gateway further west, into Central Asia. As China's central government consolidates development and control in Xinjiang, it does so also in Central Asia, largely inadvertently. China's future lies to its west. Its eastern seaboard will always be important, but Beijing has realized the truth in Mackinder's maxim that to control the "world island" is to control much of the world. And in a modern twist, this will help Beijing control its own wild west.

★ ★ ★

When we made this trip in 2012 Xinjiang felt relatively open. It was clear there were tensions on display and deep dislike between communities, but the security seemed dense if haphazard. Airport-style barriers tended to be turned off or not working, security guards were more often than not playing on mobile phones or staring uninterestedly into the distance. We were able to get right up to borders and into guards' bases where they offered tea and food while they picked their teeth with splinters of wood only vaguely curious about what we were doing there.

But as time went on it was clear that something was changing. On each subsequent trip to Xinjiang we would find the time required at the departing airport in Beijing or Shanghai got longer. By the time we were visiting in 2015 and 2017 the security was palpably tighter, with every mosque or Uyghur area of the town accompanied by large metal constructions at their entrances where severe looking and heavily armed Han guards would stand watch. Armored personnel carriers (APCs) were posted at major intersections with a quad of armed men staring out. The shoddy airport-style barriers were gone, replaced with early attempts at facial recognition technology, and everywhere you went people would search through your belongings and demand identification. Urumqi felt like a city under siege or on the brink of conflict.

As it turned out, this was simply the beginning. Subsequent independent reporting, confirmed in a number of cases by Chinese and foreign contacts who visited Xinjiang, have described a police state in which Uyghurs are seen as a threat whenever they articulate any sort of strong views on religion or their ethnicity, or voice complaints against the state. While there was no doubt that more attacks and threats were materializing within China emanating from Xinjiang during the early period we were working on this book, it was also clear that something had changed in the Chinese mindset toward the region. In retrospect, it appears that a visit in 2014 by President Xi Jinping was a major turning point in China's focus on the region. Frustrated by the fact that the problems in Xinjiang were not going away and worried about what could happen if trouble from Afghanistan was to spill into the region, the green light was given for state security to ramp up its efforts.[1]

In fact, traces of President Xi's hard line can be found earlier than that in speeches he made in 2013, in the wake of the attack in Tiananmen Square in October that year.[2] In that incident a family, reportedly angry at their treatment in Xinjiang, had decided to launch an attack against the crowds in Tiananmen Square. The resulting images of a car with an Islamist banner flowing from the back and a flaming vehicle under the famous Mao Zedong picture in the Square were beamed around the world to the great embarrassment of the authorities. Senior officials were sacked and focus increased on security. While evidence of the impact of these statements was hard to find, retrospectively, it helped clarify what we had been hearing from experts we were talking to in Beijing at the time.

Seen from Beijing's perspective, the problems China was facing from Uyghur militancy had only escalated in the years since those riots. In talking to Chinese security experts as part of the regular engagements and conferences we were involved in, we noticed that during the period 2014–16 their concern about terrorism was becoming heightened. Incidents in Tiananmen Square in 2013, Kunming in 2014, Thailand in 2015, and Kyrgyzstan in 2016 painted a worrying pattern in their minds which demanded a response. A significant moment came in August 2016 when Chen Quanguo was appointed Communist Party secretary for the region. This should have been a clarifying point to the world given Chen's recent past in subduing Tibet. Chen was known for developing and deploying measures which penetrated into every household in a region deemed a security risk, creating a monitoring web across the entire region. Tibet had notably quietened while he was in charge. Clearly, the leadership in Beijing saw in Chen a man who was able to subdue restive regions.

Stories of the clamp-down that was going on in Xinjiang started to emerge soon afterwards (they had already started to appear before, but after Chen took charge these stories indicated something far more systematic), and the narrative we started to hear in Beijing was that the idea was ultimately to roll out a similarly structured police state across other troublesome parts of the country. When we asked others about how long such a clamp-down could be sustained, they would talk about the need to "keep a tight lid on the pot." The point was that Beijing had concluded that a draconian approach was now necessary. As one of the *apparatchiks* sent to the region was reported as saying, it was going to be necessary to "wipe them out completely... destroy them root and branch."[3] Others painted an even starker picture of what Beijing thought it was facing: "If religious extremist thought is not rooted out," an internal party memo concluded at the time, "violent terrorist acts will continually multiply like cancer cells."[4]

If this was indeed their view, then the approach that we have subsequently seen taken makes sense. If one's aim is to eradicate the danger to this level and the tools to do it appear to be available, then it seems to make sense to deploy any means necessary to ensure that any shadow of the danger is indeed removed. This in part helps explain the extreme nature of what we have subsequently seen happen in the region. Beijing is not merely trying to manage a terrorist problem or disrupt a network, it is trying to eradicate the problem by re-educating the population to be subservient, rejecting separatist or extremist ideas at a more fundamental level, and so maintaining the Party's control on power.

But while a hardline security approach might manage the problem down, in the longer term a change in Xinjiang's environment is necessary. No matter how long you might want to keep a "tight lid on the pot," at some point this approach is going to stop working. Cracks were already visible; the occasional Han that we met from Xinjiang would tell us of their desire to never return to the region. This is where the heavy investment comes into play. From Beijing's perspective, long-term stability comes from prosperity. And this is where Central Asia becomes part of the picture, but it is quite clearly not the focus of attention. Reports of Chen's priority list when he came to power identified security as his main focus, with development and the Belt and Road Initiative (BRI) placed as lesser priorities.[5] Nevertheless, it was still the case that if China needs Xinjiang to become prosperous for it to become permanently stable, this would require an equally rich and stable wider neighborhood.

But in the wake of the violence in 2013 onward, this was now Beijing's secondary concern. The first priority did have to be Xinjiang's stability, and with this came the so-called "strike hard" campaigns aimed at eradicating enemies. Some echo of this pressure might have been seen in Central Asia through the expansion of the People's Armed Police (PAP) forces into the region. These were at the frontline in fighting the internal conflict in Xinjiang (and Tibet). Given the potential cross-border links with networks and groups that China's Xinjiang could have in Central Asia, it makes sense for them to forge closer links across the border. That the PAP would also help local security forces across the border improve their own capabilities and therefore be more effective partners would be a useful additional benefit.

But the real key in the longer term has always been about economics. Hence the desire for the Shanghai Cooperation Organization (SCO) to push in more economically minded directions, and hence the vision of the Silk Road Economic Belt (SREB). These larger projects are part of a vision which stretches far into the future and are about trying to reshape the Eurasian landmass to ultimately help China achieve its goals. From its earliest interactions with the five Central Asian countries in the wake of the collapse of the Soviet Union, China has looked to the region as an economic opportunity, first as a place from which it could benefit through higher commodity exports and, second, from the perspective of helping to bring prosperity and stability to Xinjiang. In the future, through controlling this territory, China would be able to extend its reach across the entire Eurasian heartland.

The impact all of this might have on Central Asia is somewhat incidental from Beijing's perspective. The focus is on how what happens there helps China, everything else is subsidiary. But given China's size and weight, the impact on its neighborhood would be substantial, and in particular in Central Asia. Beijing's activities have been ending up displacing the other great regional power, Russia. In the absence of the reliable presence of the US, Europe, or others, the field is being left open for China. Beijing is becoming a significant strategic player in the region no matter how hesitant it may be over it's role there. Whatever Beijing thinkers say, this role is also being foisted upon China and is likely increasingly to be the case over time.

★ ★ ★

China's push into Central Asia is happening in many ways incidentally to China's narrower ambitions for Xinjiang, but it is nevertheless a game-changer for the region. The holistic nature of China's entry into these markets, education systems, security structures, and more, all under the auspices of the SREB, has given China deep hooks into society in the region. And as Beijing's firms, money, forces, and equipment rewire the region, a longer-term effect on Central Asia will be seen as the region increasingly gravitates toward China.

But China is a detached regional power. As long as its economic interests are being served, the direct security threats are being managed, and its borders are secure, China does not seem to care that much about internal Central Asian dynamics. The non-interference principle still holds true and is for the most part appreciated by Central Asian governments. They might worry about what China is doing in their countries and about their growing dependence on China, but it is hard to see serious policymakers and planners worrying about Chinese invasion. This contrasts with their underlying concerns about long-term Russian goals in the region. They need only look to what Russia has done in Georgia and Ukraine to have a sense of how Russian intervention could play out.

But there is a bigger problem with China's non-interference, and that is the degree to which Beijing would be willing to step in to help resolve problems in the region when they emerge between any of the countries. In 2020, relations between Kyrgyzstan and Tajikistan worsened as the two countries exchanged fire across each other's disputed borders, leading to casualties on both sides. On the other side of Kyrgyzstan, the country was embroiled in a dispute with Kazakhstan as the Kazakhs complained of cross-border goods fraud. The supposedly open border guaranteed by the Eurasian Economic Union (EAEU) was blocked. These were situations where things could be left to the countries themselves to determine bilaterally, but in the case of the Kyrgyz–Tajik clash, it was not clear that the two governments were able to resolve the problem on their own. These are long-standing and intractable issues that could potentially disrupt regional trade and are not likely to improve without some kind of intervention. At this point, it would be useful for an outside power to step in to support a dialogue process and to provide an independent voice to help the two sides steer a way through the dilemma.

Traditionally, Moscow would likely have been called on to take on this role, but over time it could be that Beijing will be expected to step in instead. China after all is the one that is trying to build economic corridors across the region and is therefore among the most interested in ensuring that the region has open borders and free transit. And yet, this approach is something still apparently not in China's geopolitical make-up. The SCO has explicitly written into its constitution that members will not interfere in each other's internal affairs, and while this works as a logic when governments are seeking to manage internal political issues, sometimes they could benefit from some help from outside when it comes to external ones. But Beijing has no interest in playing this role. In neighboring Afghanistan where China has stepped in to offer itself as a platform for dialogue between sides, it has not followed through on this role by forcing people to work out their differences. It has instead merely provided a neutral forum for warring factions to meet. And while this is an important role, it is not likely to actually deal with any underlying conflict to help bring peace.

In fact, consistently, our sense from engaging with experts around the region throughout the project was that a Chinese engagement with Afghanistan would provide a huge opportunity for Beijing. At the time of writing, Afghanistan's perennial war has slowed down and the United States has finally left. Beijing has responded as it did during the Obama years by accelerating its engagement and building its defenses. But China this time seems more confident, and is instead focused on throwing brickbats at the United States for its failures in Afghanistan. Their diplomatic narrative has gone even further, accusing the US of going into Afghanistan with the sole intention of manipulating groups there to attack China. The idea of cooperation with the United States has ended; Beijing is clear that Washington should get out of its back yard. And yet, it is not clear that China sees a need to step into whatever vacuum might follow this exit. Afghanistan watchers we knew in Beijing were sanguine about having a Taliban return to power, while senior Afghans we spoke to seemed content with behind the scenes agreements they were carving out with the Chinese. There was no evidence that China planned to try to step in to fix the problems—they seemed content to simply glide behind others' initiatives and wait and see what happened.

It is perhaps an arrogant Western perspective to suggest that outside powers need to come in to resolve problems between or within warring countries, but the reality is that this is sometimes what is indeed needed. In some cases, this intervention can make the situation worse, but in other cases the mediator can play an important peacebroker role. As was seen in Afghanistan in the early 2000s, without such intervention, and in worst case scenarios, the danger is that such unstable countries can eventually become exporters of threats to others.

The dilemma for China is that through its BRI it is increasingly becoming the power with the greatest (or at least very significant) interests and geopolitical weight present on the ground in a growing number of places. This is sometimes welcome and sometimes not. It will sometimes bring clashes with other powers, but it will bring great opportunity in others. Whatever the case, though, China is becoming a significant actor. If Beijing is the one providing all the future economic opportunities within a neighboring country, and is doing so by using institutions associated with the state (like national policy banks and state-owned enterprises), then it can come as little shock that Beijing will end up becoming a significant political actor on the ground there as well. This sets China up as a natural fit, in some cases, to play the role of honest broker or at least significant player in local dynamics. But Beijing seems little interested in playing this role. Rather, China prefers to stand back from any situation, to wait and see who comes out on top, and to then make deals with them. Should there be a period of uncertainty or chaos, their answer has been simply to make deals with everybody, refusing to make value judgment choices about the actors on the ground. Unfortunately, given China's size, this is not an approach without any impact. However, it does allow China to retain uninterrupted relations with countries. Egypt is a good example of this. Here, China has managed to move effortlessly from having good relations with the government under President Mubarak to then transferring this relationship to the Muslim Brotherhood that briefly led government under President Morsi, to having a very effective relationship with President al Sisi's regime today: seamlessly moving from one side of the country's political spectrum to the other.

Closer to home in Central Asia, Beijing has managed to maintain a working relationship with whoever has been in power in Kabul, as well as with all of the various warring factions in the conflict. When senior Chinese officials visit, they are pictured in turn with each of the major power-brokers at that moment. China has continued to maintain its relations with the Taliban, both directly and through Islamabad. The five Central Asian countries have not faced the same sort of conflict recently, but even in Kyrgyzstan where there has been some instability, there has been a consistent relationship with Beijing, no matter who has been in power.

Beijing is setting itself up as the player who will support whoever comes to power with little value judgment about what their plan might be while they are in control. And doubtless for many countries the lack of criticism is appreciated as an alternative to the moralizing West, with its demands that they change their governance and practice to fulfill criteria that these countries might not feel to be relevant for their context. The West offers support, but only in exchange for an adherence to their standards. For countries in the developing world who are struggling with meeting these high standards, the arrival of China in the mix can be appreciated.

And maybe this is good. These countries do need economic and political development. However, it might also incentivize bad behavior. Beijing's lack of interest in the detail of who is in power, its focus being simply on who can deliver outcomes China seeks, will naturally attract the more authoritarian leaders who also ignore complaints in favor of results. It is also a real challenge to the Western notion of viewing countries' histories in terms of an arc toward greater democracy and openness. Western support for the developing world is often predicated on the notion that through helping these countries to develop in the same direction as the West, they will eventually naturally achieve the same openness and democratic norms found in Western countries. This might seem arrogant and overbearing to some, but it is nonetheless what underpins much of Western thinking: the primacy of the Western model of democracy over all else, and the assumption that most other countries will want to achieve this model in the long run. It is a vision that many in the West had for China, but they have now shed this optimism as they have watched Xi Jinping's power grow.

The challenge China poses through the BRI is that it is showing through its own experience and its outward investments that things do not need to be this way. Beijing is offering an opportunity which is ground-up, focused on helping countries develop all of the trappings of statehood without their having to build the institutions that would provide the public with the guarantee of a system ensuring accountability and good governance. From Beijing's perspective, governance is delivered through economic opportunity, strong security, and stability. This can be seen most clearly in the broad contours of the vision laid out for Xinjiang. It is not necessarily delivered through transparency and rule of law.

But this in itself also highlights the failure of the Chinese model. Notwithstanding China's massive investments and efforts in Xinjiang, Beijing continues to face the problem of an unhappy public. And while Chinese experts point to the new stability and lack of attacks in Xinjiang as evidence of how successful the model has been, the fact they have to continue to run mass re-education camps with hundreds of thousands of people in them is a clear signal that the public in Xinjiang has yet to be persuaded. Some of the most recent reports from Xinjiang suggest that the levels of policing in the region might be decreasing, as the authorities feel they have broken the back of the problem they face. But there is little evidence that a lighter police presence is going to equate to a lessening of control. Rather, the control has now become so pervasive it seems like the authorities feel they do not need the same physical displays as before.

The question for the world posed by the BRI is the degree to which China is going to seek to impose this similar outcome or model elsewhere. So far there is little evidence of this. Notwithstanding fears and complaints, the degree to which China has sought to impose its goals on others is quite limited—admittedly, in overseas Chinese communities there has been evidence of interference, but this is quite frequently focused on matters that ultimately are directly relevant to China (like governance in Hong Kong, Taiwan, and Xinjiang, or with political dissidents). The *Wolf Warrior* mood that is currently in vogue in Beijing—drawing on a jingoistic set of films in which a heroic Chinese soldier stands up to drug lords in Xinjiang in episode one, and Western mercenaries in Africa in episode two—has pushed China in a more aggressive outward-facing appearance. But in reality it is not clear whether this applies to those who are not directly threatening the integrity of China's borders. It is notable that the issues on which Beijing is choosing to pick fights are all related to nationhood and China's direct borders.

It has nevertheless set a particular tone with China's diplomats. In Central Asia, the embassy in Kazakhstan set up an online presence and started to aggressively push back on Facebook and Twitter against any narratives it disagreed with. When accusations came in that Chinese websites were stirring fake news against Kazakhstan—for example, that the country wanted to "return" to China; that the COVID-19 virus had originated in a US-Defense-Department-supported biolab in Kazakhstan (a story that had originated with the Russian Ministry of Foreign Affairs and was further fanned by their Chinese counterparts); or that there was a pneumonia outbreak circulating in the country which was more lethal than COVID-19—the Chinese embassy pushed back aggressively, accusing Western media of stirring the stories up. In Tajikistan, we heard stories of how the Chinese ambassador had at one point grown so angry with a local junior diplomat in a meeting at the Ministry in Dushanbe that he had demanded that this diplomat leave the meeting, despite it being held in his own building. In Kyrgyzstan, we were told that after a prominent local Chinese businessman had been murdered, the Chinese embassy had called in the Kyrgyz Ministry of Foreign Affairs for an explanation—an unheard-of breach of protocol. Many of these events took place prior to the *Wolf Warrior* mood becoming so public in China, reflecting how China's diplomats were already sometimes behaving in an overbearing way in Central Asia even before this latest more aggressive Chinese cultural trend.

But while these events speak to an increasingly assertive and arrogant power, they do not speak to a desire to invade or control. Rather, they point to a demanding partner that believes that, as a large power, these are the rights that are its due. The challenge that the BRI represents for the world is that a newly rising power is displacing the current order and doing it in a manner which challenges the advance of the democratic system that the West has been offering up to this point. And this is being done in a manner that does not necessarily show consideration for what the local political outcome or result might be, but is single-mindedly focused on that power's own interests. Local commons are not a priority unless they impact directly on China's investments or interests. This approach has been playing out in Central Asia for the past few decades, and now we are seeing it globalized under the BRI. China is no longer exporting its Marxist revolution, but it is showing how its use of brute economic power can transform countries and keep governments in power.

★ ★ ★

As we wrote the final stages of this book, COVID-19 has appeared and ravaged the planet. Emanating from China, it arrived at a moment when the world was convulsed by a geostrategic clash between China and the US. Shortly before it enveloped the globe, in late 2019 we made a trip across Central Asia to all five capitals. The purpose of the trip was not focused on China, but the country and topic still came up at every visit in different ways. The discussion on China in Central Asia has moved from the fringes of research conversations to become a central focus. When we first published on this topic, experts in the region angrily dismissed our interest in China's focus on Central Asia, saying it was not likely to last. It is now the core topic in the region today. Beijing's interests are tangible across many aspects of Central Asian life. Chinese influence is ubiquitous and evident. China is no longer a distant power of the future, but increasingly the dominant player now.

Against this backdrop, it was interesting to see how the discourse around COVID-19 played out in the region. What was most striking was the timeline. It was not until mid-March 2020 that the Central Asians started to report they had cases of the disease, and all three of those who admitted cases (Kazakhstan, Kyrgyzstan, and Uzbekistan) did it at around the same time and accusing their first COVID-19 patients as having come from Europe or Saudi Arabia. This was not to say that during the preceding two months the region had not been rife with rumors of sick Chinese people bringing the disease to the region. Watching from afar, we saw stories on social media and in local outlets of Chinese people being chased at markets, of their being thrown off trains, and of a general fear of Chinese disease carriers.

We also heard stories from contacts on the ground about people being sick and hospitals being full of patients. In Tajikistan, which waited until mid-April 2020 to formally admit they had cases (Turkmenistan has yet to admit having any at time of writing, although there have been consistent rumors appearing on dissident media outlets since February 2020), reports have emerged of Chinese workers who had grown so concerned about the government's handling of the disease that they had started to riot, demanding to be sent home. Yet it was interesting to see that during January and February, the local authorities refused to say whether they had any cases, and instead sent aid packages to China.

Once they did admit that the disease had spread to within their borders, everything changed. Soon, aid from China was flowing in. It came from across China, with different regions offering money, doctors, personal protective equipment, and more. Chinese companies that were invested in the countries started to hand over checks and medical equipment through local embassies. The People's Liberation Army (PLA) sent planeloads of aid to their counterparts, while the local embassy in Bishkek reached out to the Kyrgyz Border Guard Service to offer them protective equipment. Jack Ma's Foundation sent planeloads of aid to all of the countries except Turkmenistan.

Chinese doctors went over offering training based on their own experience of managing COVID-19, webinars were set up, as well as online facilities to enable Central Asians to ask Chinese doctors questions directly. In Khujand, the staff at the Confucius Institute took it upon themselves to work with colleagues back in China to translate a manual about how to manage the spread of the virus. In Tashkent, the local Ministry of Public Security (MPS) representative at the embassy gathered information and experiences from home which he then took to share with his counterparts trying to manage lockdown in Tashkent. Some of these stories have appeared earlier in the text, but the point in listing them again is to highlight how comprehensive Chinese "medical" or "mask" diplomacy really was.

But most interesting in many ways was the role taken by the SCO that started to emerge from the ashes of the virus. As we saw in an earlier chapter, during COVID the new SCO Secretary General Vladimir Norov clearly saw an opportunity to help commercial Chinese firms focused on providing e-goods in the region. The SCO worked closely with Alibaba to co-host seminars for doctors across the region and with Weidong Cloud Computing to help Central Asian children stuck at home continue learning remotely during lockdown. At the same time, he seems to have focused a substantial portion of his time building up further the e-commercial relationship between China and the Russian-speaking SCO countries. The opening of the Qingdao SCO demonstration center (with housing for Chinese tech and e-commerce firms to develop their projects in the region in late 2020) highlighted an additional physical aspect to this link.

Back in mid-2019, Alibaba founder Jack Ma met with Secretary General Norov in Chongqing during the SMART EXPO-2019. During this meeting he boasted of how his firm was going to create some hundred million new jobs, and support around ten million new enterprises over the next few years in the SCO space. While where exactly this would happen was not specified (and by this point, of course, the SCO has links with almost half of the world's population), nevertheless the boosterism does seem to have been matched by a subsequent surge in contacts and activity between the SCO and the firm. The firm's senior managers are recorded as making numerous visits to the Secretariat in Beijing over the subsequent year, while the SCO hosted various functions focused on seeing how Alibaba's e-payments and e-commerce platforms could be better used throughout the SCO region.

But Secretary General Norov seems to have decided to not stop there, building connections with other prominent Chinese online providers like JD.com or Giushi technology. The aim overall seems to have been to push the SCO firmly in a more e-commerce direction and ultimately fulfilling the goal that Beijing had long wanted the organization to achieve.

Russia during the pandemic has proven a disastrous partner for the Central Asians, hurting their economies through the mass repatriation of the migrant labor workforce that had been providing crucial remittances to the Central Asian economies. Focused on fixing itself, Russia failed to come up with anything much by way of aid for the region. Over time this changed, but in the meantime China and the SCO had been consistently forthcoming with aid and support, using the opportunity to build even deeper links with these local economies and societies.

China's goal may, once again, have been primarily commercial, but the net result was to bind the countries even closer to China. And while it is difficult to discern exactly what the benefit to Xinjiang is of all of this e-commerce, creating a more prosperous and stable environment around the region, according to the Chinese conception, is always going to be positive for it in the longer term. Unmentioned so far is the potential data mine to which Chinese firms are gaining access across the region. While there is no evidence at the moment of any nefarious use being planned, these technology links provide Chinese firms with unprecedented access and understanding of the region. Concerns around Chinese technologies have been among the most prominent issues in the press at the time of writing, with paranoia and fear abounding. Certainly, without any oversight in place, abuse of data privacy is an issue which has already caused huge damage in the West. But this digital and tech investment into Central Asia has come at a moment when the world is reeling from the COVID-19 pandemic, meaning any positive economic opportunity has been particularly appreciated by the COVID-stricken Central Asian economies.

Longer term, it remains to be seen what the full impact of the pandemic will be, but in the short and medium term, it is clear that it is going to strengthen China's footprint in Central Asia. It is the latest in a series of steps that China has taken in its long march toward prominence in the region, steps that provide a possible hint of what China's global footprint might ultimately look like.

China's inadvertent empire in Central Asia will have geopolitical consequences in terms of Western influence in what remains one of the most pivotal geographic zones of the planet. Should Washington (and by extension its allies) become preoccupied solely with the so-called Indo-Pacific in its China policy, not only will it be missing the more profound manifestation of China's global posture, it could also quickly find it far more difficult to cultivate relationships with the countries of Central Asia and beyond, across a growing chunk of the Eurasian landmass. And as we have seen with the growth of the SCO and China's BRI more generally, the region tends to act as a testing ground for Chinese activities in other areas of the world. China may not be seeking an empire in the region, but it is the only power that is active here in any comprehensive, long-term-oriented manner. If other outside powers do not also engage, China's lock on Central Asia to the exclusion of others will not only be inadvertent but inevitable.

Endnotes

INTRODUCTION

1. Xi Jinping, "Promote Friendship Between Our People and Work Together to Build a Bright Future," Speech by H.E. Xi Jinping, President of the People's Republic of China at Nazarbayev University, Astana, *Foreign Ministry of People's Republic of China*, September 7, 2013 https://www.fmprc.gov.cn/mfa_eng/wjdt_665385/zyjh_665391/t1078088.shtml
2. Xi Jinping, "Speech by President Xi Jinping to Indonesian Parliament," *ASEAN-China Centre*, October 3, 2013 http://www.asean-china-center.org/english/2013-10/03/c_133062675.htm
3. Belt and Road Initiative (BRI) has gone through numerous name changes in English. Papers have been written about why this is so—what is most significant in our view is that the Chinese name has stayed consistently the same, reflecting Beijing's unflinching view.
4. Barack Obama, "Remarks by President Barack Obama at Suntory Hall," *Obama White House Archives*, November 14, 2009 https://obamawhite-house.archives.gov/the-press-office/remarks-president-barack-obama-suntory-hall
5. Barack Obama, "Statement by the President on the Signing of the Trans-Pacific Partnership," *Obama White House Archives*, February 3, 2016 https://obamawhitehouse.archives.gov/the-press-office/2016/02/03/statement-president-signing-trans-pacific-partnership
6. "Grassley, Senators Express Concerns Over China's 'Debt Trap' Diplomacy With Developing Countries," *Chuck Grassley Senate Website*, August 10, 2018 https://www.grassley.senate.gov/news/news-releases/grassley-senators-express-concerns-over-china-s-debt-trap-diplomacy-developing
7. "A Conversation with Ambassador Alice Wells on the China-Pakistan Economic Corridor," *Wilson Center*, November 21, 2019 https://www.wilsoncenter.org/event/conversation-ambassador-alice-wells-the-china-pakistan-economic-corridor

8. RFE/RL, "Pompeo Urges Kazakhstan to Press China Over Xinjiang Crackdown," *VOA News*, February 2, 2020 https://www.voanews.com/a/south-central-asia_pompeo-urges-kazakhstan-press-china-over-xinjiang-crackdown/6183571.html

9. Sir Halford Mackinder, an English geographer, academic, and politician, who is regarded as a founding father of both geopolitics and geostrategy, proposed the Heartland theory: whoever controls Eastern Europe controls the Heartland—stretching from the Volga to the Yangtze and from the Himalayas to the Arctic—and in turn whoever controls the Heartland, commands the World-Island, the land mass which stretches between the Atlantic and the Pacific oceans, and hence the world.

    American Admiral Mahan's approach in the 19th-century had emphasized the importance of strength in the seas: the United States needed greater control over its seaborne commerce to protect its economic interests. Mahan's theory on the importance of sea power as the main cause of Britain's rise to world power neglected diplomacy and land arms. It also did not explain the rise of land empires, such as Bismarck's Germany or the Russian Empire.

10. Liu Xiaoming, "New Silk Road is an opportunity not a threat," *Financial Times*, May 24, 2015 https://www.ft.com/content/c8f58a7c-ffd6-11e4-bc30-00144feabdc0

11. "This is what happens when no English speakers are in the room," as one Russian official put it to us as we all chuckled about the nomenclature.

12. Wang Jisi (王缉思), "'西进', 中国地缘战略的再平衡," ("Going West": China's Rebalancing Strategy), 环球时报 *(Global Times)*, October 17, 2012 https://opinion.huanqiu.com/article/9CaKrnJxoLS

13. Yu Hongjun (于洪君), "阿富汗: 名不虚传的帝国坟场," (Afghanistan: Deservedly Called a Graveyard of Empires), 察哈尔评论 *(Charhar Review)*, March 6, 2020 http://www.charhar.org.cn/newsinfo.aspx?newsid=15791

14. See Alexandros Petersen's first book, *The World Island: Eurasian Geopolitics and the Fate of the West* (Praeger, 2011) for a discussion of this concept.

CHAPTER 1

1. *Records of the Grand Historian: Han Dynasty I*, translated by Burton Watson (Columbia University, rev. edn, 1993).

2. Christopher I. Beckwith, *Empires of the Silk Road: A History of Central Eurasia from the Bronze Age to the Present* (Princeton University Press, 2009).

3. *Records of the Grand Historian: Han Dynasty I*, translated by Burton Watson (Columbia University, rev. edn, 1993).

4. Shouyi Bai et al., *A History of Chinese Muslims* (Zhonghua Books, 2003).

5. Wan Lei, "The First Chinese Travel Record on the Arab World: Commercial and Diplomatic Communications during the Islamic Golden Age," Qiraat (King Faisal Center for Research and Islamic Studies, December 2016) https://kfcris.com/pdf/c2508c385dd7671ac18676b7178a955a58e09505 b194a.pdf

6. Wilhelm Baum, *The Church of the East: A Concise History* (Routledge, 2010).

7. Shouyi Bai et al., *A History of Chinese Muslims* (Zhonghua Books, 2003).

8. Shouyi Bai et al., *A History of Chinese Muslims* (Zhonghua Books, 2003).

9. Hasan H. Karrar, *The New Silk Road Diplomacy: China's Central Asian Foreign Policy since the Cold War* (UBC Press, 2009).

10. Svat Soucek, *A History of Inner Asia* (Cambridge University Press, 2000).

11. Sven Hedin, *My Life as an Explorer* (Kodansha, 1996).

12. Owen Lattimore, *Frontier History* (Oxford University Press, 1962).

13. This book generally uses "Russian" instead of "Soviet" to more accurately reflect the reality of the colonial rule by Moscow in Central Asia until 1991.

CHAPTER 2

1. Wen Jiabao, "Chinese Premier Wen Jiabao's speech at opening session of second China-Eurasia Expo," *Ministry of Commerce of People's Republic of China*, September 3, 2012 http://english.mofcom.gov.cn/article/news-release/significantnews/201209/20120908320465.shtml

2. This short paragraph summarizes what is a spectacularly rich history. For readers interested in more detail, please see David Brophy's *Uyghur Nation* (Harvard University Press, 2016) or Justin Jacobs' *Xinjiang and the Modern Chinese State* (University of Washington Press, 2017), among many other excellent texts.

3. Hasan H. Karrar, *The New Silk Road Diplomacy: China's Central Asian Foreign Policy since the Cold War* (UBC Press, 2009), p. 36.

4. Dr Yajun Bao, "The Xinjiang Production and Construction Corps: An Insider's Perspective," *Blavatnik School of Government Working Paper Series*, January 2018 https://www.bsg.ox.ac.uk/sites/default/files/2018-05/BSG-WP-2018-023.pdf

5. Wiens, Herold, "Cultivation Development and Expansion in China's Colonial Realm in Central Asia," *Journal of Asian Studies* 26 (1966), p. 1. http://english.mofcom.gov.cn/article/newsrelease/significant-news/201209/20120908320465.shtml

6. Cheng Li, "Hu's Followers: Provincial Leaders with Backgrounds in the Youth League," *China Leadership Monitor*, No. 3, Summer 2002, https://www.hoover.org/research/hus-followers-provincial-leaders-background-communist-youth-league

7. Michael Wines, "A Strongman is China's Rock in Ethnic Strife," *New York Times*, July 10, 2009 https://www.nytimes.com/2009/07/11/world/asia/11xinjiang.html

8. David Holley, "An Islamic Challenge to China: Officials fear the spread of fundamentalism in the westernmost region. They toughen controls on religious life and suppress secessionist activities," *Los Angeles Times*, November 12, 1990 https://www.latimes.com/archives/la-xpm-1990-11-12-mn-3265-story.html

9. Patrick E. Tyler, "Ethnic Muslims Boil Over in Riots and Bombings," *New York Times*, February 28, 1997 https://www.nytimes.com/1997/02/28/world/in-china-s-far-west-tensions-with-ethnic-muslims-boil-over-in-riots-and-bombings.html

10. Xinhua, "Chinese central government to step up support for Xinjiang: senior leader," *People's Daily*, March 31, 2010 http://en.people.cn/90001/90776/90785/6935452.html

11. Author interview, Shanghai, 2012.

12. Author interview, Urumqi, 2012.

13. Jenni Marsh, "My life: Josh Summers," *South China Morning Post*, June 8, 2014 https://www.scmp.com/magazines/post-magazine/article/1525810/my-life-josh-summers

14. In fact, a 2015 census of the entire Ili prefecture states that Han are the majority (41.2%), with Kazakhs next (26.8%), and Uyghurs third (17.45%). http://www.xjtj.gov.cn/sjcx/tjnj_3415/2016xjtjnj/rkjy/201707/t20170714_539450.html

15. Joey Wang, "Shanghai-Volkswagen Starts Work on New Factory in Xinjiang, China," *Car News China*, May 29, 2012.

16. Vicky Xiuzhong Xu, Danielle Cave, Dr. James Liebold, Kelsey Munro, and Nathan Riser, "Uyghurs for sale," *Australian Strategic Policy Institute International Cyber Policy Centre Report*, March 1, 2020 https://www.aspi.org.au/report/uyghurs-sale

17. "Chinese contractor cleared to start next phase of £700m Middlewood Locks," *The Construction Index*, September 29, 2021 https://www.theconstructionindex.co.uk/news/view/chinese-contractor-cleared-to-start-next-phase-of-700m-middlewood-locks

18. Vicky Xiuzhong Xu, Danielle Cave, Dr. James Liebold, Kelsey Munro, and Nathan Riser, "Uyghurs for sale," *Australian Strategic Policy Institute International Cyber Policy Centre Report*, March 1, 2020 https://www.aspi.org.au/report/uyghurs-sale

19. "Chinese city bans, destroys matches to fight terror," *Reuters*, July 15, 2014 https://www.reuters.com/article/us-china-xinjiang/chinese-city-bans-destroys-matches-to-fight-terror-idUSKBN0FK0RN20140715

20. Sophie Beach, "In Xinjiang, Household Knives must be ID'd," *China Digital Times*, October 10, 2017 https://chinadigitaltimes.net/2017/10/xinjiang-household-knives-must-ided/

21. Chris Buckley and Austin Ramzy, "China Is Erasing Mosques and Precious Shrines in Xinjiang," *New York Times*, September 25, 2020 https://www.nytimes.com/interactive/2020/09/25/world/asia/xinjiang-china-religious-site.html

22. Adrian Zenz and James Leibold, "Xinjiang's Rapidly Evolving Security State," *China Brief*, March 14, 2017 https://jamestown.org/program/xinjiangs-rapidly-evolving-security-state/

23. "Xinjiang Introduces 'Convenience Police Stations' to Closely Monitor Uyghurs," *Radio Free Asia*, 2017 https://www.rfa.org/english/news/special/uyghur-oppression/ChenPolicy1.html

24. Confusingly, Kazakhstan's capital city has gone through a number of name changes during its recent life. From 1998 to 2019 (the period during which much of the research for this book was undertaken), the city was called Astana. Then in March 2019, a unanimous vote changed the city's name to Nursultan in honor of leader Nursultan Nazarbayev. Prior to being called Astana, the city was called Akmola.

25. Adrian Zenz, "Sterilizations, IUDs, and Mandatory Birth Control," *Jamestown Foundation*, June 2020 https://jamestown.org/press-releases/sterilizations-iuds-and-mandatory-birth-control-the-ccps-campaign-to-suppress-uyghur-birthrates-in-xinjiang/

CHAPTER 3

1. Author interviews, August, November, December 2012.

2. China Daily, "China, Kazakhstan Discuss Cross-Border Gas Pipeline," *China.org*, August 25, 2004 http://www.china.org.cn/english/BAT/105031.htm

3. Guy Chazan, "Turkmenistan Gas Field is One of the World's Largest," *Wall Street Journal*, October 16, 2008 https://www.wsj.com/articles/SB122409510811337137

4. Song Yen Ling, "Fourth link of Central Asia-China gas pipeline to start construction this year," *S&P Global, Platts*, March 10, 2014 https://www.spglobal.com/platts/en/market-insights/latest-news/natural-gas/031014-fourth-link-of-central-asia-china-gas-pipeline-to-start-construction-this-year

5. Author interviews, August, November 2012.

6. Alexandros Petersen, "Did China just win the Caspian Gas War?," *Foreign Policy*, July 7, 2010 https://foreignpolicy.com/2010/07/07/did-china-just-win-the-caspian-gas-war/

7. Author interviews, Aktobe, Astana, May 2012.

8. Author interviews, February 2013.

9. Wu Jiao, "Deal signed to expand Sino-Kazakh oil pipeline," *China Daily*, April 7, 2013 https://www.chinadaily.com.cn/china/2013-04/07/content_16379084.htm

10. Xinhua, "China-Kazakhstan oil pipeline transports 10.88 mln tonnes in 2019," *Hellenic Shipping News*, January 10, 2020 https://www.hellenicshippingnews.com/china-kazakhstan-oil-pipeline-transports-10-88-mln-tonnes-in-2019/

11. Alexandros Petersen, "Afghanistan has what China wants," *South Asia Channel, Foreign Policy*, April 18, 2013 https://foreignpolicy.com/2013/4/18/afghanistan-has-what-china-wants/

12. Alexandros Petersen, "China's Strategy in Afghanistan," *The Atlantic*, May 21, 2013 https://www.theatlantic.com/china/archive/2013/05/chinas-strategy-in-afghanistan/276052/

13. Erica Downs, "China Buys into Afghanistan," *SAIS Review*, Vol. XXXIII, No. 2 (Summer-Fall 2012) https://www.brookings.edu/wp-content/uploads/2016/06/China-Buys-into-Afghanistan-Erica-Downs.pdf

14. Ayrizek Imanaliyeva, "Kyrgyzstan: Living in the shadow of a sleeping Chinese oil refinery," *Eurasianet*, October 22, 2020 https://eurasianet.org/kyrgyzstan-living-in-the-shadow-of-a-sleeping-chinese-oil-refinery

15. Author interview, April 2013.

16. Ayrizek Imanaliyeva, "Kyrgyzstan: Living in the shadow of a sleeping Chinese oil refinery," *Eurasianet*, October 22, 2020 https://eurasianet.org/kyrgyzstan-living-in-the-shadow-of-a-sleeping-chinese-oil-refinery

17. Author interview, Bishkek, 2013.

18. "Chinese-funded project gives Kyrgyzstan its first independent power transmission line," *Asia News*, August 28, 2015 http://www.asianews.it/news-en/Chinese-funded-project-gives-Kyrgyzstan-its-first-independent-power-transmission-line-35168.html

19. Catherine Putz, "China-Kazakhstan Copper Mine Brawl: Food for Thought?," *The Diplomat*, July 14, 2015 https://thediplomat.com/2015/07/china-kazakhstan-copper-mine-brawl-food-for-thought/

20. RFE/RL Tajik Service, "Tajik Police Use Firearms to Disperse Rare Protest by Chinese Workers," *Radio Free Europe/Radio Liberty*, May 22, 2020 https://www.rferl.org/a/tajik-police-use-firearms-to-disperse-rare-protest-by-chinese-workers/30627748.html

21. Dirk van der Kley, "Chinese Companies' Localization in Kyrgyzstan and Tajikistan," *Problems of Post-Communism*, vol. 67, 2020, Issue 3 (published

online June 2, 2020) https://www.tandfonline.com/doi/full/10.1080/10758216.2020.1755314

22. Marlene Laruelle and Sebastien Peyrouse, *The Chinese Question in Central Asia: Domestic Order, Social Change, and the Chinese Factor* (Hurst, December 2012).

23. "Tajikistan cedes land to China," *BBC News*, January 13, 2011 https://www.bbc.com/news/world-asia-pacific-12180567

24. Rayhan Demytrie, "Kazakhs protest against China farmland lease," *BBC News*, January 30, 2010 http://news.bbc.co.uk/2/hi/asia-pacific/8489024.stm

25. Mark Vinson, "Tajikistan to Lease 6,000 Hectares of Land to China," *Eurasia Daily Monitor*, vol. 9, Issue 30, February 13, 2012 https://jamestown.org/program/tajikistan-to-lease-6000-hectares-of-land-to-china/

CHAPTER 4

1. A brief note on names. The "Belt and Road Initiative" is a term used which brings together in rhetorical terms the two speeches with which President Xi launched his keynote foreign policy vision. These were delivered in Astana in September 2013 where he spoke of a "Silk Road Economic Belt," and a month later in Jakarta where he spoke of a "21st-Century Maritime Silk Road." These were brought together as the "Belt and Road Initiative," though the term went through a few iterations before it landed on this phrase. Initially, it was referred to as the "One Belt, One Road" (which is a more faithful translation of the Mandarin "Yi Dai, Yi Lu"), but this was felt to be too restrictive in English. It is worth noting that the Mandarin version has stayed the same throughout.

2. See, for example, Yun Sun's "March West: China's Response to the U.S. Rebalancing", January 31, 2013 https://www.brookings.edu/blog/upfront/2013/01/31/march-west-chinas-response-to-the-u-s-rebalancing/

3. Liu Xiaoming, "New Silk Road is an opportunity not a threat," *Financial Times*, May 24, 2015 https://www.ft.com/content/c8f58a7c-ffd6-11e4-bc30-00144feabdc0

4. William H. McNeill, *Plagues and Peoples* (Anchor Books, 1989).

5. Marlene Laruelle and Sebastien Peyrouse, *The Chinese Question in Central Asia: Domestic Order, Social Change, and the Chinese Factor* (Hurst, December 2012).

6. Raffaello Pantucci and Li Lifan, "Decision time for Central Asia: Russia or China?," *Open Democracy*, January 24, 2013 https://www.opendemocracy.net/en/odr/decision-time-for-central-asia-russia-or-china/

7. Data from Observatory of Economic Complexity (World Bank). https://oec.world/

8. Data from Observatory of Economic Complexity (World Bank). https://oec.world/

9. Author interviews, Bishkek, 2012.

10. Kijin Kim and Paul Mariano, "Trade Impact of Reducing Time and Costs at Borders in the Central Asia Regional Economic Cooperation Region," *ADBI Working Paper Series*, No. 1106, March 2020 https://www.adb.org/sites/default/files/publication/575606/adbi-wp1106.pdf

11. Catherine Putz, "A New Slowdown at the Kazakh-Kyrgyz Border," *The Diplomat*, April 8, 2019 https://thediplomat.com/2019/04/a-new-slowdown-at-the-kazakh-kyrgyz-border/

12. "A quick guide to SCO's interconnectivity," *CGTN*, June 7, 2018 https://news.cgtn.com/news/3d3d514f3159544f77457a6333566d54/share_p.html

13. Author interview, Kyrgyzstan, 2019.

CHAPTER 5

1. Author interview, Beijing, June 2013.

2. Joseph S. Nye, "Soft Power," *Foreign Policy* 80 (Autumn 1990), pp. 153–71.

3. In 2020, reflecting a global pushback against the Confucius Institutes Hanban was abandoned and the Chinese International Education Foundation was established to manage the Confucius Institutes. As a result the Hanban website was abandoned. This quote came from the introduction page of the old website, and can still be found through the Web Archive: http://web.archive.org/web/20200118050700/http://english.hanban.org/node_7719.htm

4. A number of times in our research we heard about a Confucius Institute (CI) off-shoot in Naryn; however, we were unable to get confirmation from CI staff, or to visit it, or to find much evidence of it on the Hanban website.

5. "Chinese Universities Compile the First New Crown Prevention Manual for Tajikistan," *news.sciencenet.cn*, April 15, 2020.

6. Raffaello Pantucci and Alexandros Petersen, "Beijing Lays the Groundwork in Tajikistan: A View from the Ground," *China Brief*, vol. 12, Issue 11, May 25, 2012 https://jamestown.org/program/beijing-lays-the-groundwork-in-tajikistan-a-view-from-the-ground/

7. "Chinese aid to Kyrgyzstan bus handover ceremony was held in Bishkek," *YaXing Press Release*, September 3, 2009 (original link dead,

webarchive retained the release: http://web.archive.org/web/
20101017203542/http://www.yaxingkeche.com.cn:80/en/News.aspx?i
d=9e5e7e19-76cc-47e5-8e8b-7d16ab378210)

8. "China to provide $14.3 million to Kyrgyzstan for implementation of
   specific projects," AKIpress News Agency (Kyrgyzstan), June 20, 2011

9. "Chinese Red Cross Society Allocates Humanitarian Aid to Kyrgyzstan
   in Sum of $200,000," AKIpress News Agency (Kyrgyzstan), Tuesday,
   April 16, 2013.

10. Interview: "Kyrgyzstan-China Agricultural Cooperation Flourishing:
    Minister," *Xinhua General News Service*, Monday 9:47a.m. (EST),
    May 30, 2016.

11. http://www.cablegatesearch.net/cable.php?id=10BISHKEK56

12. Author interviews, Osh, 2014.

13. Tatiana C. Gfoeller, "Chinese soft power in Kyrgyzstan," *US State
    Department Diplomatic Cable*, January 22, 2010 released by Wikileaks:
    https://wikileaks.org/plusd/cables/10BISHKEK56_a.html

14. Dirk van der Kley, "Chinese Companies' Localization in Kyrgyzstan and
    Tajikistan," *Problems of Post-Communism*, vol. 67, 2020, Issue 3 (published
    online June 2, 2020) https://www.tandfonline.com/doi/full/10.1080/
    10758216.2020.1755314

15. "Uyghurs," *World Directory of Minorities and Indigenous Peoples,* Minority
    Rights Group International, June 2015 https://minorityrights.org/
    minorities/uyghurs-2/

16. Author interview, Astana, 2012.

17. Marlene Laruelle, Gerard Toal, John O'Loughlin, and Kristin M. Bakke,
    "Kazakhs are wary of neighbours bearing gifts," *Open Democracy*, April
    30, 2020 https://www.opendemocracy.net/en/odr/kazakhs-are-wary-
    neighbours-bearing-gifts/

18. Brian Spegele and Lukas I. Alpert, "Jennifer Lopez Turkmenistan Gig
    Shines Light on Chinese Oil Firm," *Wall Street Journal,* July 1, 2013 https://
    www.wsj.com/articles/SB10001424127887324251504578579484286462430

19. "Xi Jinping and President Emomali Rahmon of Tajikistan jointly attend
    the groundbreaking ceremony of China-Tajikistan electricity and China-
    Central Asia natural gas pipeline cooperative projects stressing to carry for-
    ward the spirit of the Silk Road, construct the monument of friendship and
    build the bond of cooperation," *Foreign Ministry of People's Republic of China*,
    September 14, 2014 https://www.fmprc.gov.cn/mfa_eng/topics_665678/
    zjpcxshzzcygyslshdsschybdtjkstmedfsllkydjxgsfw/t1191503.shtml

20. "Confucius Institute," the introduction is no longer available on the
    University website, but can be found through the WayBack Machine,

http://web.archive.org/web/20200814230723/http://cie.upc.edu.cn/admission_en/About_Us/Confucius_Institute.htm

21. Joseph S. Nye, "Soft Power," *Foreign Policy* 80 (Autumn 1990), pp. 153–71.
22. Author interview, Tashkent, 2011.

CHAPTER 6

1. "Shanghai Cooperation Organisation: A Vehicle for Human Rights Violations," *FIDH*, September 3, 2012 https://www.fidh.org/IMG/pdf/sco_report.pdf
2. "Shanghai Cooperation Organisation: A Vehicle for Human Rights Violations," *FIDH*, September 3, 2012 https://www.fidh.org/IMG/pdf/sco_report.pdf
3. Peter Brookes, "Club for Dictators: An ugly agenda for Asia," *Commentary, Heritage Foundation*, June 12, 2006 https://www.heritage.org/defense/commentary/club-dictators-ugly-agenda-asia
4. Alexander Cooley, "The League of Authoritarian Gentlemen," *Foreign Policy*, January 30, 2013 https://foreignpolicy.com/2013/01/30/the-league-of-authoritarian-gentlemen/
5. "Kazakhstan proposes to establish cyber-police within SCO," *Intellinews*, April 25, 2012.
6. Xinhua, "Chinese Premier addresses Uzbekistan Parliament," *Xinhua*, April 19, 1994.
7. RFE/RL, "Russia, China, Kazakhstan, Kyrgyzstan and Tajikistan Sign Treaty," *Radio Free Europe/Radio Liberty*, April 9, 1996 https://www.rferl.org/a/1080434.html
8. "Li Peng Meets Participants of International Symposium," *Xinhua*, FBIS-CHI, May 9, 1996, p. 1.
9. "Declaration on the establishment of the Shanghai Cooperation Organization," *Xinhua*, May 28, 2003 http://www.chinadaily.com.cn/en/doc/2003-05/28/content_239254.htm
10. Melissa Akin, "Shanghai Give Lure Yeltsin to Bishkek," *Moscow Times*, August 24, 1999.
11. Aleksandr Chudodeyev, "Boris Yeltsin Rehearses 'Primakov U-Turn' and is ready to do battle with 'Westerners'," *Current Digest of the Post-Soviet Press*, No. 34, vol. 51, September 22, 1999 https://dlib.eastview.com/browse/doc/19928150
12. Author interview, Shanghai, 2012.
13. Bates Gill, "Shanghai Give: An Attempt to Counter US Influence in Asia?," *Brookings Institute*, May 4, 2001 https://www.brookings.edu/opinions/shanghai-five-an-attempt-to-counter-u-s-influence-in-asia/

14. Yury Sigov and Sergei Guly, "The Five Diluted by the Addition of Islam Karimov," *Current Digest of the Post-Soviet Press*, No. 24, vol. 53, July 11, 2001 https://dlib.eastview.com/browse/doc/19930649

15. "Commentary: 'Shanghai Spirit' – New Banner of International Cooperation," *People's Daily*, June 15, 2001 http://en.people.cn/english/200106/15/eng20010615_72746.html

16. "Commentary: 'Shanghai Spirit' – New Banner of International Cooperation," *People's Daily*, June 15, 2001 http://en.people.cn/english/200106/15/eng20010615_72746.html

17. "Shanghai Summit Concludes with 'Moscow Nights'," *Current Digest of the Post-Soviet Press*, No. 24, vol. 53, July 11, 2001 https://dlib.eastview.com/browse/doc/19930546

18. Zhao Huasheng, "The Shanghai Cooperation Organization at 5: Achievements and the Challenges Ahead," *The China and Eurasia Forum Quarterly* 4/3 (2006), pp. 105–23.

19. Author interview, London, 2009.

20. "Third SCO Summit Meeting Held in Moscow," *Foreign Ministry of the People's Republic of China*, May 30, 2003 https://www.fmprc.gov.cn/mfa_eng/topics_665678/hjtcf_665940/t23117.shtml

21. Author interview, Shanghai, 2013.

22. "Billions involved in new projects in China-SCO demonstration zone," *Xinhua*, November 20, 2020 http://www.xinhuanet.com/english/2020-11/20/c_139531322.htm

23. Author interview, Beijing 2012.

24. Author interview, Shanghai, 2012.

25. Author interview, Beijing, 2011.

26. Author interview, Urumqi, 2012.

27. Author interviews, Beijing and Shanghai, 2012.

28. Author interview, Beijing, 2013.

29. Author interview, Shanghai, 2012.

30. "China, Kyrgyzstan Pledge Cooperation in Fighting 'Three Evil Forces'," *Xinhua*, May 20, 2014.

CHAPTER 7

1. Thomas Nilsen, "78-years old former Russian navy captain, now professor on Arctic, accused of working for Chinese intelligence," *Barents Observer*, June 15, 2020 https://thebarentsobserver.com/en/2020/06/78-years-old-former-russian-navy-captain-now-professor-arctic-accused-working-china

2. Thomas Grove, "A Spy Case Exposes China's Power Play in Central Asia," *Wall Street Journal*, July 10, 2019 https://www.wsj.com/articles/a-spy-case-exposes-chinas-power-play-in-central-asia-11562756782

3. RFE/RL Kazakh Service, "Kazakh Sinologist Jailed for Treason, Stripped of Citizenship," *Radio Free Europe/Radio Liberty*, October 15, 2019 https://www.rferl.org/a/kazakh-sinologist-jailed-for-treason-stripped-of-citizenship/30217549.html

4. Kyrgyz visit to National Institute for Strategic Studies (NISS), Ministry of Economy, Ministry of Foreign Affairs, 2011.

5. Reuters, "China to build outposts for Tajik guards on Tajikistan-Afghanistan border," *South China Morning Post*, September 26, 2016 https://www.scmp.com/news/china/diplomacy-defence/article/2022718/china-build-outposts-tajik-guards-tajikistan

6. "Rivals for Authority in Tajikistan's Gorno-Badakhshan," *Crisis Group Briefing No. 87*, March 14, 2018 https://www.crisisgroup.org/europe-central-asia/central-asia/tajikistan/b87-rivals-authority-tajikistans-gorno-badakhshan

7. Gerry Shih, "In Central Asia's forbidding highlights, a quiet newcomer: Chinese troops," *Washington Post*, February 18, 2019 https://www.washingtonpost.com/world/asia_pacific/in-central-asias-forbidding-highlands-a-quiet-newcomer-chinese-troops/2019/02/18/78d4a8d0-1e62-11e9-a759-2b8541bbbe20_story.html

8. Craig Nelson and Thomas Grove, "Russia, China Vie for Influence in Central Asia as US Plans Afghan Exit," *Wall Street Journal*, June 18, 2019 https://www.wsj.com/articles/russia-china-vie-for-influence-in-central-asia-as-u-s-plans-afghan-exit-11560850203

9. Angela Stanzel, "Fear and loathing on the New Silk Road: Chinese security in Afghanistan and beyond," *European Council on Foreign Relations Policy Brief*, July 12, 2018 https://ecfr.eu/publication/new_silk_road_chinese_security_in_afghanistan_beyond/ and July 2018 meetings with Academy of Military Sciences (AMS) in Beijing.

10. Sebastien Peyrouse, "Military Cooperation between China and Central Asia: Breakthrough, Limits, and Prospects," *China Brief* 20/5 (March 5, 2010).

11. "China to Give 1.3 Million Dollars in Military Aid to Kyrgyzstan," *AFP*, March 15, 2002.

12. Sebastien Peyrouse, "Military Cooperation between China and Central Asia: Breakthrough, Limits, and Prospects," *China Brief* 20/5 (March 5, 2010). https://jamestown.org/program/military-cooperation-between-china-and-central-asia-breakthrough-limits-and-prospects/

13. Sebastien Peyrouse, "Military Cooperation between China and Central Asia: Breakthrough, Limits, and Prospects," *China Brief* 20/5 (March 5, 2010). https://jamestown.org/program/military-cooperation-between-china-and-central-asia-breakthrough-limits-and-prospects/

14. Temur Umarov, "China Looms Large in Central Asia," *Carnegie Moscow Center*, March 30, 2020 https://carnegiemoscow.org/commentary/81402

15. There have been some limited reports, including an article in the Russian press, "China Boosts Influence in Central Asia through Loans," *Nezavisimaya Gazeta*, November 28, 2007, quoting the Turkmen defense minister saying the country had received a loan of $3 million.

16. Sebastien Peyrouse, "Military Cooperation between China and Central Asia: Breakthrough, Limits, and Prospects," *China Brief* 20/5 (March 5, 2010). https://jamestown.org/program/military-cooperation-between-china-and-central-asia-breakthrough-limits-and-prospects/

17. For example, in November 2007, the head of border guards under the Chinese minister for public security, Cheng Sheng, met the secretary of the Kyrgyz National Security Council Tokon Mamytov and handed over RMB 4 million, and "communications facilities, computer equipment" and more "Kyrgyzstan to Get 0.5m Dollars Worth of Chinese Military Aid," *Kabar.kg*, November 12, 2007.

18. "Kyrgyzstan Receives Military Aid from China," *24.kg*, November 12, 2013.

19. "People's Liberation Army of China to Allocate 100mn Yuan for Needs of Kyrgyzstan's Armed Forces," *AKI Press*, September 4, 2014; "China's Defence Minister to Pay Official Visit to Tajikistan," *Asia-Plus*, March 28, 2014.

20. "China Promises Multimillion Military-Technological Aid Package to Tajikistan," *Interfax*, March 31, 2014.

21. "People's Liberation Army of China to Allocate 100mn Yuan for Needs of Kyrgyzstan's Armed Forces," *AKI Press*, September 4, 2014.

22. "Chinese, Kyrgyz Armies to Step Up Cooperation in Regional Security Issues," *Interfax*, March 22, 2017.

23. "China, Kyrgyzstan to enhance security cooperation," *Xinhua*, September 8, 2018 http://www.xinhuanet.com/english/2018-09/08/c_137454384.htm

24. "Tajikistan: new military vehicles for GKNB border troops," *Global Defense Security*, December 11, 2018 https://www.armyrecognition.com/december_2018_global_defense_security_army_news_industry/tajikistan_new_military_vehicles_for_gknb_border_troops.html

25. "China to Provide Police Equipment to Interior Ministry," *AKI Press*, May 14, 2019.

26. Ma Yao, "In-depth: How China becomes third-largest supplier of weapons worldwide," *China Military Online*, February 27, 2018 http://english. chinamil.com.cn/view/2018-02/27/content_7953754.htm

27. Catherine Putz, "Kazakhstan Wants to Sell You an Armoured Vehicle," *The Diplomat*, December 9, 2015.

28. Almas Zheksenbekov, "Nursultan Nazarbayev: KADEX 2018 has become a global-scale event," *KazInform*, May 23, 2018 https://www. inform.kz/qz/nursultan-nazarbayev-kadex-2018-has-become-a-global-scale-event_a3262191

29. "Kazakhstan Unveils New 'Pterodactyl' Unmanned Combat Aerial Vehicle at KADEX 2016," *Defence-blog.com*, August 22, 2016. https:// defence-blog.com/news/kazakhstan-unveil-new-chengdu-pterodactyl-unmanned-combat-aerial-vehicle-at-kadex-2016.html

30. "Kazakhstan Receives First Y-8 Military Transport Aircraft from China," *Defence-blog.com*, September 23, 2018. https://defence-blog.com/news/ kazakhstan-receives-first-y-8-military-transport-aircraft.html

31. "Military Parade Reveals Turkmenistan's New Chinese-Built UAVs," *IHS Jane's Defence Weekly*, November 2, 2016.

32. Joshua Kucera, "Turkmenistan Shows Off New Chinese Rockets," *The Bug Pit*, April 2, 2016. https://eurasianet.org/turkmenistan-shows-off-new-chinese-rockets

33. "New Chinese-Built MANPADS Has Entered Service with Turkmenistan Army," *Defence-blog.com*, January 16, 2018. https://defence-blog.com/army/new-chinese-built-manpads-has-entered-service-with-turkmenistan-army.html

34. Sebastien Peyrouse, "Military Cooperation between China and Central Asia: Breakthrough, Limits, and Prospects," *China Brief* 20/5 (March 5, 2010).

35. This has been reported on military blogs; and a Facebook page captured an image from Uzbek television showing them in 2018 (https://www.facebook.com/pladupdate/photos/a.1017098351660426/1896705360366383/? type=1&theater). Earlier reports of the potential sale can be found at: Joshua Kucera, "Has China Made Its First Big Military Sale in Central Asia?," *The Bug Pit*, February 6, 2015. https://eurasianet.org/has-china-made-its-first-big-military-sale-in-central-asia

36. "Uzbekistan Purchases Military Drones from China," *AKI Press*, June 5, 2014.

37. "China to Help Uzbekistan Manufacture Drones," *Trend*, July 5, 2018.

38. Huawei since 1999 (https://www.huawei.com/uz/about-huawei/local-states) and ZTE since 2004 (http://zte.ru/company/zte-in-uzbekistan/).

39. "ZTE Corporation Expands Cooperation with Uzbekistan," *Oreanda News*, November 8, 2011.
40. "ZTE Opens Plant on Mobile Handsets Production in Uzbekistan," *UzDaily.com*, March 7, 2013. https://www.uzdaily.uz/en/post/23782
41. "Uzbekistan, China's Huawei to Produce CDMA-450 Phones," *China Telecoms Newswire*, July 6, 2006.
42. "Tajik President Has Highly Appreciated the Huawei Project 'Safe City,'" *Asia-Plus*, September 3, 2015.
43. Dipanjan Roy Chaudhury, "Huawei Under Radar of Many Countries Fearing Espionage," *Economic Times*, February 1, 2019.
44. Niva Yau, "China taking Big Brother to Central Asia," *Eurasianet*, September 6, 2019 https://eurasianet.org/china-taking-big-brother-to-central-asia
45. Sébastien Peyrouse, "The Central Asian Armies Facing the Challenge of Formation," *The Journal of Power Institutions in Post-Soviet Societies*, Issue 11, 2010 https://journals.openedition.org/pipss/3799
46. https://jamestown.org/program/military-cooperation-between-china-and-central-asia-breakthrough-limits-and-prospects/
47. "10 Kyrgyz Border Guards to Receive Training in China Annually," *AKI Press*, December 25, 2008.
48. "China Plans to Train Tajik Border Guards," *Asia-Plus*, July 26, 2006.
49. Sébastien Peyrouse, "Military Cooperation between China and Central Asia: Breakthrough, Limits, and Prospects," *China Brief* 20/5 (March 5, 2010). https://jamestown.org/program/military-cooperation-between-china-and-central-asia-breakthrough-limits-and-prospects/
50. Dirk van der Kley, "China's Security Activities in Tajikistan and Afghanistan's Wakhan Corridor," in Nadège Rolland (ed.), *Securing the Belt and Road Initiative: China's Evolving Military Engagement along the Silk Roads*, Special Report No. 80, September (National Bureau of Asian Research, 2019). https://www.nbr.org/wp-content/uploads/pdfs/publications/sr80_securing_the_belt_and_road_sep2019.pdf
51. Author interview, Shanghai, 2018.
52. Umida Hashimova, "Uzbekistan Looks to China for Policing Experience," *The Diplomat*, September 10, 2018 https://thediplomat.com/2018/09/uzbekistan-looks-to-china-for-policing-experience/
53. Raffaello Pantucci, "Beijing Binds: COVID-19 and the China-Central Relationship," *Central Asia Program*, June 19, 2020 https://www.central-asiaprogram.org/archives/16339
54. Alzhanova Raushan, "Delegation of Chinese People's Armed Police arrives in Kazakhstan," *KazInform*, September 5, 2014 https://www.

inform.kz/en/delegation-of-chinese-people-s-armed-police-arrives-in-kazakhstan_a2694022; "China, Kazakhstan start joint border law enforcement," *China Military*, October 14, 2016 http://eng.chinamil. com.cn/view/2016-10/14/content_7301841.htm; Xinhua, "China, Kyrgyzstan conclude joint counter-terrorism drill," *Global Times*, August 14, 2019 https://www.globaltimes.cn/content/1161381.shtml; Li Jiayao, "Uzbekistan, China wrap up joint anti-terror drills," *Xinhua*, May 17, 2019 http://eng.chinamil.com.cn/view/2019-05/17/content_9505397.htm

55. Lianyungang Forum, "Forum Introduction," http://www.lygforum. gov.cn/js

56. Thomas Grove, "A Spy Case Exposes China's Power Play in Central Asia," *Wall Street Journal*, July 10, 2019 https://www.wsj.com/articles/a-spy-case-exposes-chinas-power-play-in-central-asia-11562756782

57. Niva Yau and Dirk can der Kley, "The Growth, Adaptation and Limitations of Chinese Private Security Companies in Central Asia," *The Oxus Society*, October 13, 2020 https://oxussociety.org/ the-growth-adaptation-and-limitations-of-chinese-private-security-companies-in-central-asia/

58. Austin Ramzy and Chris Buckley, "'Absolutely No Mercy': Leaked Files Expose How China Organized Mass Detentions of Muslims," *New York Times*, November 16, 2019 https://www.nytimes.com/interactive/ 2019/11/16/world/asia/china-xinjiang-documents.html

CHAPTER 8

1. Austin Ramzy and Chris Buckley, "'Absolutely No Mercy': Leaked Files Expose How China Organized Mass Detentions of Muslims," *New York Times*, November 16, 2019 https://www.nytimes.com/interactive/ 2019/11/16/world/asia/china-xinjiang-documents.html

2. Erica Downs, "China Buys into Afghanistan," *SAIS Review*, Vol. XXXIII, No. 2 (Summer-Fall 2012) https://www.brookings.edu/wp-content/ uploads/2016/06/China-Buys-into-Afghanistan-Erica-Downs.pdf

3. Raffaello Pantucci, "China's Non-Intervention in Afghanistan," *Oxus Society*, November 18, 2020 https://oxussociety.org/chinas-non-intervention-in-afghanistan/

4. "Utilisation of certain idle proceeds raised from IPO for temporary sup-plementation of working capital," *Metallurgical Corporation of China Ltd. Press Release*, March 29, 2016 https://www1.hkexnews.hk/listedco/ listconews/sehk/2016/0329/ltn201603291303.pdf

5. Michael Wines, "China Willing to Spend Big on Afghan Commerce," *New York Times*, December 29, 2009 https://www.nytimes.com/2009/ 12/30/world/asia/30mine.html

6. Erica Downs, "China Buys into Afghanistan," *SAIS Review*, Vol. XXXIII, No. 2 (Summer-Fall 2012) https://www.brookings.edu/wp-content/uploads/2016/06/China-Buys-into-Afghanistan-Erica-Downs.pdf

7. Andrew Small, "Tea with the Taliban," *The China-Pakistan Axis: Asia's New Geopolitics* (Oxford University Press, 2014).

8. Hannah Bloch, "Mega Copper Deal in Afghanistan Fuels Rush to Save Ancient Treasures," *National Geographic*, September 15 https://www.nationalgeographic.com/magazine/article/mes-aynak-buddhist-archaeology-afghanistan

9. Mohsin Amin, "The Story Behind China's Long-Stalled Mine in Afghanistan," *The Diplomat*, January 7, 2017 https://thediplomat.com/2017/01/the-story-behind-chinas-long-stalled-mine-in-afghanistan/

10. Author interview, Kabul, 2013. Mohsin Amin, "The Story Behind China's Long-Stalled Mine in Afghanistan," *The Diplomat*, January 7, 2017 https://thediplomat.com/2017/01/the-story-behind-chinas-long-stalled-mine-in-afghanistan/

11. "Afghan Taliban offer security for copper, gas projects," *Reuters*, November 29, 2016 https://www.yahoo.com/news/afghan-taliban-offer-security-copper-gas-projects-105029614.html?ref=gs

12. Author interview, Beijing, 2015.

13. Vanda Felbab-Brown, "A BRI(dge) too far: The unfulfilled promise and limitations of China's involvement in Afghanistan," *Brookings Institution*, June 2020 https://www.brookings.edu/research/a-bridge-too-far-the-unfulfilled-promise-and-limitations-of-chinas-involvement-in-afghanistan/

14. Author interview, Kabul, 2012.

15. Author interview, Beijing, 2015.

16. "Utilisation of certain idle proceeds raised from IPO for temporary supplementation of working capital," *Metallurgical Corporation of China Ltd. Press Release*, March 29, 2016 https://www1.hkexnews.hk/listedco/listconews/sehk/2016/0329/ltn201603291303.pdf

17. Andrew Small, "Tea with the Taliban," *The China-Pakistan Axis: Asia's New Geopolitics* (Oxford University Press, 2014), p. 137.

18. Michael Martina and Mirwais Harooni, "Slow road from Kabul highlights China's challenge in Afghanistan," *Reuters*, November 23, 2015 https://www.reuters.com/article/us-afghanistan-china-road-idUSKBN0TB0X520151122

19. Author interview, Beijing, 2015.

20. Andrew Small, "Tea with the Taliban," *The China-Pakistan Axis: Asia's New Geopolitics* (Oxford University Press, 2014), p. 129.

21. "Huawei's Link to Taliban Groundless," *China Daily*, December 14, 2001 http://www.china.org.cn/english/FR/23721.htm

22. Afghan Communication Ministry, "Chinese Companies Sign Agreement," *BBC Summary of World Broadcasts*, Friday, August 22, 2003.

23. "Afghanistan to Roll Out CDMA Network," *2.5-3G*, September 2007.

24. "Afghan Telecom Signs Agreement of GSM and 3G Equipment with ZTE Company," *Ministry of Communications and Information Technology of Afghanistan*, November 20, 2012 https://www.mcit.gov.af/en/afghan-telecom-signs-agreement-gsm-and-3g-equipment-zte-company-0

25. Nick Paton Walsh, "Uzbekistan kicks US out of military base," *Guardian*, August 1, 2005 https://www.theguardian.com/world/2005/aug/01/usa.nickpatonwalsh

26. Andrew Kuchins and Zhao Huasheng, "China and Afghanistan: China's Interests, Stances, and Perspectives," *CSIS Russia and Eurasia Program*, March 2012 https://csis-website-prod.s3.amazonaws.com/s3fs-public/legacy_files/files/publication/120322_Zhao_ChinaAfghan_web.pdf

27. "China appoints special envoy for Afghanistan," *Reuters*, July 18, 2014 https://www.reuters.com/article/us-china-afghanistan-idUSKBN0FN11Z20140718

28. "Afghanistan's new president starts landmark China visit," *BBC News*, October 28, 2014 https://www.bbc.com/news/world-asia-29803768

29. Author interviews in Beijing, 2015. "China Favours Role in Afghan Peace Talks, Appreciates Pakistan's Efforts," *Dawn*, August 15, 2015 http://www.dawn.com/news/1200627

30. Edward Wong and Mujib Mashal, "Taliban and Afghan Peace Officials Have Secret Talks in China," *New York Times*, May 25, 2015 https://www.nytimes.com/2015/05/26/world/asia/taliban-and-afghan-peace-officials-have-secret-talks-in-china.html

31. Jon Boone, "Afghanistan and Taliban peace talks end with promise to meet again," *Guardian*, July 8, 2015 https://www.theguardian.com/world/2015/jul/08/afghanistan-and-taliban-peace-talks-end-with-promise-to-meet-again

32. "Afghan, Taliban delegates attend Oslo talks on ending conflicts," *Reuters*, June 16, 2015 https://www.reuters.com/article/us-norway-afghanistan-idUSKBN0OW17B20150616

33. Author interview, Beijing, July 2015.

34. Author interviews, Beijing and London, 2016. The detail of Uyghur militants being present is confirmed by a number of sources including other foreign militants who were in Afghanistan at the time.

35. Mullah Abdul Salam Zaeef, *My Life with the Taliban* (C. Hurst Ltd, 2011).

36. Author interview, Tashkent, March 2019.

37. Author interview, Delhi, 2014.

38. Author interview, Delhi, 2014.
39. http://eng.mod.gov.cn/DefenseNews/2016–08/04/content_4707451 .htm
40. Author interview, Bishkek, 2015.
41. Author interview, Moscow, 2017.
42. Author interview, Beijing, 2017.

CHAPTER 9

1. Wang Jisi, "Marching Westwards: The Rebalancing of China's Geostrategy," *International and Strategic Studies Report*, No. 73, October 7, 2012 http:// en.iiss.pku.edu.cn/research/bulletin/1604.html (it was first laid out in Chinese: Wang Jisi (王缉思), "'西进', 中国地缘战略的再平衡," ("Going West": China's Rebalancing Strategy), 环球时报 *(Global Times)*, October 17, 2012 https://opinion.huanqiu.com/article/9CaKrnJxoLS).

2. Wang Jisi, "Marching Westwards: The Rebalancing of China's Geostrategy," *International and Strategic Studies Report*, No. 73, October 7, 2012. http://en.iiss.pku.edu.cn/research/bulletin/1604.html

3. Wang Jisi, "Marching Westwards: The Rebalancing of China's Geostrategy," *International and Strategic Studies Report*, No. 73, October 7, 2012. http://en.iiss.pku.edu.cn/research/bulletin/1604.html

4. Hillary Clinton, "America's Pacific Century," *Foreign Policy,* October 11, 2011 https://foreignpolicy.com/2011/10/11/americas-pacific-century/

5. "Li Peng Addresses Uzbek Parliament on China's Relations with Central Asia," *Xinhua*, Beijing, 19 April, 1994 (as reported on *BBC Monitoring*, April 22, 1994).

6. "China Wants to Promote Relations with Central Asian States," *TASS*, April 27, 1994.

7. "Uzbekistan-China: 'Silk Road' Neighbours Sign Major Loan Agreement," *IPS-Inter Press Service*, April 19, 1994.

8. "China-Japan to Study New Gas Pipeline," *Reuters*, February 17, 1993.

9. "China-Turkmenistan Joint Statement Issued," *Xinhua*, July 6, 2000.

10. "Kunming Initiative," signed in Kunming, China, on August 17, 1999.

11. *People's Daily*, June 19, 1999.

12. Wang Jisi, "Marching Westwards: The Rebalancing of China's Geostrategy," *International and Strategic Studies Report*, No. 73, October 7, 2012. http://en.iiss.pku.edu.cn/research/bulletin/1604.html

13. Halford John Mackinder, "The Geographical Pivot of History," *The Geographical Journal* 170/4 (1904), pp. 298–321; Peter Frankopan, *The Silk Roads: A New History of the World* (Bloomsbury Publishing, 2018).

14. Hillary Rodham Clinton, "Remarks on India and the United States: A Vision for the 21ˢᵗ Century," *US Department of State*, July 20, 2011 https://2009-2017.state.gov/secretary/20092013clinton/rm/2011/07/168840.htm

15. Hillary Rodham Clinton, "Remarks on India and the United States: A Vision for the 21ˢᵗ Century," *US Department of State*, July 20, 2011 https://2009-2017.state.gov/secretary/20092013clinton/rm/2011/07/168840.htm

16. "Putin Warns of Losing Far Eastern Region to the Orient," *Agence France Presse*, July 21, 2000.

17. Vladimir Putin, "A New Integration Project for Eurasia: The Future in the Making," *Izvestia*, October 3, 2011.

18. Author interview, Moscow, 2015.

19. Wang Jisi, "Marching Westwards: The Rebalancing of China's Geostrategy," *International and Strategic Studies Report*, No. 73, October 7, 2012. http://en.iiss.pku.edu.cn/research/bulletin/1604.html

20. Alexei Anishchuk and Timothy Heritage, "China's new leader welcomes Russia's Putin as a friend," *Reuters*, March 22, 2013 https://www.reuters.com/article/us-china-russia/chinas-new-leader-welcomes-russias-putin-as-a-friend-idUSBRE92L0KE20130322

21. Marlene Laruelle, Gerard Toal, John O'Loughlin, Kristin M. Bakke, "Kazakhs are wary of neighbours bearing gifts," *Open Democracy*, April 30, 2020 https://www.opendemocracy.net/en/odr/kazakhs-are-wary-neighbours-bearing-gifts/

22. "Xi Jinping Holds Talks with President Vladimir Putin of Russia," *Foreign Ministry of the People's Republic of China,* May 8, 2015 https://www.fmprc.gov.cn/mfa_eng/topics_665678/xjpcxelsjnwgzzsl7oznqdbfelshskstbels/t1263258.shtml

23. "Address by Prime Minister Ryutaro Hashimoto to the Japan Association of Corporate Executives," July 24, 1997 https://japan.kantei.go.jp/0731douyukai.html

24. "Address by Prime Minister Ryutaro Hashimoto to the Japan Association of Corporate Executives," July 24, 1997 https://japan.kantei.go.jp/0731douyukai.html

25. Michael D. Swaine, "Chinese Views and Commentary on Periphery Diplomacy," *China Leadership Monitor*, Issue 44, Summer 2014 https://www.hoover.org/research/chinese-views-and-commentary-periphery-diplomacy

26. "Important Speech of Xi Jinping at Peripheral Diplomacy Work Conference," *China Council for International Cooperation on Environment*

and Development, October 30, 2013 http://www.cciced.net/cciceden/NEWSCENTER/LatestEnvironmentalandDevelopmentNews/201310/t20131030_82626.html

27. Cited in: Michael D. Swaine, "Chinese Views and Commentary on Periphery Diplomacy," *China Leadership Monitor,* Issue 44, Summer 2014 https://www.hoover.org/research/chinese-views-and-commentary-periphery-diplomacy

28. Robert Zoellick, "'Whither China? From Membership to Responsibility," *National Committee on US-China Relations,* September 21, 2005 https://www.ncuscr.org/sites/default/files/migration/Zoellick_remarks_notes06_winter_spring.pdf

29. Stephanie Kleine-Ahlbrandt, "Beijing, Global Free-Rider," *Foreign Policy,* November 12, 2009 https://www.crisisgroup.org/asia/north-east-asia/china/beijing-global-free-rider

30. Author interview, Beijing, 2016.

31. "Premier Li Keqiang Arrives in Islamabad for Official Visit to Pakistan," *Foreign Ministry of the People's Republic of China,* May 22, 2013 https://www.fmprc.gov.cn/mfa_eng/wjb_663304/zzjg_663340/yzs_663350/gjlb_663354/2757_663518/2759_663522/t1044069.shtml

32. "Xi Jinping Holds talks with Prime Minister Narendra Modi of India Building Closer Partnership for Development and Achieving Peaceful Development and Cooperative Development Together," *Foreign Ministry of the People's Republic of China,* September 18, 2014 https://www.fmprc.gov.cn/mfa_eng/topics_665678/zjpcxshzzcygyslshdsschybdtjkst-medfsllkydjxgsfw/t1193332.shtml

33. Raffaello Pantucci, "China's development lenders embrace multilateral co-operation," *Beyond BRICS Financial Times,* November 1, 2016 https://www.ft.com/content/a3192fa0-c59a-30cc-968a-6651ca9310b9

34. Author interview, Delhi, 2015.

35. Author interview, SCO Secretariat, 2014.

CONCLUSION

1. Austin Ramzy and Chris Buckley, "'Absolutely No Mercy': Leaked Files Expose How China Organized Mass Detentions of Muslims," *New York Times,* November 16, 2019 https://www.nytimes.com/interactive/2019/11/16/world/asia/china-xinjiang-documents.html

2. James Leibold, "The Spectre of Insecurity: The CCP's Mass Internment Strategy in Xinjiang," *China Leadership Monitor,* March 2019 https://www.prcleader.org/leibold

3. Austin Ramzy and Chris Buckley, "'Absolutely No Mercy': Leaked Files Expose How China Organized Mass Detentions of Muslims," *New York Times*, November 16, 2019 https://www.nytimes.com/interactive/2019/11/16/world/asia/china-xinjiang-documents.html

4. James Leibold, "The Spectre of Insecurity: The CCP's Mass Internment Strategy in Xinjiang," *China Leadership Monitor*, March 2019 https://www.prcleader.org/leibold

5. James Leibold, "The Spectre of Insecurity: The CCP's Mass Internment Strategy in Xinjiang," *China Leadership Monitor*, March 2019 https://www.prcleader.org/leibold

List of Acronyms

ADB	Asian Development Bank
AI	artificial intelligence
AIIB	Asian Infrastructure Investment Bank
ANPR	automatic number plate recognition
APC	armored personnel carriers
B3W	Build Back Better World
BCIM-EC	Bangladesh-China-India-Myanmar Economic Corridor
BG	British Gas
BRI	Belt and Road Initiative
BRICS	Brazil, Russia, India, China, and South Africa [Bank]
CAREC	Asian Development Bank's Central Asia Regional Economic Cooperation
CASA	Central Asia–South Asia electricity connectivity projects
CCP	Chinese Communist Party
CCTV	China Central Television (which now uses the acronym CGTN, China Global Television Network for its international broadcasts); *also* closed-circuit television
CDB	China Development Bank
CDMA	code-division multiple access
CEIEC	China National Electronics Import & Export Corporation
CI	Confucius Institute
CICIR	China Institutes for Contemporary International Relations
CIS	Commonwealth of Independent States
CNISCO	China National Institute for SCO International Exchange and Judicial Cooperation

CNOOC	China National Offshore Oil Corporation
CNPC	China National Petroleum Corporation
CPEC	China–Pakistan Economic Corridor
CRBC	China Road and Bridge Corporation
CSTO	Collective Security Treaty Organization
DAFA	Délégation archéologique française en Afghanistan
EAEU	Eurasian Economic Union
EDZ	Economic Development Zone
EEU	European Economic Union
ETR	East Turkestan Republic
EU	European Union
FIDH	International Federation for Human Rights
FSB	Russian internal security service
FTA	free trade area
G7	Group of Seven
G8	Group of Eight
GDP	gross domestic product
ICPVTR	International Centre for Political Violence and Terrorism
ID	identity [cards]
IMF	International Monetary Fund
JCC	Jiangxi Copper Corporation
KGB	Committee for State Security
KMG	KazMunaiGas (Kazakhstan's national oil company)
LNG	liquefied natural gas
MCC	Metallurgical Corporation of China
MPS	Ministry of Public Security
MSS	Ministry of State Security
NATO	North Atlantic Treaty Organization
NFC	China Non Ferrous Metal Industry's Foreign Engineering and Construction Co., Ltd
OBOR	One Belt One Road (an earlier articulation of BRI)
OPIC	Overseas Private Investment Corporation
PAP	People's Armed Police

PLA	People's Liberation Army
PLAN	People's Liberation Army Navy
PSB	Public Security Bureau
QCCM	Quadrilateral Coordination and Cooperation Mechanism
QCG	Quadrilateral Coordination Group
QR	quick response
RATS	Regional Anti-Terrorism Structure
RDIF	Russia's Direct Investment Fund
RMB	renminbi
SAMS	surface to air missile systems
SASS	Shanghai Academy of Social Sciences
SCO	Shanghai Cooperation Organization
SEZ	special economic zones
SOE	state-owned enterprise
SREB	Silk Road Economic Belt
TAPI	Turkmenistan-Afghanistan-Pakistan-India
TIRET	Turkic Islamic Republic of East Turkestan
TPP	Trans-Pacific Partnership
VPN	virtual private network
UAV	unmanned aerial vehicle
UK	United Kingdom
UN	United Nations
US	United States
XJASS	Xinjiang branch, Chinese Academy of Social Sciences
XPCC	Xinjiang Production and Construction Corps
YASS	Yunnan Academy of Social Sciences
ZTE	Zhongxing Telecommunications Equipment

Photographs and Maps

Index